STUDIES IN 5
COMPARATIVE ECONOMICS

Studies in Comparative Economics

THE ECONOMICS OF
SOVIET PLANNING

by Abram Bergson

NEW HAVEN AND LONDON
YALE UNIVERSITY PRESS
1964

B 6501025

C D

301203

For R.M.B.

FOREWORD

Modern economics has been bred chiefly in Western Europe and the United States, and despite its aspiration toward generality it bears the stamp of institutions and issues characteristic of these areas.

But the economic world no longer revolves about London and New York. Dozens of new nations are struggling toward economic independence and industrial growth under institutional arrangements quite unlike those of the West. Economies of a novel type also extend eastward from central Europe to the Bering Strait and have been busily developing their own principles as a by-product of administrative experience. It is asserted that "Western economics" has only limited analytical value in these other countries.

The problem of the content and relevance of economics thus arises inescapably. Are the economic principles taught in the West really susceptible of general application? Or are they culture-bound and relevant mainly to industrial capitalist countries? Is it possible to create a general economics which would be as useful in Poland or India as in Canada or France? Or must we be content with several species of economics which will remain distinct in intellectual content and applicability?

"Comparative economics" has been regarded as a separate area of the economics curriculum, consisting of a botanical classification of national economies into a few loosely labeled boxes. But surely any course in economics is potentially comparative. A concern with comparative experience

vii

can profitably be infused into any of the standard branches of economic study. This series is inspired by the hope that a rethinking of particular branches of economics in world perspective, combined with a bibliography of available material from many countries, may help teachers to give their courses a broader and more comparative orientation.

In pursuing this objective, we deliberately chose autonomy over standardization. Each author was left free to determine his own approach and method of treatment. The essays thus differ considerably in length, analytical as against descriptive emphasis, geographical coverage, and other respects. How far the original intent of the series has been accomplished is for the profession to judge.

We are grateful to the authors who have struggled with possibly insoluble problems, to the Ford Foundation for its support of the enterprise, and to the staff of the Yale University Press for their helpful cooperation.

The Inter-University Committee on Comparative Economics: Abram Bergson, Arthur R. Burns, Kermit Gordon, Richard Musgrave, William Nicholls, Lloyd Reynolds (Chairman)

ACKNOWLEDGMENTS

I am happy to express my indebtedness to Alexander Erlich and Leon Smolinski, who read and commented on a preliminary version, and to Alexander Gerschenkron and Nancy Nimitz, who read and commented on parts of it. Professor Smolinski also supplied apt examples to illustrate a number of points. The volume has benefited throughout from the exceptionally thorough and skillful editing given it by Lillian Weksler.

The study was aided at different stages by opportunities for research provided by a Faculty Fellowship of the Ford Foundation and a Fellowship at the Center for Advanced Study in the Behavioral Sciences. I have also benefited much from access to the facilities of the Russian Research Center at Harvard.

Translations of Soviet publications appearing in the *Current Digest of the Soviet Press* have been quoted with the kind permission of this periodical, which is published weekly at Columbia University by the Joint Committee of Slavic Studies.

Abram Bergson

Stanford, California
February 1964

ix

CONTENTS

Contents

Contents

TABLES

Tables

ABBREVIATIONS

Comparisons: Joint Economic Committee, Congress of the United States, *Comparisons of the United States and Soviet Economies*

Current Digest: The Current Digest of the Soviet Press

Dimensions: Joint Economic Committee, Congress of the United States, *Dimensions of Soviet Economic Power* (Washington, D.C., 1962)

Direktivy: Direktivy KPSS i sovetskogo pravitel'stava po khoziaistvennym voprosam

Gosplan: Gosudarstvenny Komitet Planirovaniia SSSR (State Planning Committee of the U.S.S.R.)

Narkhoz, 1956: TSU, *Narodnoe khoziaistvo SSSR v 1956 godu* (Moscow, 1957)

Narkhoz, 1958: TSU, *Narodnoe khoziaistvo SSSR v 1958 godu* (Moscow, 1959)

Narkhoz, 1959: TSU, *Narodnoe khoziaistvo SSSR v 1959 godu* (Moscow, 1960)

Narkhoz, 1960: TSU, *Narodnoe khoziaistvo SSSR v 1960 godu* (Moscow, 1961)

Narkhoz, 1961: TSU, *Narodnoe khoziaistvo SSSR v 1961 godu* (Moscow, 1962)

RAND: The RAND Corporation, Santa Monica, California

Real SNIP: Abram Bergson, *The Real National Income of Soviet Russia Since 1928* (Cambridge, Mass., 1961)

Tsentrosoiuz: Tsentral'nyi Soiuz Potrebitel'skikh Obshchestv (Central Union of Consumers' Societies)

TSU: Tsentral'noe Statisticheskoe Upravlenie (Central Statistical Administration)

TSUNKHU: Tsentral'noe Upravlenie Narodno-khoziaistvennogo Ucheta (Central Administration of National Economic Accounting)

VSNKH: Vyshii Sovet Narodnogo Khoziaistva (Supreme Economic Council)

Zakonodatel'nye akty: Zakonodatel'nye akty po voprosam narodnogo khoziaistva SSSR

THE ECONOMICS OF
SOVIET PLANNING

1 INTRODUCTION

In the fifth decade since November 1917 the economic system of Soviet Russia is no longer a very novel theme, but it is still not easy for the Western scholar to penetrate beyond familiar rudiments. Despite the difficulties, however, a number of illuminating studies of different facets have now been published. A summary survey which takes account of these writings may contribute to understanding of a society and a way of economic life which are of interest almost everywhere.

Any community, the primers tell us, has to deal with a pervasive economic problem: how to determine the uses of available resources, including not only goods and services that can be employed productively but also other scarce supplies. How is this matter dealt with in Soviet Russia? Particularly, what are the relevant institutions? How do they function to determine resource use? The economic system of the U.S.S.R. might be examined from different standpoints, but for the student of economics this survey may gain in value if it focuses, somewhat more explicitly than is often done, on questions such as these.

The way of economic life of concern here is socialism; indeed, the U.S.S.R. is today the foremost example of this form of economic organization. The economic merit of a socialist system is not quite as controversial a topic in the West as it once was, and it is generally understood that positions taken on either side in the famous theoretic debate on this matter have often been untenably extreme. But within these bounds the economic case regarding socialism remains an open issue. The first concern of the present study is to grasp the nature of working arrangements for resource use in the U.S.S.R., but in such an inquiry we wish to become aware of pertinent behavior patterns and, where possible, to understand them. In seeking awareness and understanding, we may also gain further insight into the issue of economic merit.

A way of economic life, it is true, has noneconomic consequences; and in view of the experience with socialism to date no one who values human life, freedom, and dignity will be inclined to judge this system solely or even primarily in economic terms. Nevertheless the economic merit of socialism remains a weighty issue.

The Soviet economic system is still evolving; in fact it seems to have been even more in flux lately than it had been for a long time. But while truths about such a system thus may only prove to be temporal, we cannot refrain from seeking them. Although we must focus primarily on recent circumstances, we may be able by referring to earlier phases to gain some understanding of the meaning and permanency of the features being considered. From this standpoint, the period of particular interest is that since 1928, the year when the First Five Year Plan was initiated.

4

Introduction

Occasionally, we must also consider the period of the New Economic Policy (1921–28) and even that of War Communism (1918–21).

While the Soviet economic system has been changing much, Soviet economic thought recently has been changing even more. To the Western student of economics the latter has an interest of its own. I focus here, however, on the system. In inquiring into it, I must touch on thought, but this theme must be left essentially to separate inquiry.

Even in respect to the economic system, our survey must sometimes be incomplete. Among other things, I shall deal only briefly with the peripheral and little-explored topic of location of economic activity, and have little to say concerning foreign trade. For the U.S.S.R. the latter has been of relatively limited consequence, although it has lately been assuming a larger role.[1]

Opinions still differ as to how the Soviet economy should be designated, but I hope I may call it "socialist," with the understanding that the reference is essentially to one out-

1. On the economics of location in the U.S.S.R., the reader may wish to consult Harry Schwartz, *Russia's Soviet Economy* (2d ed. New York, 1954), ch. 7; M. Gardner Clark, *The Economics of Soviet Steel* (Cambridge, Mass., 1956); Holland Hunter, *Soviet Transportation Policy* (Cambridge, Mass., 1957); Franklyn D. Holzman, "The Soviet Ural-Kuznetsk Combine," *Quarterly Journal of Economics, 71* (1957), 368–405. On Soviet foreign trade, reference may be made to Alexander Gerschenkron, *Economic Relations with the USSR,* Carnegie Endowment for International Peace (New York, 1943); Alexander Baykov, *Soviet Foreign Trade* (Princeton, 1946); Joseph Berliner, *Soviet Economic Aid* (New York, 1958); Horst Mendershausen, "Terms of Trade between the Soviet Union and Smaller Communist Countries," *Review of Economics and Statistics, 41* (1959), 106–18, and comments on this article by Holzman and Mendershausen in the same journal, *44,* (1962) 134–47, 493–501; Franklyn D. Holzman, "Foreign Trade," in Abram Bergson and Simon Kuznets, eds., *Economic Trends in the Soviet Union* (Cambridge, Mass., 1963); Frederic L. Pryor, *The Communist Foreign Trade System* (Cambridge, Mass., 1963).

standing feature: the predominantly public ownership of the means of production. In any case, the reader can appraise for himself the familiar issues posed, although the following pages may further illuminate them. He should consider, however, that Marx in all his voluminous writings had little to say about the precise nature of socialism and hardly envisaged that this form of society would first come into being in circumstances such as prevailed in Russia in 1917. Hence differences in opinion as to how we should designate the economic system which exists in the Soviet Union today are understandable.

In describing the system of the U.S.S.R. as socialism, we must consider that, in view of the peculiar institutions which shape and control it, it is socialism of a special sort. By implication, if the conclusions reached for the U.S.S.R. are to apply elsewhere, it must be primarily to socialist societies with similarly authoritarian political institutions. Thus far, however, authoritarianism seems nowhere to have been avoided when public ownership has been predominant, although admittedly the degree has varied in different countries and at different times. Of course, many advocates of socialism sincerely aspire to avoid authoritarianism, while some who consider themselves socialists do not seek thoroughgoing public ownership to begin with.

If, like other countries, the U.S.S.R. faces any economic problem to speak of, this can be only because it has not yet reached the ultimate stage of development that Marx envisaged for a socialist society, the one that materializes "after the enslaving subordination of individuals under division of labor, and therewith the antithesis between mental and physical labor has vanished; after labor from a mere means of life, has itself become a prime necessity of life; after the productive forces have increased with the all around development of the individual, and all the

6

springs of cooperative wealth flow more abundantly." [2] But as the directors of Soviet economic life acknowledge, in the U.S.S.R. "communism" still remains to be achieved. They also state explicitly that communism is the "higher phase of communist society" that Marx depicted. The U.S.S.R. is thus held to be an example of Marx's "first phase of communist society," in the U.S.S.R. now called socialism. So far as the absence of communism in the U.S.S.R. is concerned, no one will dispute the Soviet usage.

Under the new party program adopted in October 1961, however, realization of the ultimate goal is now held to be imminent.[3] At least, a "material basis" for communism is to be established by 1980. To what extent the program's ambitious production targets will be achieved must be a matter for another inquiry. And we may properly wait until they are approached to debate the further question: In what ways, if at all, might realization of such targets be followed by progress toward the ultimate goal?

In exploring Soviet working arrangements for resource use, we wish to discern and understand behavior patterns. In economics, one often focuses such an inquiry by means of a hypothesis.

I propose, therefore, to consider this supposition: In determining working arrangements for resource use, the system's directors in the U.S.S.R. seek diverse goals, but a cardinal concern is to assure the rapid growth of the economy. Hence, in choices between present and future, resource use is supposed to conform to some planners' preferences, which favor the future as far as seems expedient.

2. *Critique of the Gotha Programme* (New York, International Publishers Edition, n.d.), p. 10.

3. *Pravda* (November 2, 1961); *The New Soviet Society* (New York, 1962).

7

Elsewhere, however, the concern is with "consumer's welfare," understood essentially in terms of the preferences of households. Hence, except in respect to choices between present and future, the system's directors seek to determine resource use in accord with this standard.

But, if reference is to the U.S.S.R., would it not be nearer the mark to assume that planners' preferences prevail not only between present and future but generally? The system's directors are hardly apt to have any values of their own for all the myriads of alternatives that are open, but the formulation of such values, it is true, is a task that might be delegated. On the other hand, if their chief concern is with the future, one might wonder how wise the system's directors would be to insist on overriding household preferences in any comprehensive way. Thus they would only be able to favor the future the more if they used as effectively as possible in the interest of consumers' welfare whatever resources are devoted to the present.

But I do not really wish to suggest that consumers are sovereign in the U.S.S.R., even in the restricted sphere in question. Household preferences are sometimes overruled politically in any modern community, and obviously the U.S.S.R. is not an exception to this rule. The facts on the issue posed, however, may not be as simple as is often assumed. In any case, we need not prejudge just how far Soviet consumers have been removed from the throne. If I take a concern for household preferences as a point of departure except where choices are between present and future, the inquiry seems only to be facilitated, and no more can be asked of such a procedure.

Actually, in regard to resource use, what is in order in a community from the standpoint of ends of one kind frequently is no less appropriate from that of others. Among other things, for many goods more is better than less in terms of almost any ends. Therefore, in a study like this,

8

Introduction

one could make too much of the whole question of ends. But ends must still be very consequential, and the approach adopted may enable us more readily to gauge the ends that prevail.

Among goods allotted to current consumption, consumers' welfare is supposed to be the concern where supplies may be made physically available to different households more or less independently. For "collective goods" (e.g. defense, police protection, epidemic control, etc.), where supplies must instead be made available to different households jointly, obviously the system's directors seek to implement some planners' preferences.[4] Regarding Soviet resource use in the case of collective goods, however, I can add little to what is already fairly familiar. Hence I shall not say much about arrangements for dealing with them.

In resource use, household preferences can serve as a guide only regarding aspects other than income distribution, but where consumers' welfare is the end, concern for the latter is usually also involved. What is implied is subject to more than one interpretation, but so far as incomes derive from labor, they are most often understood ideally to be determined in such a way as to allow for differences in disutility, and otherwise to vary more or less with need. This is a principle which some suppose should be observed especially under socialism. But what principle is applied in the U.S.S.R. must be a question for inquiry.

Household preferences are supposed to provide a basis for the valuation of "material" aspects of resource use and, as understood here, so too are any planners' preferences

4. Contrary to a common supposition, a concern for consumers' welfare is not formally precluded from decisions regarding collective goods. At least, such supplies might still be appraised in the light of the aggregate valuation of all households together for an increment, and this is all that might properly be asked from the standpoint of consumers' welfare. But such a principle is not practical and in the real world is probably observed rarely if ever.

9

that supplant them. The material results achieved also provide a basis for evaluating the working arrangements themselves. But the system's directors can hardly be expected to decide procedures on this basis alone. Thus different procedures might be more or less popular among different groups of the population. Where these varying public reactions are due to differences in material consequences, they should be considered by the system's directors in deciding how to value such consequences. But public reactions to different procedures might vary even apart from the material consequences; the procedures may simply be approved or disapproved for their own sake. When they are, even under Soviet socialism the public reactions would represent political data that the system's directors could scarcely ignore.

Then, too, such varying public reactions might occur because some procedures are more consistent than others with prevailing ideological precepts. Hence, if only on political grounds, the system's directors must be concerned with ideology. But it would be surprising if they should not be concerned about ideology in any case. So far as they are this too becomes a consideration in its own right, and without regard to politics. Again, the system's directors would be rather exceptional persons if sometimes they did not also appraise arrangements from still another standpoint—that is, simply in terms of the personal satisfactions they derive from administering the economy through some procedures rather than others.

In deciding on working arrangements, then, the system's directors are apt to be concerned not only with material but also with diverse nonmaterial aspects. Moreover, the latter may conflict with and even override the former. But here again we must be wary of trying at the outset to be too realistic. In economics, when seeking to perceive and understand behavior patterns, one usually takes material ends[5] as primary, at least provisionally. Even if such a supposition is not always impelling here, a principal aim of a study like this must be to see to what extent patterns of conduct reflect material ends.

Depending on the degree to which conduct conforms to the material ends sought, it is usually said to be more or less economically rational. We are thus led to ask, in respect to Soviet conduct regarding resource use, the cardinal question that arises in respect to economic conduct generally: In terms of what material ends and to what extent is such behavior economically rational? And in so asking, we may at once apply a familiar body of analysis. Thus, in order for resource use to be fully rational economically, theory teaches that a community must realize an "economic optimum": With available resources, values sought must be achieved to the maximum degree feasible. And, for the ends assumed here, the economic optimum must correspond to these standards. In practice, of course, this economic optimum is hardly attainable. But we may usefully inquire whether there are any systematic tendencies toward such a use of resources or, if not, whether there may be any systematic tendencies at all.

Actually, the optimum could be realized fully only if there were perfect knowledge. But through the working arrangements employed, the system's directors may be able to generate more or less of the required knowledge. The optimum therefore represents a conceptually meaningful although practically unattainable economic desideratum. The optimum usually is defined, however, without regard to the fact that different working arrangements can be

5. I hope there will be no misunderstanding if I refer in this way to values for material aspects, although such values may reflect more ultimate goals of any and all sorts. Also, for convenience, I shall refer to values for nonmaterial aspects of the working arrangements as nonmaterial values.

11

costly to administer. For this reason it is somewhat dubious even in principle, and this fact will have to be considered.

Conformity with an economic optimum means, hence in principle may be judged from, conformity with corresponding optimum conditions. As usually formulated, however, such conditions are institutionally quite abstract. It will often be preferable, therefore, to consider related operating principles with some institutional specificity. These I shall set forth as the inquiry proceeds, though all will be fairly familiar. I have already alluded to the theoretical debate on socialist resource use. The operating principles are either taken from or suggested by well-known theoretic planning schemata that have been elaborated chiefly in contributions to this debate.

In contemporary theory the concept of economic efficiency is variously construed, but most frequently, equity apart, it comes to the same thing as economic rationality, and is so understood here. Equity in turn refers to the optimal quality of income distribution in particular. The operating principles to be considered all bear especially on efficiency, hence are designated "efficiency rules." For convenience, however, I shall also refer in this way to conventional optimum conditions bearing on efficiency. Although they lack institutional specificity, such conditions are sometimes considered.[6]

But whether reference is to conventional optimum con-

6. While I shall refer only infrequently to optimum conditions in their most general form, the reader may wish to turn to pertinent theoretic writings. For summary surveys and bibliographies, see Abram Bergson, "Socialist Economics," in Howard S. Ellis, ed., *A Survey of Contemporary Economics* (Philadelphia, 1948); Kenneth E. Boulding, "Welfare Economics," in B. F. Haley, ed., *A Survey of Contemporary Economics, 2* (Homewood, Ill., 1952); E. J. Mishan, "A Survey of Welfare Economics, 1939–1959," *Economic Journal, 70* (1960), 197–265. These writings, especially the first, also discuss theoretic schemata for socialist planning, and cite literature on them.

ditions or operating rules, the principles represent an application to socialist resource use of a particular value theory. This is the marginal value theory accepted in the West. In the U.S.S.R., however, is it not the Marxian labor value principle that is applied? Indeed, is this not in itself one of the nonmaterial aspects considered? In any event, is it not simply on this account foreordained that resource use will often diverge markedly from an economic optimum? While economic thought in the U.S.S.R. has lately been in ferment, Soviet economists still affirm that Marxian value theory is superior to its "vulgar, bourgeois" rival. As has had to be considered, however, the labor theory is not always an incisive guide to resource use. Furthermore, under Soviet socialism the government has always been held to be the master rather than the servant of "economic laws." And among the laws in question is Marx's "law of value." As we proceed, we must try to apprehend to what extent Soviet conduct actually reflects this obsolete theory; though here, too, it is best not to prejudge the outcome.

Where the law of value is violated, we must also consider that resource use may be still further from the optimum than where it is observed; for when the government is the master rather than the servant of economic law, the alternative to the labor theory may not be marginal analysis—it may only be no theory.

In sum, if we apply abstract theoretic principles to the U.S.S.R., we should not be surprised if resource use often fails to conform to them. But this is still no argument for an alternative approach often employed in respect to the U.S.S.R.: to apply no principles, or at least none to speak of. After all, one needs some principles even to discover that none prevail. As to the particular principles applied here, I can say no more than has been said already: Their use seems to facilitate the inquiry. But of this the reader will be able to judge for himself.

13

As was implied, in the U.S.S.R. most but not all the means of production are publicly owned. Such differences regarding forms of ownership as have existed have not always been of much practical import, but in Chapter 2 I comment briefly on the nature of the different ownership forms, and on the extent to which they have prevailed in the more important sectors. Economically, the U.S.S.R. is characterized first of all by the predominant public ownership, but a hardly less distinctive feature is the bureaucratic apparatus concerned with resource use. In Chapter 3 I examine this aspect. After considering both ownership forms and the administrative apparatus, we shall be ready to deal more specifically with resource use. Hence in the chapters following, through the penultimate one (13), I consider different facets of resource use and inquire how they are dealt with in the U.S.S.R. I said above that, by seeking to discern and understand Soviet behavior patterns regarding resource use, we might gain insight into the economic merit of socialism. The reason must already be evident; and, as I proceed, implications regarding economic merit will also often be clear, but a final chapter is devoted to summary comment on this theme.

2 OWNERSHIP

       Although nationalization occurred primarily during the Revolution, public ownership had not approached its present levels after a decade of War Communism and New Economic Policy and has continued to vary in scope under the five-year plans. Moreover, forms of ownership other than public have occupied differing places in relation to each other at different times since the Revolution. In examining the nature and extent of various ownership forms, we must therefore consider not only present circumstances but those prevailing under the plans generally.

In the U.S.S.R. as elsewhere ownership may convey various rights, chiefly of use and disposal, limited by law. Because in the Soviet case the latter limitation acquires novel force, the existence of forms of ownership other than public is not always of much practical consequence. But if I elucidate forms here, substance will become clear as the inquiry into working arrangements proceeds in the chapters following.

Essentially, there have been three different ownership forms: public, where ownership is vested in the government; cooperative, where it is vested in a cooperative association, the members being either workers engaged in or consumers patronizing the organization; and private, where ownership is by private persons.

Where ownership has been public, usually administration has been so too, and this is even more generally true where ownership has been cooperative or private. To this rule there is one main exception: the ownership of land, including mineral deposits, forest reserves, etc., is, and ever since the Revolution has been, vested exclusively in the government. Cooperative and private producers have been able to operate only because the government has made available for their use on appropriate terms necessary publicly owned land.

In order to gauge the scope of different forms of ownership in industry (to consider that sector first) we may refer to available data on output of corresponding organizations (Table 2.1). From this standpoint, public ownership has

TABLE 2.1.

Industrial Production by Type of Organization, U.S.S.R.
(percentages)

	1928	1937	1950	1960
Public organizations	69.4	90.3	91.8	97
Cooperatives	13.0	9.5	8.2	3
Private producers	17.6	0.2	. . .[a]	. . .
Total	100.0	100.0	100.0	100

Source: Narkhoz, 1960, p. 213.

a. Here and in later tables an ellipsis (. . .) indicates that the figures are negligible.

16

long been predominant, and in the course of time has become increasingly so. Both cooperatives (in this case largely of producers) and private producers functioned in 1928, and in terms of output were almost equally important. But soon thereafter the latter came to be represented by a zero in the official reports, and since then the dwindling residual share of industry not accounted for by public organizations has been in the hands of cooperatives alone. The residual share has fallen, for one reason, because of the relatively limited expansion of the output of organizations that were initially cooperatives. Especially in recent years, however, the role of cooperatives has also declined because of their transfer to public ownership. In consequence, by the end of 1960 producers' cooperatives had practically ceased to exist in Soviet industry.

Bearing in mind the public ownership of land, we may judge the relative importance of different ownership forms in agriculture from areas sown by different kinds of organizations (Table 2.2). On the eve of the plans private producers—here individual peasant households—were still almost unchallenged. The era of the peasant farm was to be short-lived, however, for in January 1930 the government made its famous decision on wholesale collectivization, and soon thereafter the role of the peasant farm became inconsequential. As a result of the annexation of new territories, during 1939–45 the peasant holding again assumed importance, but more recently it has been reduced to negligible proportions.

In the U.S.S.R. the collective farm (*kolkhoz*) that prevails in agriculture is often referred to as if it were *sui generis,* but legally it is a form of producers' cooperative. An integral feature, however, is the subsidiary farm plot of limited size, most often one-quarter hectare (one hectare = 2.471 acres), that is made available to a member household for its own use. On this plot the household may also raise its own

17

TABLE 2.2.

Sown Area in U.S.S.R. by Type of Farm Holding
(percentages)

	1928	1937	1940	1950	1955	1961
State farms; other government farm undertakings	1.5	9.0	8.8	10.9	15.8	42.6
Collective farms	1.2	85.7	78.3	82.7	80.2	54.1
Subsidiary holdings of collective farm households	1.0	3.7	3.0	4.0	3.1	2.1
Subsidiary holdings of wage earners and salaried workers	. . .	0.8	0.5	1.1	0.9	1.2
Peasant farms	96.2	0.8	9.4	1.3	. . .	. . .
Total	100.0	100.0	100.0	100.0	100.0	100.0

Sources: Gosplan, *Itogi vypolneniia vtorogo piatiletnego plana razvitiia narodnogo khoziaistva Soiuza S.S.R.* (Moscow, 1939), p. 92; *Narkhoz, 1956,* p. 116; *Narkhoz, 1961,* p. 316. Subsidiary holdings of wage earners and salaried workers for 1937 are calculated from 1938 data in Naum Jasny, *The Socialized Agriculture of the U.S.S.R.* (Stanford, Calif., 1949), p. 48.

livestock, although the number of heads of each type is also limited—for example, in grain regions, the member household may hold only one cow, no more than two calves, and so on. No limit is specified for rabbits.[1]

The collective farm already existed on the eve of the five-year plans, but until January 1930 it occupied only a limited place. After that date it became consequential. Thus collective farms in 1937 tilled 85.7 per cent of the sown area. They have continued to play a major role, although the government has operated its own farms since before 1928, chiefly through an organization formed especially for this purpose, the state farm (*sovkhoz*). While these have long operated on a limited scale, they recently have come much to the fore, chiefly under the New Land Program for the

1. The collective farm historically has been organized in diverse ways. I refer exclusively to the *artel'*, which has long been the only one in extensive use.

wholesale plowing of previously untilled land, which was initiated in 1954. In the last few years the state farm has gained importance simply through the conversion of collective farms in older areas. Public farms have also been operated as subsidiary enterprises of organizations engaged primarily in nonagricultural fields.

While the private peasant has vanished from the scene, private ownership has continued on the collective farm household's subsidiary plot. Depending on the government's policy, such ownership has varied in extent, but in terms of sown area it has always been limited and recently has tended to decline. To some extent private ownership has also continued elsewhere, particularly on small plots worked by employees of state farms and other government workers.

In the foregoing we have characterized different forms of agricultural ownership in terms of sown area. In gauging the roles of the diverse forms, we must also consider holdings of other assets, particularly livestock, for the relative roles depend to a marked degree on the yardstick used. For example, although the subsidiary plots of collective farm households represent but a small fraction of the total sown area, the households raise on these plots a good part of the livestock herds of the U.S.S.R. Because there are so many households, even the small holdings of each household become consequential in the aggregate (Table 2.3). The share of Soviet livestock herds owned by the collective farm households reached its peak long ago and, while it has fluctuated since, lately it has been on the decline. But such holdings still represent one of the most important survivals of private ownership of the means of production in the U.S.S.R.

There is no need to explore machinery holdings, but it should be observed that machinery generally is held and operated by the collective as well as by the state farm. This has only been true, however, since March 1958. Before that date the larger machines were held by a government organ-

TABLE 2.3.

Livestock Herds in U.S.S.R. by Type of Farm Holding
(million head)

	SUMMER 1928			JANUARY 1, 1938			JANUARY 1, 1951			JANUARY 1, 1962		
	Cattle	Hogs	Sheep and Goats	Cattle	Hogs	Sheep and Goats	Cattle	Hogs	Sheep and Goats	Cattle	Hogs	Sheep and Goats
State farms; other government farm enterprises	n.a.[a]	n.a.	n.a.[a]	5.3	4.1	8.4	3.9	3.4	8.7	21.4	19.3	41.1
Collective farms	0.2	0.1	0.2	14.8	6.3	22.7	28.1	12.3	68.3	36.8	30.1	68.0
Subsidiary holdings of collective farm households	0.8	0.3	0.8	25.1	12.8	30.7	18.3	6.3	16.2	14.7	10.9	22.2
Peasant farms; workers' plots; other	69.5[b]	25.6[b]	145.7[b]	5.7	2.5	4.8	6.8	2.4	5.8	9.2	6.4	13.1
Total	70.5	26.0	146.7	50.9	25.7	66.6	57.1	24.4	99.0	82.1	66.7	144.4

Sources: Nancy Nimitz, *Statistics of Soviet Agriculture*, RAND RM-1250 (May 7, 1954), p. 43; Jasny, *Socialized Agriculture*, p. 789; Harry Schwartz, *Russia's Soviet Economy* (New York, 1950), p. 325; *Narkhoz, 1956*, pp. 129–30; *Narkhoz, 1961*, pp. 382–83. "Peasant farms; workers' plots; other" calculated as a residual for 1928, 1951, and 1962. "State farms; other government farm enterprises" calculated as a residual for 1938.

a. Here and in later tables "n.a." indicates that the data are not available or not applicable.

b. Including state farms, etc.

ization, the machine-tractor station (MTS), which serviced the collective farm on a contractual basis. Under the law of March 1958, which initiated the transfer of MTS machinery to the collective farm, the MTS was not fully liquidated, but was converted into a repair-technical station (RTS), which serviced the collective farm in the more limited way that its name implies. But through another reorganization announced on February 21, 1961, the RTS in turn was absorbed by a newly created All-Union Farm Machinery Association. Through local associations, including collective farm and state farm representatives, this agency now provides repair services formerly performed by the MTS. It also has other responsibilities regarding provision of machinery and supplies to agriculture.

On the eve of the plans, railway transport was entirely in the hands of the government, and so it has remained.[2] Most other forms of public transport have also been predominantly under government ownership throughout, although at least in the early years private enterprise functioned on a very modest scale, especially in carting.

In retail trade, the private middleman was still of some consequence in 1928, but soon thereafter he ceased to appear in the official reports on sales. It is to these data that we must turn in order to appraise ownership forms in this sphere (Table 2.4).[3] The figures for private trade probably represent only sales by professional middlemen, hence exclude those made by peasants in the bazaars that were an inevitable concomitant of the peasant agriculture of the time.

2. Actually, over two-thirds of the Russian railway mileage belonged to the government even under tsarism, and the balance was nationalized soon after the Bolsheviks seized power.

3. In January 1961 the Soviet government instituted a monetary reform under which one new ruble was given the value of ten old rubles. The figures in Table 4 are in terms of new rubles but generally, unless otherwise indicated, monetary data cited in this study are in terms of rubles of the date to which they refer.

TABLE 2.4.

Retail Sales in the U.S.S.R. by Trade Outlet
(billions of rubles)

	All Outlets	Government Shops	Cooperative Shops	Cooperative Commission Trade	Collective Farm Markets	Private Outlets
1928	1.54	0.25	0.93	...	...	0.36
1932	4.79	1.46	2.58	...	0.75	...
1937	14.37	9.28	3.31	...	1.78	...
1940	20.42	12.81	4.70	...	2.91	...
1950	40.88	26.11	9.85	...	4.92	...
1955	55.08	34.73	14.97	0.49	4.89	...
1961	84.99	56.84	23.37	0.86	3.91	...

Sources: TSU, *Sovetskaia torgovlia* (Moscow, 1956), pp. 14, 24, 179; Gosplan, *Itogi vypolneniia vtorogo piatiletnego plana* . . . (Moscow, 1939), p. 107; *Narkhoz, 1960,* pp. 673 ff.; *Narkhoz, 1961,* pp. 629 ff.

Soviet official figures of "retail sales," which relate primarily to transfers of foodstuffs and manufactures, have in recent years also included transfers of some services, particularly custom manufacture and repair work. Especially between 1928 and later years, the figures vary in the extent to which intrarural sales are included, and also in other ways. Then, too, the official figures include, in addition to sales to households, appreciable marketings to organizations like collective farms and education and health care institutions. All figures are in post-January 1, 1961, rubles.

With the initiation of wholesale collectivization this trade too was soon extinguished. In the process, however, it was replaced by the collective farm market, familiar to all tourists in the U.S.S.R. As we shall see (Chapters 4 and 9), both the collective farms and their members have had to turn over much of their produce to the government, but after meeting these and other requirements they have been allowed to dispose of any surpluses in this market. The collective farm market, thus exemplifying both cooperative and private trade, is found not only in rural but extensively in urban localities. Although it has occupied only a relatively limited and indeed, lately, even declining place in retail trade, it is almost exclusively a supplier of foodstuffs. Hence in this area it is more consequential than its share in total sales might suggest.

While collective farm sales in the collective farm market exemplify cooperative ownership in retail trade, other cooperative organizations, chiefly of consumers but in some degree also of producers, play a much greater role. Indeed, on the eve of the plans such organizations (in the official reports used here they alone are designated as cooperatives, and unless otherwise indicated I adhere to the same usage) conducted the bulk of retail trade. Yet public organizations were already functioning here too, and in the course of time they came to overshadow all others, including the cooperatives. In comparison with the latter, public organizations gained ground progressively, but their predominance dates from October 1935, when the government nationalized all shops of the consumers' cooperatives in urban localities, and decreed that thenceforth such cooperatives should operate only in rural localities. Recently, however, the consumers' cooperatives have again been allowed to conduct some retail trade in cities. Among other things, since 1953 they have been permitted to conduct trade on a commission basis in the urban collective farm market and elsewhere on behalf of collective farms and collective farm members.

While conducting retail trade, both public organizations and cooperatives have also engaged extensively in wholesale operations, but the private middleman, before his extinction, conducted little wholesale trade. Reference is to trade in processed foods and manufactures. In agricultural procurements, in 1928 all three forms of enterprise were active and each on some scale; but here, too, the private middleman was soon eliminated, while public organizations soon

23

The Economics of Soviet Planning

became predominant and have remained so ever since. The cooperatives, however, still play a role, especially in the procurement of eggs, vegetables, and certain other crops.

In foreign trade the government has maintained a monopoly throughout in theory and, except in the earliest years, also in practice. The cooperatives seemingly have also participated in a small way.

Housing is usually thought of more as a means of consumption than as a means of production, but it should be observed that here, too, private ownership has prevailed throughout the period of the plans, and on a large scale. In the country, at least among private and collective farmers, housing almost always has been and still is owned by its occupants. In the city, private ownership of housing intended primarily for own use has also been permitted, and such housing has constituted a major though varying part of the total available urban housing space throughout (Table 2.5).

TABLE 2.5.

Urban Housing Space by Ownership, U.S.S.R.
(percentages)

	1926	1940	1950	1955	1961
Public and cooperative	47.7	63.4	66.3	67.1	61.6
Private	52.3	36.6	33.7	32.9	38.4
Total	100.0	100.0	100.0	100.0	100.0

Sources: Narkhoz, 1958, p. 641; Narkhoz, 1961, p. 614.

The bulk of other housing in the cities has been publicly owned, but cooperatives too have had a limited role. Moreover, until 1937 the government permitted cooperatives to operate much public housing on the government's behalf.

In construction, the government throughout has been predominant, but so far as other forms of ownership have prevailed in regard to current productive activities in different sectors, they have also played some role in respect to

24

construction. Among other things, farm buildings were constructed by private peasants while the latter still held sway, and since then they have been constructed by collective farms. In housing, the government usually has allowed and sometimes has encouraged private building.

3 THE ADMINISTRATIVE APPARATUS

The bureaucratic apparatus concerned with resource use in the U.S.S.R. is extraordinarily intricate. Under the five-year plans, and especially of late, it has also been subject to very frequent change. Our concern here is with essentials, some of which will be elaborated in following chapters.

The apparatus has been formed from many component organizations, but the general organs of government have necessarily been of cardinal importance. The U.S.S.R. is nominally a federation of republics, but the governments of these republics represent only one of several strata in a complex political hierarchy.[1] Thus at the apex is the central or all-union government, with authority extending over the

1. At present there are fifteen republics: the Russian (by far the largest), Ukrainian, Uzbek, Kazakh, Belorussian, Georgian, Azer-

whole of the U.S.S.R. Subordinate to this are the governments of the different republics, each holding sway in the republic concerned. Within each republic there are still further political strata of a local sort. Most often, although not always, the highest of these is at the level of the province (*oblast'*), while under the provincial government is that of the district (*raion*). Subordinate to the latter are political authorities concerned with towns, villages, and hamlets. A city has its own government, which, depending on its size, may be directly subordinate to that of the province or even the republic.

Virtually all the different general organs constituting these diverse governments are in some degree concerned with resource use, but from this standpoint the most important by far are bodies wielding executive power: in the all-union government, the Council of Ministers; at the republican level, the body with the same name; and at the local level, the executive committee. Headed by a chairman, the all-union council has a diverse membership, including chiefly persons occupying senior posts in subordinate organizations. Among the latter have been not only the inevitable ministries or executive departments, but usually various commissions, committees, subsidiary councils, and the like which also have served the council in diverse ways. However, not all persons directing organizations of the latter sort have had seats on the council. The republican council is constituted similarly, and so too is the local executive committee, although especially in the case of the latter the number of executive departments, commissions, etc. is relatively limited. In addition to the executive organs, which are of chief interest here, there are the corresponding legis-

baidzhan, Lithuanian, Moldavian, Latvian, Kirgiz, Tadzhik, Armenian, Turkmen, and Esthonian. On governmental structure in the U.S.S.R., the standard work is Merle Fainsod, *How Russia Is Ruled* (rev. ed. Cambridge, Mass., 1963).

The Economics of Soviet Planning

lative bodies: at the all-union and republican levels, the Supreme Soviet; and at local levels, the soviet. Formally, appointments to the executive authority at each level are made by the corresponding legislative body, while the latter is constituted nominally by direct election.

I refer here to recent times, but the governmental organs have been much the same throughout the five-year plans, except that before 1946 the Council of Ministers in the all-union and republican governments was known as the Council of People's Commissars, and individual executive departments were designated correspondingly. Also, the Supreme Soviet came into existence only with the constitutional change of 1936. Previously the legislature at both the all-union and republican levels had been the indirectly elected Congress of Soviets. In the course of time, the nature and comparative importance of different local government bodies have also varied. Although generally such changes are of little consequence here, it should be observed that since November 1962 the local governmental structure has been in process of substantial reorganization. Thus rural districts have been extensively amalgamated, while separate soviets and related organs are being established at the levels of the province and the district to deal with affairs of the industrial and agricultural population. This reorganization of local governmental organs is but one of many sweeping changes which have recently been introduced into the Soviet bureaucratic structure. Other changes will be discussed below. The reforms in good part implement proposals made in a report by Khrushchev to the party Central Committee in November 1962.

AGENCIES FOR OPERATIONAL CONTROL

The general organs of government, so far as they have had to deal with resource use, have been concerned

28

with economic activity almost everywhere, though particularly where use has been made of publicly owned productive assets. In overseeing this sphere, they have employed a host of additional organizations. At the highest level, most of these have been agencies like those referred to above: executive departments, committees, commissions, councils, and similar bodies immediately subordinate to the general executive organs at different levels of government. Very broadly, however, these organizations, together with still others that have served them, have been of two rather different types: on the one hand, those which on behalf of the general executive organs have exercised operational control over publicly owned productive assets in different economic sectors and regions; on the other, those which on behalf of the general executive organs have borne functional and often staff responsibilities.

To begin with the former group of organizations, among the economic sectors involved, industry has been especially important. Here the bureaucratic structure has changed hardly less than that for Soviet economic administration generally, but until 1932 practically all publicly owned industry was administered through a hierarchy of economic councils paralleling the governmental one just described. Thus at the apex was the Supreme Economic Council of the U.S.S.R., or VSNKH.[2] Subordinate to this were corresponding republican economic councils, and subordinate to them were still other local economic councils. At each level the economic council was also under the corresponding general executive organ of government, but according to a principle observed in the U.S.S.R. in such circumstances, subordination was primarily to the economic council at the next higher governmental level.

At each governmental level, the corresponding economic

2. For the expansion of this and other abbreviations see the Abbreviations list, above, p. xvii.

council administered publicly owned production assets
either with or without the mediation of a subordinate economic council, but in either case still further bureaucratic
strata were used. These varied in the course of time, but under relatively perfected arrangements that prevailed toward
the end of the period in question, at least at the all-union
and republican levels, the economic council itself usually
was subdivided into "chief administrations" (*glavki*) for the
direction of different industrial branches and regions. Subordinate to each *glavk* there might be additional strata consisting of agencies of diverse sorts expressly established to
deal with successively smaller industrial or regional spheres.
The most important of these different kinds of agencies
were the "combine" (*ob'edinenie*) and the "trust" (*trest*).
Ultimately in any case the individual plant or mine was
placed in charge of still another organization, formed for
this purpose—the government "enterprise" (*predpriiatie*).

The all-union VSNKH and corresponding republican and
local economic councils were liquidated in January 1932,
and various new superior administrative organs were established that continued to prevail until industry was again
reorganized in a wholesale way in May 1957. The two chief
kinds of organs that replaced the economic councils were
the "all-union" ministry and the "union-republican" ministry. In both cases, either for the U.S.S.R. as a whole or for
a region, a ministry in the all-union government administered some or all of the enterprises in one branch of industry; but in the case of the all-union ministry this was done
without—and in the case of the union-republican ministry
it was done with—the help of corresponding ministries at
the republican level.

While these two kinds of organization prevailed generally, the number of ministries of either sort changed in the
course of time. Thus initially there were only three; but
these were progressively split up, and by the early postwar

period there were as many as 33. Subsequently the number fluctuated, but early in 1957 there were 28 all-union and union-republican industrial ministries. In this way the initial three that had held sway over such grand spheres as heavy industry, light industry, and the timber industry were in time supplanted by ministries concerned with restricted sectors like the machine-tool industry, transport machine building, automobile industry, and coal industry.

There were also shifts between the two kinds of ministries. Thus the all-union ministry was sharply on the decline and the union-republican sharply on the increase for a period before May 1957.

The replacement of the economic councils by the two types of ministries still left the individual plant or mine in the hands of the enterprise, and each continued to be so thereafter. Inevitably, there were changes in the intermediate links. Most importantly, as the number of ministries increased, the need for further coordinating links declined. In the course of time these also evolved in character, but the ministry most often came to manage with the *glavk* alone, the latter now a division of the ministry rather than of the economic council. Occasionally the ministry might even dispense with the *glavk;* on the other hand, it sometimes used not only the *glavk* but also another body, the survivor of the trust that had prevailed under VSNKH.

Through these arrangements, operational control was exercised over the bulk of publicly owned industry. However, some industrial enterprises were subordinated either to republican ministries, which prevailed where there was no counterpart at the all-union level, or to executive departments in local governments.

As a result of the reorganization of May 1957, the all-union and union-republican ministries have been liquidated, in their turn, and, curiously, have been replaced by an organization reminiscent of the economic councils of the early 1930s: a new regional economic council (*sovnark-hoz*). Subordinate to the Council of Ministers in the republic in which it is located, the new council administers publicly owned industry within the limits of the region assigned to it. As before, the individual plant or mine is immediately the responsibility of an enterprise, but different enterprises in a given branch are now grouped under a corresponding division of the council.

Under the reform of May 1957, all-union and union-republican ministries were to be liquidated only in the course of time, but by December 1962 only two such ministries remained: that for medium machine building, which reportedly is concerned with atomic matters, and that for electric power.[3] Since the reform was directed at the all-union and union-republican ministries, for a time it left largely untouched the arrangements previously prevailing whereby enterprises were subordinated to republican ministries and local executive departments; but recently much of this industry too has been transferred to the councils. As a result, in late 1962 the councils controlled some 85 per cent of the output of all industry in the U.S.S.R.

The new form of organization, even as it has been extended in scope, has been subject to the inevitable changes. Thus, as initially established, each regional council usually administered industry within the limits of a province. As a result, the councils were numerous; in the latter part of 1961 they numbered 101. In late 1962, however, the regional scope of the council was generally much increased, and their number correspondingly was reduced. It is now 47.

As already stated, the regional council is subordinate to the Council of Ministers in the republic where it is located, but since 1960 in the three largest republics (the Russian,

3. In March 1963, both ministries were transformed into "state production committees" and made subordinate to the newly formed Supreme Economic Council of the U.S.S.R. See below, pp. 33, 39.

32

Ukrainian, and Kazakh) it has been more immediately sub-ordinate to a republican economic council that was estab-lished in that year. The republican council has had diverse functions, but a principal one has been, on behalf of the Council of Ministers of the republic concerned, to coordi-nate the work of regional economic councils. Then, too, in accord with a resolution of the party Central Committee in November 1962, the government has now established a similar agency at the all-union level, the Council of the National Economy of the U.S.S.R. This agency also has various functions, but—as symbolized by its union-republi-can status—a major one apparently is to oversee the work of republican and regional economic councils.[4]

The Council of the National Economy of the U.S.S.R. is not the last of the superior coordinating agencies recently created, for on March 13, 1963, the government decreed the formation of the Supreme Economic Council of the U.S.S.R. It has thus revived the name of the highest author-ity administering industry up to 1932, and has also granted the new agency supreme power in this sphere. Thus under the Council of Ministers the new Supreme Council in re-spect of industry even reigns over the U.S.S.R. Council of the National Economy. The authority of the former agency, however, also extends to construction. In view of other re-sponsibilities to appear, the Supreme Economic Council might itself be considered a general executive organ of gov-ernment, rather than simply an agency for operational con-trol.

4. Before 1960 the need for an intermediate republican organ to coordinate regional councils in eleven of the smaller republics was obviated, since there was only one regional council to begin with. More-over, in a twelfth republic (Uzbek S.S.R.), instead of creating a new intermediate council the government found it expedient to merge five economic councils that had previously functioned there. More recently, the government has consolidated into one the four councils in the four Central Asian republics.

While the enterprise remains the entity at the lowest level of the bureaucratic structure administering industry, recently there has been a tendency to group enterprises into a new agency, the "firm." The enterprises that are so grouped frequently are in the same locality. Often a successor to the old trust, the firm is nevertheless somewhat novel in that several small enterprises are placed under the tutelage of a single leading one. The management of the latter administers the affairs of the firm generally.

As regards the bureaucratic arrangements through which the general executive organs of government have exercised operational control over publicly owned sectors other than industry, it may suffice to say that usually these have been broadly similar to those that prevailed in industry between 1932 and 1957. Thus operational control has been exercised most often through an executive department of one of the diverse kinds then found in industry: the all-union, union-republican, and republican ministries, and the corresponding local government department. Also, where operational control has been exercised through a ministry, the ministry itself, at least in recent years, has often come to be subdivided into branch and regional departments like the industrial *glavki,* and the government enterprise charged with administration of some restricted individual economic activity, e.g. a farm, shop, etc., has been subordinate to all.

The arrangements have often differed among sectors, and here, too, change has been the rule rather than the exception, but we need only observe here that, as a result of a reorganization initiated by the party Central Committee in March 1962, state farms are now subordinate to a rather novel administrative structure, which is also used to direct the affairs of collective farms. This apparatus is discussed below when I come to authorities concerned with the latter. It should be noted that the government enterprise has often varied from sector to sector, and in a few instances the differences have been consequential. Also, the enterprise has sometimes had a special name. For agriculture, I have already referred to the state farm and the machine-tractor station. There is also the trading "corporation," found in foreign trade.[5]

FUNCTIONAL AGENCIES

We have been considering one type of agency through which general organs of government at different levels have directed the use of publicly owned productive assets: those agencies through which operational control has been exercised over different economic sectors and regions. The second type is the agency with responsibilities more nearly of functional, and frequently also of staff, kind. One of the chief organizations in question has been mainly responsible for the formulation of the five-year and other economic plans. With a regional structure paralleling that of the government generally, Gosplan throughout the period of the five-year plans has been subordinate to and has formulated plans under the direction and for the approval of its corresponding general executive authority. At the all-union level, however, Gosplan has now been made subordinate also to the Supreme Economic Council that was formed in March 1963. At least, this is so in respect of its activities regarding industry and construction.[6]

5. The Soviet designation for this agency, *ob'edinenie*, might be translated as "combine," but here I follow accepted Western usage. In any event, I believe I am right in considering the agency more or less a counterpart of the government enterprise found elsewhere in the Soviet economy at the lowest bureaucratic level.

6. Gosplan has been the short form of reference for a number of different titles for the agency, the changes apparently being associated with changes in responsibilities. Its separate units at different governmental levels have also been variously named. At present, at the all-union level, the agency is the Gosudarstvennyi Komitet

While generally the main organization concerned with the formulation of plans in the U.S.S.R., Gosplan in recent years has experienced notable changes in its responsibilities. But for present purposes the complex shifts, which on several occasions were made only to be reversed soon after, are of limited interest. Indeed, there should be no loss if, unless otherwise explained, Gosplan is understood elliptically to include not only the entity so designated in the U.S.S.R. but diverse other organizations which at one time or another have shared with it responsibilities for plan formation.[7]

Planirovaniia SSSR, or the State Committee for Planning in the U.S.S.R.

Although Gosplan has been subordinated to the Supreme Economic Council in regard to industry and construction, one might think that it continues to be immediately responsible to the Council of Ministers in regard to the economy generally. Some Soviet sources, however, appear to imply the contrary. See *Current Digest* (February 12, 1964), pp. 3 ff.

7. The first reorganization occurred in December 1947, when responsibilities for the formulation of plans for materials supply were transferred from Gosplan to the new State Committee for Materials Supply (Gossnab). Responsibilities of Gossnab for consumers' goods were transferred to still another agency in 1951. But in 1953 both agencies were merged with Gosplan, and the latter once more formulated plans for materials supply along with those for the economy generally.

This it continued to do until 1955 when, under another reorganization, it was confined primarily to construction of long-term plans, while responsibility for formulation of annual plans (which, as we shall see, are, if anything, more consequential for operational purposes than those for longer periods) was placed in the hands of a new body, the State Economic Commission (Gosek). This rearrangement too, however, was soon reversed; for in 1957, in connection with the reorganization of industry, Gosek was transferred to Gosplan, and the latter once more was responsible for planning generally.

Still another reorganization took place in 1960, when responsibilities for construction of long-term plans were transferred from Gosplan to Gosekonomsovet, the State Scientific-Economic Council. But, as a

Administrative Apparatus

There have also been changes in the relation between Gosplan U.S.S.R. and the corresponding agencies at republican levels. Among other things, these organizations only recently have been endowed with a union-republican status, which makes the republican agencies formally subordinate to Gosplan U.S.S.R. For convenience, however, the entire structure of planning organizations that obtained before and has obtained since this reorganization will be referred to simply as Gosplan.

In addition to formulating plans, Gosplan has also been a continuing source of economic information and counsel for the over-all executive authorities. While it is organized regionally after the patterns that prevail for general government organs, in May 1961 new authorities were established to aid in the work of coordinating regional councils in major economic regions. These authorities were to report to Gosplan and to Gosekonomsovet, another agency then sharing with it responsibilities for plan formulation. Presumably they still report at least to the former.

Closely related to the task of plan formulation is that of compiling statistical data. Under the five-year plans major responsibilities for the latter work have been borne by an organization long known as the Central Statistical Administration.[8] At one time under Gosplan, the Central Statis-

---

result of decisions taken by the party Central Committee in November 1962, Gosekonomsovet has now been abolished and Gosplan once more has responsibility for long-term planning. Although the contrary has been reported, I believe Gosplan still has primary responsibility also for formulating the annual plans. This task, however, is shared with other agencies, including the new Council of the National Economy of the U.S.S.R. and corresponding republican organs.

8. For Tsentral'noe Statisticheskoe Upravlenie, or TSU, the name of the agency since 1939 and also before 1930; but in the period between 1930 and 1939 it was known as Central Administration of National-Economic Accounting, for Tsentral'noe Upravlenie Narodno-Khoziaistvennogo Ucheta, or TSUNKHU.

37

tical Administration has for some years been immediately subordinate to the Council of Ministers. I refer to the arrangements at the all-union level. As with Gosplan, there are also republican and local entities, each subordinate to the corresponding general executive authority.

Among the organizations now under consideration, an important place must also be accorded to several concerned with credit and finance. One of the chief of these is the Ministry of Finance, which has long been a union-republican ministry. On behalf of the all-union and republican ministerial councils and corresponding local authorities, it oversees government financial affairs generally and the inevitable government budgetary process in particular. Another major agency concerned with credit and finance is the State Bank. During some periods subordinate to the U.S.S.R. Ministry of Finance, but now immediately subject to the U.S.S.R. Council of Ministers, the State Bank through a nationwide organization has in effect served as banker to the economy generally. It has had special responsibilities, however, for short-term credit. Long subordinate to the Ministry of Finance but also deserving separate mention is a complex of other banking institutions operating in restricted spheres. Among these have been diverse banks concerned mainly with long-term finance in the economy. Until 1959 the most important of these was the Industrial Bank of the U.S.S.R., or the Prombank, especially concerned with industry. In 1959 all were merged into a new institution, the all-union Bank for Financing Capital Investment, or Stroibank, which serves the economy generally. Reference should also be made to the network of banks where the public hold savings accounts.

Problems of labor and wages have also been the concern of special agencies, including at one time a union-republic Ministry of Labor and most recently a Committee on Labor and Wages attached to the all-union Council of Ministers. The latter was established in 1955 in association with one of the reorganizations of Gosplan. Necessarily, organizations administering education often have been concerned with these problems, but among these it may suffice to mention another committee attached to the all-union Council—that on Professional-Technical Education. Formed in 1959, this committee appears to bear some responsibilities for vocational training such as were once exercised by the Chief Administration (later Ministry) of Labor Reserves. Another committee, formed in 1955, is that for the Coordination of Scientific Research. While this has responsibilities corresponding to its name, in the course of time general executive organs of government have also employed other bodies to aid them in the realm of research and technology. Thus, since the industrial reorganization a number of special committees have been formed at the all-union level, apparently for the most part in behalf of the all-union Council of Ministers, to coordinate activities concerning technology in different industries. Although still concerned primarily with technology, these committees have been endowed with increased responsibilities since November 1962. Interestingly, the committees are often headed by former industrial ministers. In March 1963, however, these committees, together with a number of others concerned with economic affairs, were made subordinate to either Gosplan or the Supreme Economic Council.

Also to be mentioned here are various organizations whose chief responsibilities have been the control over the use of public property and the implementation of governmental decisions. For some time before November 1962 these tasks had been performed chiefly by the all-union Commission of Soviet Control, an organization under the all-union Council of Ministers, and at inferior levels by corresponding bodies. More recently, however, control has been entrusted to joint party-governmental bodies, of which the chief is a new Party-State Control Committee.

Then, too, there are the agencies which have been concerned with internal security. Responsibilities in this sphere have been variously organized at different times; suffice it to say that throughout there have been all-union and republican authorities with regional and local offices, including "special sections" in most important economic agencies and often even in individual enterprises. Although we cannot inquire here into the functioning of these agencies, their ubiquitous presence must be kept in mind. No doubt it has been so kept by those immediately responsible for administration of resource use in the U.S.S.R. By all accounts, however, the internal security agencies have suffered a decline in influence since Stalin's death on March 5, 1953. Of course, through their notorious "correctional labor," the agencies have themselves been engaged in production, and at one time certainly on a large scale.

APPARATUS FOR THE PUBLIC SECTOR FURTHER CONSIDERED

In addition to general organs of government, reference has been made to two types of government organizations concerned with the use of publicly owned productive assets: those which have exercised operational control over such assets within different economic sectors and regions, and those with responsibilities of a functional and often also of a staff character. Within their respective sectoral and regional spheres, organizations of the first type have also participated in tasks which for the economy as a whole have been the responsibility of agencies of the second type. By the same token, depending on the volume of such work performed by organizations exercising operational control, those with functional responsibilities have themselves had a varying burden to bear. The overlapping of function has been pervasive but perhaps is nowhere exemplified better than in the sphere of plan formulation. Thus Gosplan has always had major responsibilities in this sphere, but agencies exercising operational control necessarily have also participated substantially. The comparative roles of Gosplan and the latter, however, have varied. For example, responsibilities regarding plan formulation, which before the industrial reorganization of May 1957 were borne by the industrial ministries, often devolved thereafter on Gosplan, not on the regional economic councils that replaced them. But this trend appears to have been reversed with the formation of republican and all-union councils of the national economy. The all-union council, at least, now shares in an important way with Gosplan the task of plan formulation. Then, too, the Supreme Economic Council not only is to be the highest authority in the U.S.S.R. to exercise operational control over industry and construction, but it has also been endowed with plenary powers in these spheres. Hence it even has responsibility to coordinate the relevant work of agencies engaged in plan formulation, including Gosplan itself.

I have also said that the responsibilities of the functional agencies have often been of a staff character. To what extent this has been so is not always clear, but there have sometimes been significant changes in this regard. The most important developments again concern Gosplan. Specifically, until May 1957 Gosplan essentially had only a staff character, but it then acquired operational responsibilities, and these it still retains in some spheres, particularly price fixing.

Government organizations administering publicly owned productive assets have been classified thus far in terms of the general nature of their responsibilities. I alluded above to the budget of the Soviet government. Discussion of this feature is postponed, but if it is understood that there is a budget, and moreover that to a great extent revenues are broadly of a conventional sort, we may also classify these government organizations in another useful way. On the one hand, some are budgetary, in that they are supported largely out of the general government budgetary revenues. On the other, some are extrabudgetary, in that they are largely self-financing, their expenditures being met for the most part from revenues derived from their own current productive activities. At least, such is ordinarily expected to be the case.

All general government organs that have been considered have been of the former sort. So also have been all the organizations with functional responsibilities, except the State Bank. Among agencies exercising operational control, those at superior levels usually have been budgetary and those at inferior levels extrabudgetary. In industry, for example, under the arrangements prevailing before 1957 the ministry invariably, and the *glavk* usually, were budgetary, while organizations below the level of the *glavk* were not. Under the arrangements prevailing since 1957, republican and regional economic councils and their branch divisions have been budgetary. Government enterprises, as before, have been extrabudgetary.

While useful generally, the foregoing scheme incidentally provides the basis for a distinction which might otherwise be difficult to make, that, in the economic sphere, between government organizations which may be viewed as institutions constituting the government as such, and economic agencies acting on their behalf in the conduct of economic affairs. Thus budgetary organizations may be viewed as of the former kind, and extrabudgetary as of the latter. Indeed, I do no more here than record a principle which is observed by Soviet authorities themselves. Exceptions, however, are sometimes made. Thus an enterprise may be very largely or entirely supported from government funds and yet not be considered a government institution as such. The outstanding case in point is the machine-tractor station, which, while it existed, was supported primarily from general revenues in the government budget. Also, the State Bank is self-financing but seems to be considered a government institution.[9]

If in the U.S.S.R. lower level agencies exercising operational control are extrabudgetary, this is not accidental. Rather, the arrangement prevails as part of a larger system of economic practice, the system of *khozraschet* (for *khoziaistvennyi raschet,* "economic calculation") which has long been employed in the U.S.S.R. and which Soviet economists stress as a cardinal feature in the economic sphere. We shall often have occasion to refer to this aspect.

Reference thus far has been to diverse governmental agencies concerned with publicly owned productive assets in the U.S.S.R. Although these agencies have been primarily responsible for the administration of such assets, an account of the bureaucratic apparatus for dealing with this task must also refer to the trade union. The resemblance to corresponding Western entities in this case is only formal, but trade unions have been permitted in the U.S.S.R. to participate in diverse ways in the administration of matters concerning labor and wages. As with other organizations, the unions have had an elaborate bureaucratic structure of their own, ranging from the factory unit in a single enterprises to the All-Union Central Council of Trade Unions (VTSSPS), which oversees union affairs in the U.S.S.R. as a whole.

And last but hardly least, there is the Communist Party.

9. It may seem like circular reasoning generally to determine that an organization is a government institution because it is supported out of governmental budgetary revenues, but the latter revenues are clearly of a special nature, and this suffices for the distinction.

The system's directors have relied on this organization in seeking to impose their will everywhere, and the party has been appropriately organized to this end. With cells in individual offices, enterprises, and farms, there have usually been superior organs at successively higher levels paralleling those found among general organs of government. At the top has been the Presidium (since 1952; before then the supreme body was the Politburo) of the all-union Central Committee, the latter being nominally the creature of the all-union Congress. The parallelism between the party and governmental structure prevailed before the reorganization of the local governmental organs in November 1962, and has persisted since. Thus, just as with governmental organs, lower-level party agencies have been subdivided into two structures, one concerned with industrial and the other with agricultural affairs.

In using the party hierarchy to administer resource use in the public sector, the system's directors generally have found it expedient to employ it more as an instrument of control than as an apparatus with primary responsibilities. Recently, however, they have departed to some extent from this practice and have assigned to party officials executive responsibilities in party-governmental committees that form a portion of the newly constituted structure for administering agriculture.[10] Although not unprecedented, the reorganization of the all-union Commission of Soviet Control, together with its subordinate agencies, into a hierarchy of joint party-governmental agencies represents a similar variation from past practice.

ADMINISTRATION OF COOPERATIVE AFFAIRS

In the U.S.S.R. cooperatively or privately owned productive assets supposedly have been managed by corre-

10. See below, p. 46.

sponding entities, particularly enterprises of the producers'
cooperatives in industry, the collective farm in agriculture,
the consumers' cooperative enterprises in trade, and the private enterprise wherever the latter has functioned. Moreover, the party and the government supposedly "guide"
(*rukovodit'*), but do not "administer" (*upravliat'*) such
agencies.[11]

If we put aside for the present the question of the precise
relationship, no one will be surprised that general organs
of government have been concerned with cooperative and
private as well as public economic activities, that subordinate government organizations with functional responsibilities regarding publicly owned productive assets have
often had similar responsibilities regarding cooperatively
and privately owned assets, and that at higher levels governmental bodies exercising operational control over the
former in a given sector or region often have also supervised
in some degree the latter in the same sphere, although sometimes governmental agencies have been formed especially to
deal with nonpublic activities. And the party has been as
active with cooperative and private enterprise as with public.

Of particular interest are the arrangements that have prevailed regarding collectivized agriculture. Here, as elsewhere, resource use has been a continuing concern of
general organs of government and of subordinate agencies
with functional responsibilities. At the same time, among
organizations administering different sectors and regions,
until 1958 the task of overseeing collective farms was a chief
task of the union-republican Ministry of Agriculture. This
organization also had jurisdiction over the machine-tractor
station, which in itself was an instrument of control over
the collective farm. In 1958 the machine-tractor station was

11. Since land is formally the property of the government, it is only
other productive assets that are subject to other forms of ownership.

45

liquidated and its agricultural machinery transferred to the collective farm, but the new repair-technical station that was organized in its place continued to be subordinate to the Ministry of Agriculture.

In 1961, however, the task of supplying machinery to the collective farm, which had been vested in the Ministry of Agriculture, was transferred to new farm machinery associations established under the general executive organs at different governmental levels, and machinery-repair facilities were also transferred to the new agencies. Actually, even before 1961 the Ministry of Agriculture found its responsibilities for collective farm agriculture curtailed generally, a principal gainer in this sphere being Gosplan, and in that year this process was brought to its culmination when the ministry was reorganized into little more than a glorified extension service. Then, in March 1962, the party announced still another reorganization, and it is the entirely new apparatus thus created that directs collective farm agriculture. It also administers state farm agriculture, for a novel feature is that the two kinds of farms have been subordinated to the same agencies.

At the lowest level, these include the Interdistrict Territorial-Production Administration (TPU), which oversees the work of collective as well as state farms in an area assigned it, generally one comprising several governmental districts. Within each province the TPU is directed by a corresponding regional administration, while the latter is subordinate to a republican Ministry of Production and Procurement of Agricultural Products. And this entire network is itself subject to supervision by another more or less parallel one consisting of party-government committees. At the apex is the all-union Agricultural Committee.

In recognition of the cooperative nature of the collective farm, the TPU is still held to be an agency for "guidance," although it is designated an administration. Also, though

the TPU is run by a full-time staff, it has been endowed
with a "democratic" cast felt to be appropriate in the circumstances through attachment to it of a council consisting
of officials of collective and state farms as well as of local
party and governmental organs.

At one time, collective farms were themselves organized
through successive regional associations into an all-union
body, but these organizations have long been dormant, if
they have continued to exist at all.

As with the collective farms, so with producers' and consumers' cooperatives, economic conduct has been a subject
of continuing concern to government organs, but here all-
union, republican, and local cooperative bodies have had
a more substantial existence; and at least in the case of
the consumers' cooperatives these organizations, within limits permitted by the government, have at each level exercised operational control over subordinate bodies. At the
apex of this hierarchy is the Tsentrosoiuz, while at the base
is the individual cooperative. The latter, however, has sometimes administered more than one enterprise.

In the U.S.S.R. cooperatives of all sorts are formally organized according to principles that prevail in the West.
Among other things, officers supposedly are elected by the
membership. Although the resemblance to Western cooperatives nevertheless is only nominal, it is wrong to conclude
that all are therefore simply governmental enterprises under another name. In any case, as has been implied already
and will become clear, the alternative form is sometimes
consequential for resource use.

Especially of late, the bureaucratic apparatus concerned
with resource use in the U.S.S.R. has frequently changed.
What is the explanation? To inquire into each reorganization that has occurred would quickly take us beyond the
scope of this study, but without doing so it is not easy to
appraise them generally. Nevertheless, changing political

and economic circumstances manifestly must have been an important cause, and among these circumstances not the least is the death of Stalin. Also, the impact of these changes must often have been compounded so far as reorganizations serve in the U.S.S.R., as elsewhere, as a convenient means of disposing of incompetent or politically doubtful personnel, and as a device to create a suitable image of dynamic leadership. But with due allowance for all these aspects, obviously the system's directors have also been dissatisfied with resource use in the U.S.S.R. So they themselves have affirmed again and again, and there is no reason to doubt their word at this point. Evidently, too, the system's directors attach great importance to purely organizational ways of repairing deficiencies in this sphere. But resource use is a matter into which we must inquire more expressly in the following chapters, and the discussion there may illuminate more clearly such deficiencies as have prevailed. As it has turned out, the successive reorganizations often have also involved some redistribution of authority between superior and inferior agencies. But comment on the interesting question that is thus posed regarding the extent and import of such shifts in centralization and decentralization is also best postponed.

4 DISPOSITION OF CONSUMERS' GOODS

In inquiring further into working arrangements for resource use, I propose to begin with a facet with which the economic process usually is thought to culminate. In a modern society, supplies of goods that become available in any period may be disposed of in diverse ways, but some must be allocated to current consumption by the community. Suppose, provisionally, that in the U.S.S.R. the supplies of each good to be so disposed of have been determined. (Here and elsewhere, employment of this familiar device of abstraction may often make the discussion seem oddly incomplete, but it is unavoidable if we are to consider each facet of resource use separately.) Because of their physical nature, some goods will be of a collective kind, and hence must be made available to the community generally as free communal consumption. For the rest, however, the supplies will consist of consumers' goods, and for these

49

the task remains actually to distribute the amounts available among households. How is this accomplished?

One outstanding and familiar feature already is implied: money. Thus, if under the *khozraschet* system the government enterprise is more or less self-financing, obviously the cooperative and private enterprises are also. And for such arrangements money is a prerequisite. Hence, to a great extent, although by no means completely, consumers' goods are made available to households at established money "prices," while each household meets the resultant charges out of some money income at its disposal. By the same token, disposition of supplies becomes intertwined with determination of money income. For the present let us merely observe that the household receives a money income, and that this for the most part is earned, in the sense that it represents a return for productive services rendered.[1]

In the distribution of consumers' goods, where money is *not* used, some dispositions take the form of free communal consumption; for in the U.S.S.R. as elsewhere, along with collective goods some consumers' goods are distributed in this way. In fact, such dispositions have been made chiefly for provision of two familiar kinds of services: health care and education. Why in the U.S.S.R. these services have been supplied as free communal consumption is still an interesting question; so too is that concerning the precise manner in which the services have been distributed; for so far as supplies inevitably have fallen short of requirements at zero prices, some restrictions on household access to the services have been unavoidable. But both questions must be left to separate study.[2]

1. Strictly speaking, what counts here is not so much the household's money income but its money outlays on consumers' goods. The latter may differ from the former by savings and taxes, which though found in the U.S.S.R., need not now detain us.

2. It should be observed, however, that in the U.S.S.R. neither health care nor education has been provided entirely in the form of

Consumers' Goods

In addition to communal consumption, moneyless distribution has taken the form of earned income in kind,
including chiefly military subsistence, penal labor subsistence, and farm consumption of own production. Important as defense has been in the U.S.S.R., I cannot explore
here resource use in that sphere. I cannot say much about
penal labor either, although it may be observed that by all
accounts this is no longer as important as it was under
Stalin. Farm consumption of own production will be discussed in a later chapter.[3]

We are left with supplies made available at money prices.
These have been of diverse sorts and, money apart, there
have been differences in working arrangements used to distribute them, but the great bulk of such supplies have consisted of foodstuffs and manufactures, and I shall focus
here on these goods. While making such supplies available
to households on a monetary basis, the government[4] has

free communal consumption. Thus the government has supplied
health care generally without charge, but it has also long permitted
medical personnel that it employs to engage in some private practice,
and this they have done, though on a limited and probably declining
scale. Drugs, at least in part, are also supplied at money prices. Education, too, has generally been free, but during protracted periods
in the past (most recently from 1940 to 1956) limited fees were
levied on many students. See Mark Field, *Doctor and Patient in
Soviet Russia* (Cambridge, Mass., 1957), pp. 21–22, 30, 103; Abram
Bergson, *The Structure of Soviet Wages* (Cambridge, Mass., 1944),
pp. 26 ff., 234 ff.; Nicholas DeWitt, *Soviet Professional Manpower*
(Washington, 1955), pp. 142 ff.; DeWitt, *Educational and Professional
Employment in the USSR* (Washington, 1961), pp. 64 ff.; and Janet
Chapman, *Real Wages in Soviet Russia since 1928* (Cambridge, Mass.,
1963), pp. 129 ff.

3. See below, Ch. 9.

4. In this essay reference to the "government" of the U.S.S.R. is
conveniently understood either as reference to the system's directors
or to institutions, such as were delineated above, p. 42. The sense
implied in any particular case will be sufficiently evident from the
context.

been able to choose between two alternative distributional procedures: the open market, where households exercise freedom of choice in determining their purchases; and rationing, where purchases are prescribed administratively.

For the period of the five-year plans, the government in fact has employed both procedures. Moreover, while at present only the open market is used, rationing was employed during two protracted intervals: from the latter part of 1928 to 1935–36, and from shortly after the German attack to December 1947. But the latter interval embraced the war and the beginning of reconstruction, while even by Soviet standards the circumstances that prevailed during the former period (especially under the First Five Year Plan) were unusual to say the least. Of course, if circumstances were unusual, the government itself was largely responsible.[5] But Soviet economists have some basis to hold (as they do) that in the distribution of marketed foodstuffs and manufactures rationing has been a rather special expedient. Hence the open market is not only the contemporary procedure for disposing of these products but the one normally applied.

We may therefore focus on the experience with this form of distribution. Also, for the period of the five-year plans, if we pass by the two intervals of rationing, we are left with three intervals during which the open market prevailed, of which the only protracted one is also the most recent, the period since December 1947. For present purposes, therefore, the experience during this interval is by far of chief interest.

Turning, then, to this aspect, it is time to consider the first of the efficiency rules referred to at the outset:[6] Where an open market prevails for consumers' goods, prices ideally

5. On the experience under the early five-year plans, see below, Ch. 13.

6. See above, p. 12.

are such as to limit demand for each product to available supplies. If prices approach such clearing levels, they must tend to be uniform among different sellers in any market area, but according to the rule prices are supposed also to be nondiscriminatory between households. In the U.S.S.R., to what extent have prices tended to conform to this principle? Where they have diverged from it, what other principle or principles have been observed?

COLLECTIVE FARM MARKET PRICE FORMATION

Disposition of foodstuffs and manufactures among households that involves sale at a price represents a form of trade, and although in the U.S.S.R. as elsewhere households probably can sometimes buy at wholesale, such trade is virtually always retail. Prior to their final disposition, supplies are often transferred in a wholesale way among different organizations. But we are concerned here primarily with prices prevailing in retail trade.

Retail trade, however, has been conducted through different sorts of outlets.[7] Also, retail prices have sometimes been formed differently, depending on this aspect. The collective farm market has been quantitatively the least important outlet, but we may conveniently begin by considering fairly familiar essentials as to price formation in this sector: While the government through its procurement policy ultimately limits supplies offered for sale, it does not endeavor to fix directly the prices at which the available supplies are sold. Rather, prices are left to the suppliers themselves to determine, and the latter are usually numerous. In other words, regarding collective farm market prices, for practical purposes we deal simply with a farmers' bazaar, such as is familiar in other countries. Even so, like any other market the collective farm market is hardly comparable to a theoretic

7. See above, pp. 21 ff.

model in which prices always neatly equate demand to supply. But presumably a tendency in that direction has prevailed, and well-known facts about the continual fluctuations of collective farm market prices in response to changing conditions of supply and demand corroborate this view.

If prices have tended toward clearing levels, they should also have tended to be uniform among sellers within any market area. At least this should have been so within any one collective farm market, and perhaps some such tendency also prevailed even within a larger locality, like a city, so far as households have had the opportunity to shop at several markets. Whether farmers, too, have been able to move about from market to market is not known. While prevailing generally, the tendency toward uniformity has sometimes been impeded. Thus, because of the arrangements between the collective farms and their marketing representatives, sales by the latter may sometimes have been made "below the market."[8] This source of price variation can have been of only limited consequence, however, since the bulk of the produce sold on the collective farm market is supplied not by the collective farm but by member households. Then, too, in conducting "commission trade" on behalf of the collective farms and farmers,[9] consumers' cooperatives have been required to dispose of the produce at a prescribed discount from prices prevailing in sales by other participants in the collective farm market. Here, again, the volume of sales involved has been limited.[10]

8. John T. Whitman, "The Kolkhoz Market," *Soviet Studies,* 7 (1955–56), 388.

9. See above, p. 23.

10. See Table 2.4. According to Whitman, p. 402, commission sales are supposed to be made at prices 10–15 per cent below those in the collective farm market. In fact, during recent years prices in commission sales appear to have been reduced sometimes by less than 10 and sometimes by more than 15 per cent, but the available price

Consumers' Goods

Where within any market area prices for similar goods have varied, this is a fact of interest in itself; but, as was implied, produce has been made available at different prices to households more or less generally. In other words, there has been no systematic variation in prices between different households or groups of households. Accordingly, there is still no basis to speak of discrimination among households in any meaningful sense.

OFFICIAL RETAIL PRICES VERSUS CLEARING LEVELS

Exclusive of the collective farm market, during the open market period on which we focus (i.e. since December 1947) foodstuffs and manufactured goods have been made available to households entirely through publicly or cooperatively owned retail shops. The cooperatives have been predominantly those of consumers, although some retail shops have also been owned by producers' cooperatives. The government and cooperative outlets have far overshadowed the collective farm market in importance (Table 2.4).

As to determination of prices charged in these shops (and reason to consider them together will become evident), no one will expect to find here a process like that in the collective farm market, where prices are fixed in the first instance by many competitive profit-seeking suppliers. But in trade as elsewhere operational control of government productive assets has been exercised by a many-tiered bu-

data may reflect differences in quality. See TSU, *Sovetskaia torgovlia* (Moscow, 1956), p. 134; *Narkhoz, 1958,* p. 774; *Narkhoz, 1960,* pp. 718–19. While commission trade dates from 1953, there was something of a precedent for it during 1946–49. During this period consumers' cooperatives were allowed to procure from collective farms and member households produce for resale at prices which after a time had to be 10 per cent below those prevailing in the collective farm market.

reaucratic structure. Also, organizations at lower levels have been extrabudgetary, and although the import of this feature has yet to be explored, not surprisingly such organizations are in some degree also profit-seeking. Perhaps, therefore, it is advisable to observe first that, for the government retail shop, prices almost always have been fixed neither by the individual enterprise administering it nor by immediately superior agencies of an extrabudgetary sort (there have been such), but by government institutions.[11] Furthermore, even among government institutions this task has been dealt with in a highly centralized manner. Thus the all-union Council of Ministers itself not only has overseen this work generally but, directly or through all-union executive agencies acting in its behalf, has established the actual prices to be charged for a substantial volume of goods sold. Until its abolition in 1959, the chief department aiding the Council was the Ministry of Trade; more recently Gosplan seems to have gained responsibilities in this sphere. Especially since 1957, republican and local government institutions have also participated in retail price fixing; but here, too, apparently general executive organs have played a leading role.

Retail prices sometimes have been fixed not as such but by the addition of some given trade-margins to separately fixed

11. On price formation in government and cooperative retail trade, a number of summary surveys are now available. Among these, I have found particularly useful A. I. Maizenberg, *Tsenoobrazovanie v narodnom khoziaistve SSSR* (Moscow, 1953), ch. 4; D. D. Kondrashev, *Tsenoobrazovanie v promyshlennosti SSSR* (Moscow, 1956), ch. 4; Sh. Ia. Turetskii, *Ocherki planovogo tsenoobrazovaniia v SSSR* (Moscow, 1959), ch. VII; Chapman, *Real Wages in Soviet Russia since 1928*, ch. II; Marshall Goldman, *Soviet Marketing* (Glencoe, Ill., 1963), ch. 4; M. M. Lifits, ed., *Ekonomika Sovetskoi torgovli* (Moscow, 1950), ch. XIV, and (Moscow, 1955), ch. XIII. I am indebted to Dr. Goldman for aid on a number of points.

wholesale prices. The same authorities have fixed these margins as have fixed retail prices. Then, too, under long-standing accounting arrangements, determination of the retail price has meant in any case determination of its margin over costs. It goes without saying that the role of superior government authorities in retail price fixing has been in no way diminished by the fact that this margin has been constituted in good part of separately determined sales taxes, including the notorious turnover tax (*nalog s oborota*), to which I shall refer later.[12]

While retail prices generally have been fixed by superior agencies, subordinate ones, including even individual retail shops, have not been entirely lacking in discretion. Thus, lately, the retail shop has been permitted, within very narrow limits, to cut prices of goods which it holds in excessive stock.

Nevertheless, the individual enterprise has had a very limited role in fixing prices, and this has hardly been less true of retail trade of the consumers' cooperatives than of retail trade of the government. In fact, in consumers' cooperative trade not only the individual enterprise but organizations generally have lacked authority; for though departures from the rule of public ownership of productive assets have sometimes been consequential for resource use, consumers' cooperatives have not been much of a case in point. Except in name, it is not easy to perceive how administration in their sphere has differed from that in the government's own. At any rate, this has been so in respect of prices. As already noted, the consumers' cooperatives have been subjected to only limited government control regarding prices of the small volume of produce that they have been selling recently on a commission basis in behalf of collective farms and member households. But for the rest, prices in

12. Below, pp. 118 ff.

retail outlets of consumers' cooperatives have almost always been fixed by the government organs that have fixed prices in government shops, and indeed often by the same action.

In retail trade the producers' cooperative has played only a limited role, and lately hardly any at all, but here, too, government price fixing has been the rule. Nevertheless, for some goods, especially where extensive use has been made of materials procured by the cooperative itself or of materials consisting of waste products, some autonomy has been allowed to the cooperatives. Interestingly, the responsible agency is not the individual association but a superior body.

Granting that the "official" retail prices (as we may conveniently refer to those charged in government and cooperative retail shops) have been fixed in the foregoing manner, on what basis has this been done? Of particular interest is the extent to which such prices have been established at clearing levels. According to limited evidence, during the open market period on which I focus, prices no doubt conformed in some degree to clearing levels, but again and again they diverged markedly from them. I consider these facts:

1. As was stated, in order for prices to be at clearing levels, they must be uniform among different sellers in any market area. Essentially this has been true of official retail prices. These prices often have differed between major geographical zones, and also between urban and rural localities, but such differentials are not of much concern here. The same product sometimes has also sold at varying prices even within urban or rural localities, but such cases appear to occur chiefly in special circumstances, especially where there are sales by producers' cooperatives.[13]

2. There is no necessary relation between the degree to which prices balance supply and demand at any time and the frequency and variety of price change, but for a dynamic

13. See Chapman, pp. 11 ff.; Turetskii, pp. 459 ff.

economy like that of the U.S.S.R. it is illuminating that from December 1947 until 1954, official prices generally were changed each spring, but since 1954 they have been held more or less constant. The government, it is true, sharply increased the prices of meat products and butter on June 1, 1962 (on the average by 30 and 25 per cent, respectively), and has varied some prices more or less markedly otherwise, but generally it has either held prices constant or altered them only infrequently. As was explained, however, the government lately has allowed individual shops very limited discretion to cut prices on overstocked goods. I shall return to the June 1, 1962, increase later.[14] Since December 1947, prices that have varied usually have varied differently for different products, but within broad categories (for example, bread and grain products, fish and fish products, meat and meat products) changes often have been uniform.[15]

3. If clearing levels are realized, prices of consumers' goods should depend not only on quantities supplied but on other factors, particularly price and income elasticities and the real income level. But as a rule such prices might be expected to vary to some extent inversely with quantities supplied. In the U.S.S.R. the relation is positive for official retail prices; at any rate, there is no systematic relation to speak of, of one sort or the other:[16]

14. Below, p. 66. I refer to goods other than of a seasonal sort. For a few products subject to sharp seasonal fluctuations in supplies, particularly milk products, eggs, potatoes, vegetables, and fruits, official retail prices have been changed seasonally for some time. This has been so even since 1954, when prices generally have been more or less stable.

15. On the frequency and variability of official retail price changes, see Chapman, particularly ch. II and appendix A; Turetskii, ch. VII; TSU, *Sovetskaia torgovlia*, p. 132; *Narkhoz, 1958*, p. 771; *Narkhoz, 1960*, p. 717; *Narkhoz, 1961*, p. 653; *Pravda* (June 1, 1962).

16. The absence of an inverse relation is surprising, for alternative index numbers computed in prices of alternative years indicate that

	Coefficient of correlation, changes in official retail prices and in quantities disposed of
1950–55	+0.21
1955–60	+0.42

4. During the open market period of concern, for comparable goods, prices in the collective farm market often have been markedly above those charged in government and cooperative outlets (Tables 4.1 and 4.2). Since prices in the collective farm market should have related demand there to available supplies, an *agio* of those prices over official retail prices signifies that the latter are too low to limit demand to available supplies in the government and cooperative outlets; for only if supplies were insufficient in the latter outlets would consumers be willing to pay such an *agio*.

Details are often lacking on the manner of compilation of the official and other figures that underlie the tabulated data. While comparisons of collective farm market and official retail price levels must have been made for similar goods in the same locality, almost certainly these are affected by differences in quality and location. Furthermore, not too much is known about the latter, although one suspects that they operate in diverse ways for different products, tending

---

an inverse relation has often prevailed for Soviet retail prices. See *Real SNIP*, ch. 12 and pp. 305 ff. Statistical limitations in the calculations may have been a factor in the result observed here. In the calculation of the coefficients of correlation, changes in official retail prices are related to the volume of sales in both government and cooperative outlets. It was not possible, however, to extend the calculation of quantities, as might have been desirable, to include sales on the collective farm market. Also, the coefficients are derived from relatives of official retail prices and corresponding quantities of broad categories of consumers' goods. For the underlying index numbers of prices and quantities, see TSU, *Sovetskaia torgovlia*, pp. 52–55; *Narkhoz, 1958*, pp. 703–04; *Narkhoz, 1960*, pp. 678, 717.

TABLE 4.1

Relation of Collective Farm Market to Official Retail Prices, U.S.S.R.
(official retail prices = 100)

	U.S.S.R., Average for Year, Assuming Relation for 1956 as for 101–02 Cities[a]	101–02 Cities, Average for Year[b]	101–02 Cities, Third Quarter[c]
1948	130	n.a.	n.a.
1949	107	n.a.	n.a.
1950	109	n.a.	n.a.
1951	123	n.a.	n.a.
1952	134	n.a.	n.a.
1953	142	n.a.	n.a.
1954	161	n.a.	182
1955	167	n.a.	170
1956	145	145	143
1957	141	134	131
1958	141	138	139
1959	139	131	129
1960	n.a.	135	136

a. Compiled from Soviet official index numbers of prices in collective farm markets and of food prices in government retail shops, given in TSU, *Sovetskaia torgovlia*, pp. 131, 182; *Narkhoz, 1959*, pp. 677, 709. For 1948 and 1949 see *Real SNIP*, pp. 305 ff.

b. See *Narkhoz, 1958*, pp. 773–74; *Narkhoz, 1959*, pp. 680–81; *Narkhoz, 1960*, pp. 718–19.

c. See the sources cited in note b., and TSU, *Sovetskaia torgovlia*, pp. 133–34.

to produce sometimes a premium in the collective farm market (e.g. for vegetables, which probably are fresher there) and sometimes a discount (e.g. for milk, which is usually pasteurized in the government and cooperative store but never in the collective farm market). But at least for the comparisons in Table 4.2 such differences in quality and location should be persistent. Hence for any product they could only explain the more limited premiums observed at different times.

Even for food products, sales in collective farm markets usually are limited relatively to those in government and cooperative outlets. For this reason, the divergence of official retail prices from clearing levels necessarily is less than that of these prices from prices in the collective farm market. On the other hand, the former gap often is still appreciable, e.g. in 1954; with the same total spending on the products affected, the fixing of official retail prices at a clearing level would have required that these prices be increased 12–15 per cent. Furthermore, even where the required increase is less (as in 1958, when it might have come to 5–7 per cent), it appears to have been persistent. For individual commodities the required increase necessarily is often much larger than for commodities generally.[17]

5. Because of their limitations as to time and place, reports of travelers to the U.S.S.R. on the state of the retail market are difficult to interpret; but it is of interest that deficiencies in the supplies available for retail outlets, and the resulting queues, are a familiar theme in such accounts. Relative to the population, however, there probably are many fewer retail shops in the U.S.S.R. than in the West. Queues sometimes may be due to the insufficiency not of supplies but of trading capacity.[18]

From the foregoing one may gauge the degree of conformity to clearing levels of official retail prices generally, but reference should also be made to numerous oddities for

17. Assuming total spending is given, the required increase is readily determined if one considers the comparative shares of government and cooperative shops and of collective farm markets in sales of the commodities in question. Available data for the latter outlets apparently refer primarily to sales in urban localities. For this reason I made an alternative computation where I exclude from sales at official retail prices those made in cooperative outlets. The latter are almost exclusively in rural localities.

18. On the adequacy of trade outlets in the U.S.S.R., see Goldman, *Soviet Marketing*, pp. 177 ff.

TABLE 4.2.

Relation of Collective Farm Market to Official Retail Prices,
101–02 Cities, Third Quarter, U.S.S.R.
(official retail prices = 100)

	1954	1955	1956	1957	1958	1959	1960
Wheat flour, coarse milled	151	137	148	154	112	149	180
Wheat flour, select	173	183	189	135	135	111	118
Grits and legumes	190	176	137	112	119	120	136
Potatoes	311	246	157	138	139	122	140
Vegetables	203	216	158	149	142	155	160
Apples	303	274	204	137	154	143	138
Beef	174	177	131	135	141	133	142
Mutton	196	205	146	149	154	138	153
Pork	118	130	116	111	131	126	142
Milk	158	146	120	115	127	118	120
Butter	142	170	130	126	114	114	116
Vegetable oil	117	153	113	115	135	106	127
Eggs	167	176	159	162	172	147	143
All products	182	170	143	131	139	129	136

Sources: See Table 4.1, notes b. and c.

individual commodities. Among these are the pricing of better quality woolen cloth and furniture below corresponding articles of inferior quality, and admittedly far too low pricing of caviar in relation to herring. After an increase in the spread from 9.3:1 to 19.1:1 in 1958, the price of caviar is still considered too low.

That official retail prices have often diverged from clearing levels Soviet economists themselves have freely acknowledged. Some of the evidence cited above has been found in their expositions. Nevertheless, by considering typical circumstances for different broad categories of products, a Soviet authority recently has attempted to classify such categories according to the adequacy of supplies to meet requirements in 1961. The results (Table 4.3) also show frequent divergencies from clearing levels, though perhaps not as fre-

TABLE 4.3.

Inventories and Sales, Government and Cooperative Shops
According to State of Market, U.S.S.R.

| | Inventories, January 1, 1962 | | | Sales, 1961 | |
	In Billion Rubles	Per cent	In Days of Turnover	In Billion Rubles	Per cent
Goods for which demand is "basically satisfied" and there are no significant excess stocks	5.38	26	67	26.34	36
Goods for which demand is "basically satisfied" but for which stocks have increased and are relatively excessive	11.02	55	167	22.29	31
Goods for which supplies are insufficient	3.84	19	52	24.17	33
Total	20.24	100	94	72.80	100

Source: R. Lokshin, "Proizvodstvo tovarov i platezhesposobnyi spros," *Planovoe khoziaistvo*, No. 1 (1963), 24–25. The data, I believe, refer to retail trade other than that in restaurants.

quent as the evidence given above would suggest. Goods in short supply, however, would necessarily tend to occupy a relatively limited place in data such as are tabulated on stocks and sales, and the apparent difference in findings has to be read accordingly. While reference is to 1961, there is little basis for the belief that availabilities were greater in that year than in earlier ones on which I have focused.

OFFICIAL RETAIL PRICE FORMATION

Reference has been to the relation of official retail prices to clearing levels. Let us consider now how in general such prices have been fixed. The principles of formation of these prices have been a subject of discussion by

Soviet political figures as well as economists.[19] These expositions together with the facts set forth on the relation of such prices to clearing levels indicate that conformity to the latter has been a desideratum, but that there have been others as well, and depending on the circumstances these have often been overriding.

The alternative desiderata in part concern the relation of prices to costs. What costs consist of and what the relation of prices to costs has been generally are subjects for later discussion, but it should be observed here that the government apparently has often been interested to maintain some appropriate correspondence between these two aspects, although not necessarily proportionality. Depending on the availability of supplies, of course, this in no way need have precluded that prices also be at clearing levels. But a given relation probably has sometimes been felt desirable without regard to availabilities, as with the prices of "children's things," which seemingly have had to be low as a matter of principle. Divergencies of prices from clearing levels have also been tolerated, in the interest of maintaining some appropriate relation between prices. Thus, since the use of bread as fodder is held to be undesirable, a recurring concern in fixing meat prices has been that they not be so high as to induce city-dwellers so to use bread.

Divergencies have also been allowed because price stability is something of a virtue, especially if the alternative is a price increase. Manifestly this has been a dominant desideratum for some years. Where prices have been changed, uniformity of change among different products also has been something of a virtue. Last but not least, a divergence from clearing levels has been viewed as in some respects advantageous in and of itself—provided that it is downward, so that demand exceeds supply.

19. See above, n. 11, and below, n. 24.

The foregoing have been desiderata generally, but none has been inviolate, and the concern for stability in recent years, as already explained, did not prevent a sharp increase in the prices of meat products and butter on June 1, 1962. Apparently, the increase was deemed essential because of prevailing shortages, and because of the need to compensate for concomitant increases in procurement prices for farm products. The latter, avowedly, had been inordinately low.[20]

While intended to reflect varied desiderata, the official retail prices have been affected by administrative deficiencies. Such deficiencies are inevitable, but in order that clearing levels be approximated, the official retail prices must be fixed in the light of projections of prospective supplies of different goods and of the aggregate money income that will be available to purchase them. Such projections are and long have been customary in the U.S.S.R. but, as will become clear, they must often have been materially in error, although perhaps less so in recent years than formerly. Use of such projections in the fixing of official retail prices incidentally entails compilation of the first of many balances that we shall encounter: that of the sources and disposition of household money income. Any close approximation to clearing levels also would require estimation of demand schedules, but here too Soviet planning is still in a relatively primitive stage.[21] As Soviet economists acknowledge, administration of official retail prices often has left something to be desired in other ways. Among other things, coordination of the many agencies involved has been faulty.

In the foregoing I have commented on the manner in which official retail prices have been fixed generally, but it remains to refer to one interesting aspect: price discrimination. As already implied, during the open market period of concern here, official retail prices as a rule have been non-

20. *Pravda* (June 1, 1962).
21. See below, pp. 276 ff.

discriminatory. When supplies have been available at such prices, they have ordinarily been available to households generally. Nevertheless, there probably have been exceptions to this rule. Thus for some groups—army officers, higher officials of the government, and the like—reportedly there are special shops where sales are made at reduced prices or where supplies of deficit goods are more plentiful.

CONCLUSIONS

In distributing foodstuffs and manufactures to households at money prices, the government has long maintained an open market, but in fixing prices it has often violated an efficiency rule that is an imperative for economic rationality where consumers' welfare is the end. The rule requires that prices be nondiscriminatory and at clearing levels. While prices generally have been nondiscriminatory, especially in the government and cooperative shops they have diverged from clearing levels. The divergencies have been due partly to administrative deficiencies, but they have also been purposeful. Must we not conclude that in this sphere the system's directors in effect have often supplanted household by planners' preferences?

Conformity of prices to clearing levels must still be a desideratum even if household preferences are overruled, provided that the system's directors are still concerned about differences in intensity of desire among different households for any good.[22] Conformity to clearing levels is no longer in order, however, if the system's directors are entirely indiffer-

22. From the standpoint of consumers' welfare, in an economic optimum the relative marginal utilities of different commodities must be the same for all households. In an open market, this condition is met if there is conformity to our efficiency rule. But conformity to the rule would still be in order under planners' preferences, provided the departure from household evaluations for one or another good were uniform among different households.

ent to such differences in intensity of desire, and no doubt the chief moral is that the system's directors simply have not been very sensitive to such differences.

But, if only for clarity, it should be observed that the desiderata they have considered, other than conformity to clearing levels, reflect a concern for diverse aspects. Probably the chief of these is ease of administration, or essentially economy of administrative costs. Even where consumers' welfare is the end, such costs are a proper basis for allowing prices to diverge from clearing levels. Economic rationality depends on conformity to our efficiency rule only if one neglects costs of administration. Nevertheless, at least from the same standpoint of consumers' welfare, the concern for administrative costs in the U.S.S.R. surely has been inordinate.

Thus economy of administrative costs must be a principal reason why price stability is a virtue. Uniformity of price changes presumably is also a desideratum on the same account. If prices that depart from clearing levels most often are allowed to fall short of the latter, economy of administrative costs is again a major motive. Given the resultant excess of demand over supply, the government considers that, in order to dispose of oncoming supplies, it need not make a series of price adjustments to test the market. Since consumers are less choosy, it apparently is felt, movement of supplies is facilitated.

And in all these ways costs must be economized, for time and effort devoted to administration must be reduced. But the economy must be limited. It should not be very costly, for example, for the government to vary prices more often than it has done lately, which is not at all often. Also, where consumers' welfare is the end, the economy only seems the more limited, since consideration then must be given not only to administrative expenditures as such but to household time and energy devoted to shopping. While failure to

68

realize clearing levels is economical of the former, it magnifies the latter.[23]

The determination of individual incomes in the U.S.S.R. is yet to be considered, but here as elsewhere the government exercises substantial control. The result, however, may not always be equitable even from the government's own standpoint, and possibly this has been another reason why it has allowed prices to differ from clearing levels. One thinks particularly of the practice of limiting prices of products like children's things in relation to their costs, even though the prices fail to restrict demand to available supplies. Here, too, the divergence need not conflict with consumers' welfare. In effect, if income disposition is inequitable, a "first best" disposition of consumers' goods is already precluded, and possibly something of a "second best" sometimes may be realized when prices depart from, rather than conform to, clearing levels. This may be so even though the departure from clearing levels entails distribution through queues and the like. How far divergencies in the U.S.S.R. might be reconciled with consumers' welfare in this way is, however, conjectural.

Price cuts are popular and price increases are not. In pursuing desiderata other than conformity to clearing levels, manifestly the government is also aware of these effects. Its lengthy, apologetic explanation for the June 1, 1962, price boost only underlines this fact. Also, where the government is so motivated, consumers' welfare is not necessarily sup-

23. The suggestion is sometimes made that through its price policies the government realizes an economy not only of administrative costs but of consumers' goods inventories. With prices below clearing levels, inventories presumably are less than they would be if the government should try to "feel out" the market. But could it represent a consequential gain to the government to limit inventories when this is accomplished primarily by having goods move off the shelves rapidly in any supply period rather than more gradually, as would be the case under the alternative policy?

planted as a material end. Rather, the implication is only that a nonmaterial end—favorable political reactions—is of overriding import. But consumers' welfare suffers here no less than elsewhere because of the divergence from clearing levels.

In delineating the government's more basic objectives for allowing retail prices to diverge from clearing levels, I have tried to take into account Soviet expositions of the government's policies. The different objectives, however, all combine to support a more or less systematic practice of fixing prices below clearing levels. It is not surprising, therefore, that such a practice has been elevated to the status of an economic law in the Soviet Union, and that for this law still another ground has been found:[24] "In a socialist society demand must outstrip the supply of commodities. Increasing demand pushes forward the output of commodities." But obviously the additional ground cannot be taken at face value, and in repeating a view expressed much earlier by Stalin, Mikoyan himself makes clear that, if there is such a favorable effect on output, the outstripping of supply by demand might easily be excessive. The stated view is among the economic principles enunciated by Stalin that have lately been subject to attack by Soviet economists themselves.

In trying to understand the government's conduct, we must also consider that the theory of value that has a preferred status in the U.S.S.R. in itself might be construed as precluding manipulation of prices in order to assure conformity to clearing levels. As Soviet economists seem to be aware, however, such a construction is not necessary. Probably more important here is another aspect: from the standpoint of the labor theory it is not clear just what is lost

24. A. I. Mikoyan in XX C'ezd kommunisticheskoi partii Sovetskogo Soiuza, 1 (Moscow, 1956), 305; see also I. V. Stalin, Works, 12 (Moscow, 1955), 332; Current Digest of the Soviet Press (March 14, 1962), p. 31.

through a failure so to fix prices. In theorizing on this matter in the U.S.S.R., reasons still are found for fixing prices at clearing levels, but these only seem to underline the incomplete understanding. Thus clearing levels avowedly are a desideratum simply because, if official retail prices go above this level, available supplies will not be disposed of. If official retail prices fall short of clearing levels, peasants gain unduly from the resultant high prices in the collective farm market. There are also speculative resales and queues.[25] In allowing prices to diverge from clearing levels on any and all accounts, therefore, perhaps the government has failed to grasp fully the resultant losses. Then again, we may also observe here the phenomenon referred to at the outset: the reluctance of the system's directors to commit themselves to economic principles of any sort.

Whatever the reasons, so far as the disposition of consumers' goods is concerned, the government has not sought especially to heed household preferences, but, given the supplies of goods to be devoted to it, this sphere of resource use competes with others only regarding allocations of time and effort to administration. If the government has been especially economical of such allocations, therefore, this doubtless reflects in some degree the broader ends discussed previously, particularly the intense concern for the future relative to the present. Even in the restricted sphere in question, an initial manifestation of these ends is observed.

Probably the chief cause of the divergence of official retail prices from clearing levels lately has been the government's concern to maintain stable prices, or at least to avoid increases. Nevertheless, the government effected a major price boost in June 1962, and it has been suggested that henceforth a more flexible policy might be pursued. This may prove to be so, but the period since June 1962 has not been especially notable for variation in prices.

25. Turetskii, pp. 407 ff.; Kondrashev, pp. 158 ff.

71

5 MANAGERIAL MOTIVATION IN INDUSTRY

In the U.S.S.R. in nonfarm sectors, government enterprises have long been predominant. Furthermore, even where ownership has not been by government, resource use has been administered much as if it were. Thus, for practical purposes, operational direction has been exercised almost always by the Council of Ministers through one or another bureaucratic structure, including diverse intermediate agencies as well as enterprises, whether government-owned or other. For administrators of these agencies, therefore, the government has had to establish some controls over performance. It follows, too, that resource use in nonfarm sectors must have turned among other things on the nature of the goals sought by the administrators in the light of such success criteria. What are these criteria and what goals have they induced administrators to seek?

In this chapter I shall consider this question with special

attention to the use of labor. The discussion will serve as a preliminary to consideration in the next chapter of an interesting facet of resource use partly parallel to that concerning the disposition of consumers' goods: determination of employment in nonfarm occupations, enterprises, and industries, and of households from which such employment is recruited. Consideration of success criteria and resulting goals will also facilitate inquiry into procedures for dealing with other facets of nonfarm resource use.

INTEREST IN FULFILLMENT OF COST TARGETS, 1946–57

Although nonfarm enterprises and superior agencies under the Council of Ministers are not universally governmental, it may suffice to refer to circumstances in those that are. Actually, for a long time the only nongovernment organizations that have been at all consequential are those of the consumers' cooperatives, and I believe success criteria have been much the same for them as for governmental organizations.

Then, too, the criteria in industry have been broadly representative of those in nonfarm sectors generally. In any event, industry has been by far the most important of these sectors. It is also the one on which there is most information. If I may, therefore, focus on this sector,[1] it is advisable to be clear first about an underlying feature referred to previously: use of money. Particularly, under the *khozraschet*

1. On success criteria in industry I have profited from several studies of Soviet enterprise management, particularly G. Bienstock, S. M. Schwarz, and A. Yugow, *Management in Russian Industry and Agriculture* (New York, 1944); David Granick, *Management of the Industrial Firm in the USSR* (New York, 1954); Joseph S. Berliner, *Factory and Manager in the USSR* (Cambridge, Mass., 1957); Alec Nove, "The Problem of 'Success Indicators' in Soviet Industry," *Economica, 25* (1958), 1–13.

system the government industrial enterprise is charged for its inputs generally, and hence, at established wages, for the labor it employs. The enterprise is also paid for the output it produces and ships. In the U.S.S.R. it is held to be congruous to a socialist system if records are kept not only of costs incurred but of profits realized.

We wish to know about all motives of administrators bearing on use of labor, but of special interest is their concern for one possible goal: limitation in money costs of inputs, particularly labor, incurred in production of any given output. Therefore, we must inquire especially into the extent to which the success criteria might foster such a concern for economy in labor costs.

From this standpoint, pertinent criteria have varied in the course of time. To refer first to postwar years before the industrial reorganization of 1957, we must now be explicit regarding Soviet economic plans, at least those promulgated during this period. Thus there were different plans for different intervals. Among these the best known is that relating to an interval of five years, and during postwar years before 1957 several of these were published. Soon after the war the government also published a plan, at least of an informal sort, for a fifteen-year period. However, these plans supposedly were reflected in the plan drawn up regularly for still another interval, a year, and it is the latter that bore most immediately on current operations. For purposes of administration, however, the annual plan was usually broken down into quarterly and monthly installments.

Whatever the interval, ordinarily there was not one program but a complex of programs of varying scope and detail formulated regarding operations of agencies at different bureaucratic levels. Thus in industry at the time in question there were programs for the ministry, the *glavk,* and the individual enterprise. For the latter the annual plan was

74

called the "technical-industrial-financial plan," or tekhprom-finplan.

The task of fulfilling these plans, particularly the annual plan (and unless otherwise stated, reference is especially to this), constituted at once a basis for determining success. Not surprisingly, a long-standing principle was that implementation of the plan at any bureaucratic level was primarily the responsibility of those administering affairs generally at that level. By the same token, the plan formulated in respect of any bureaucratic level became a basis for determining success at that level. An initial question, therefore, concerns the extent to which in seeking to fulfill the annual plan those in charge at any level may have been interested in labor cost economy.

The plan included many targets, but at the level of the enterprise what seemed to count most was performance regarding output. Thus on their performance as measured by output depended the professional careers and hence the social status of the managerial personnel, including the director and his chief assistants. Moreover, for heeding this measure of success these persons had an additional and more concrete incentive. Depending on the degree of fulfillment of the target for output, the director and his chief assistants received sizable premiums over and above their basic salaries. Premium scales that prevailed in machinery, automotive transport, coal mining, and chemical enterprises are illustrative (Table 5.1). In each branch the scales were differentiated among groups of enterprises of different sizes and importance.

Understandably, fulfillment and overfulfillment of the output target was the principal preoccupation of those administering the enterprise. Reportedly, however, zeal was often tempered by the fact that large premiums could be earned merely for fulfilling the target. While further re-

TABLE 5.1.

Premiums for Plant Management, U.S.S.R.
(percentages of basic salary)

	For fulfillment of production target by			For each percentage of overfulfillment of production target by		
	Group I	Group II	Group III	Group I	Group II	Group III
Senior management (director and chief engineer)						
Machinery	37	30	22	4	3	2
Automotive transport	30	25	20	4	3	2
Coal mining	100			10		
Chemical	75			8		
Intermediate management (deputy directors, shop and department chiefs)						
Machinery	30	22	15	3	2	1½
Automotive transport	25	20	15	3	2	2
Junior management (deputy shop and department chiefs, senior engineers, senior foremen)						
Machinery	22	15	15	2	1½	1½
Automotive transport	20	15	15	3	2	2

Source: Compiled in Berliner, *Factory and Manager*, p. 30, from diverse Soviet sources dated 1948–52.

wards might be obtained for overfulfillment, an awkward feature here was that such achievement might lead to the establishment of a higher target in an ensuing period.

Motivation of managerial personnel in the *glavk* and ministry under the annual plan has still to be systematically studied. But, for these agencies as well as the enterprise, output was programmed. In respect of output, therefore, one might suppose that managerial personnel in the enterprise would only mirror attitudes prevailing at higher levels, and all the evidence does in fact point in this direction. Thus fulfillment and overfulfillment of the output target was the cardinal concern not only for the enterprise but also for the *glavk* and the ministry.

I have referred to *the* target for output. Needless to say, under the annual plan for the enterprise, there was ordinarily not one article produced but a variety. This was still more the case for the *glavk* and ministry. Moreover, at all levels for each article, quality as well as quantity had to be considered. Obviously, in formulating success criteria to grapple with these complexities the government encountered difficulties, but this is a matter for later discussion.[2]

The primary concern for output, of course, does not preclude the possibility that economy of labor costs should also have been sought. Thus if labor inputs available to different operating units were in any way restricted, the interest in output would have been translated at once into one in economy of labor costs. In any event, such economy might in itself have been the subject of a target. Under the annual plan, to what extent was this the case?

In addition to the target for output, the annual plan for the enterprise included one for per-unit costs. Such costs were also controlled in the corresponding programs for the *glavk* and the ministry. Moreover, managerial personnel in the enterprise, and no doubt those at higher levels as well, had reasons to try to excel in economizing costs, though these reasons were not always impelling. In order to receive premiums for fulfillment and overfulfillment of the output target, managerial personnel in the enterprise ordinarily were required to fulfill the target for cost per unit of output; but apparently this proviso was not always insisted on.[3]

If the enterprise failed to fulfill its target for costs, it might also be deficient regarding one for profits. In this way

2. See below, p. 155, pp. 287 ff.
3. Berliner, p. 71; P. I. Dmitrieva, *Rentabel'nost' promyshlennogo predpriiatiia i puti ee povysheniia* (Moscow, 1960), pp. 196–97.

it might impair its position as to working capital, for ordinarily profits were an important source of funds for the latter. In consequence, performance regarding the output target itself might also be impeded. However, the management could often find other means to prevent this, at least for a time. Among other things, the enterprise was supposed to pay promptly for supplies purchased from others, but in some degree payment might be postponed. Similarly, the enterprise might be tardy in repaying loans from the State Bank, the latter being an additional source of finance of working capital. For infractions of financial discipline such as these, the enterprise became liable to the imposition of credit sanctions. Such sanctions involved heightened State Bank supervision over the enterprise's affairs and, especially after a State Bank reform of 1954, more severe measures. But the risk of incurring credit sanctions must often have seemed preferable to underfulfillment of the output target, although probably not as often in later years as in August 1949, when 27 per cent of all State Bank clients owed overdue debts to one or more suppliers.[4]

The so-called "enterprise fund" (before 1956, the "fund of the director") was also financed out of profits, partly from those planned and partly from profits in excess of the plan. Since the fund could be used to finance plant modernization, housing, welfare measures, and premiums for workers generally, it provided an additional incentive for profitable operations, hence also for cost economy. But the sums involved were rather limited. In 1955, for example, the total appropriations to the fund often amounted to only 0.5 per cent of the wage bill. Partly for this reason the shortcomings of the enterprise fund as a stimulus to profitability were a subject of criticism even in the U.S.S.R.

In appraising interest in economy of labor costs, it must

4. Granick, p. 167.

78

be considered that there were further targets for employment and the wage bill. Indeed, in respect of labor costs in
particular, it might be supposed that these targets would
have been especially favorable to cost economy, for in contrast to the target for per-unit costs those for employment
and the wage bill were expressed in absolute terms, not in
relation to output. Nevertheless, if the enterprise exceeded
its output target, it was also allowed to exceed its targets for
employment and the wage bill, and seemingly this was true
of the *glavk* and the ministry. At least in the latter part of
the period in question, the excess allowed was not fully
proportional to the overfulfillment of the production target,
though it was for production workers.[5] Under the circumstances, the targets for employment and the wage bill in
themselves could make labor cost economy no more nor less
a concern than it already was. Interest in this aspect may
have been enhanced, however, by further controls of a
related sort, although these too were rather elastic.

Thus funds for payment of wages were supplied by the
State Bank, and traditionally this institution was responsible
for conformity of such expenditures with the plan. But with
the permission of a superior agency any organization might
obtain more funds than the plan provided. At least this was
so for the enterprise, and presumably it was also for the *glavk*
and the ministry, although the facts in this respect are not
clear. In any event, overexpenditures on wages are a recurring theme in Soviet financial writings in the period in question. Beginning in 1953, the ministry was allowed to create
under the annual plan a "reserve" or safety margin equal to
2 per cent of the wage bill of enterprises subordinate to it,
on which it might draw without authorization from any

5. Reference is to arrangements established by a decree of August
1954. See *Direktivy, 4* (Moscow, 1958), 279 ff.; Granick, pp. 178–81;
and *Zakonodatel'nye akty, 1* (Moscow, 1961), 220.

source. Overexpenditures by enterprises in that year perhaps were not inordinately great in this light, but they did occur. Of the industrial enterprises supervised financially by the State Bank in 1953, on the average each month 28 per cent were permitted to violate their wage targets. The average overexpenditure amounted to 4.3 per cent of the wage bill.[6] Partly as a result of countermeasures, however, particularly the reform of State Bank operations in August 1954, the overexpenditures thereafter declined. Thus, in 1957, 23 per cent of the industrial enterprises overexpended, and the sums involved totaled 2.4 per cent of the wage bill.

In order for success criteria to determine behavior, success and failure must be determined from reliable records on performance. In appraising the impetus to labor-cost economy under the annual plan, therefore, we must also consider that managerial personnel in Soviet industry could often manipulate statistical and accounting data bearing on their achievements. Of this we may judge both from reports of emigrées and from recurring criticism in the Soviet press. Contrary to a common supposition, such manipulation—or "simulation" (ochkovtiratel'stvo), as it is known in the U.S.S.R.—cannot easily be carried far. If detection and punishment are to be avoided, the perpetrator ordinarily must be content with limited distortions, e.g. "borrowing" future output in order to assure complete instead of nearly complete fulfillment of the output plan, misclassification of outlays, and the like. By implication, the opportunity to manipulate may have further dampened interest in labor cost economy during the period of concern, although probably not very materially.

6. I assume that the excess is compared with the wage bill of the firms exceeding their quotas. The source is not clear in this respect. See M. Kotkov i V. Turkovskii, "Puti usileniia kontrolia . . . ," *Den'gi i kredit,* No. 8 (1958), 12.

PLAN TARGETS, 1946–57: HOW TAUT?

In sum, to fulfill the target for costs generally, and related targets for labor costs particularly, should have been a concern of the industrial administrator, although not a highly urgent one. But what of the targets? How taxing were they to begin with?

The plan was not simply the creation of Gosplan, to be presented in final form for implementation to subordinate agencies exercising operational control. Nor was it simply a creation of Gosplan formulated with due regard to directives of the party leadership and the Council of Ministers. Rather it was the result of an intricate administrative process in which not only Gosplan, the party leadership, and the Council of Ministers, but the subordinate agencies themselves participated. Thus targets formulated for each administrative level were subject to negotiation between those in posts of responsibility there, their superiors, and, especially at higher levels, Gosplan. At any level, administrators sometimes took the initiative in proposing targets to superiors. It was their task also to elaborate general targets into detailed plans.

So far as they were able to determine the plan, the industrial administrators sought diverse aims; but one of these manifestly tended to be uppermost: to limit the task. That was the aim regarding targets generally, hence regarding those related to labor costs. In this way it was hoped to build a safety factor into the targets and so to enhance prospects of plan fulfillment. That industrial administrators have been so disposed is a familiar theme in reports of former Soviet citizens. The notorious safety factor is also the subject of continuing complaint in the U.S.S.R. Apparently referring to the mid-fifties, a Soviet work on wages informs us that:

81

The system of premiums for engineer-technical workers that is applied at the present time played a large role in the expansion of our industry, but it has serious deficiencies. Under this system the possibility of receiving a premium and the amount of such a premium depend exclusively on the attainment and overfulfillment of planned indices. Hence the workers are not interested in the preparation of demanding planned tasks and try to lower the targets.[7]

In Soviet usage, "engineer-technical workers" include the director of the enterprise and many of his chief assistants.

Of all this the party and government leaders were aware; and by formulating sufficiently demanding directives, they could hope to counteract pressures from below for limited targets. They also realized that if the final targets were much beyond reach, they might tend to lose their force. In any case, difficulties might arise in implementing the plan generally. It was Gosplan's task, as far as possible, to see that the realities were observed in an appropriate degree.

Reflecting as they did these conflicting currents, the targets, including those relating to labor costs, often must have been demanding; but often, too, they must have been otherwise. They tended to be more demanding in low- than in high-priority sectors, for under the famous Soviet practice of allocating resources through priorities, Gosplan necessarily favored high-priority sectors in adjudicating managerial claims to inputs. Hence the former were more apt than the latter to receive the inputs they asked for in order to fulfill projected targets for output. With the information at its disposal Gosplan had only a limited capacity to appraise such claims independently, so its decisions must frequently have been arbitrary. Willy-nilly the targets must often have

7. A. G. Aganbegian and B. F. Maier, *Zarabotnaia plata v SSSR* (Moscow, 1959), p. 163. For further discussion see the sources cited above, n. 1, especially Berliner, *Factory and Manager,* pp. 75 ff.

been relatively taxing even for high-priority sectors. Often, too, low-priority sectors must have retained much of the safety factor they sought.

The degree of tautness in Soviet plans is not easy to gauge. I have tried to consider available evidence that includes data on fulfillment of the plans, although admittedly these are difficult to interpret. During postwar years up to 1957, the government initiated three five-year plans (Table 5.2). The third such plan, however, had only been in operation two years in 1957, and was abandoned a year later. (It was supplanted by the Seven Year Plan, which is now in progress.) If the sample data given on output are at all indicative, use of labor tended to be greater relative to production than planned. Hence productivity projections were underfulfilled. Nevertheless, the excess use of labor may have been associated with deficiencies in use of other inputs; and in gauging how demanding the targets were to begin with, the record must be read in this light. Then, too, underfulfillment of the productivity targets may reflect their taxing nature, but in some measure it may also reflect the inferior priority accorded productivity. Of course, there must be some tendency toward underfulfillment generally since those managers who could overfulfill their targets are reluctant to do so. They are thus less apt to offset by their superior performance the underperformance of those really encountering difficulties.

The data in the table refer to five-year plans. Except for 1947, the government has not published its annual plan for any postwar year through 1956. Performance in respect to the annual plan must therefore be gauged chiefly from that concerning the five-year plans; from the government's releases regarding fulfillment of annual plans (which often refer to unstated targets and, moreover, to targets which have been revised in the course of the year considered)[8]; and

8. See below, pp. 103, 157.

TABLE 5.2.

Fulfillment of Five and Seven Year Plans, U.S.S.R., Selected Industrial Products and Employment

	Coal mil. m.t.	Oil mil. m.t.	Electric Power bil. kwt. hours	Cement mil. m.t.	Steel mil. m.t.	Cotton Cloth mil. meters	Boots and Shoes mil. pr.	Wage Earners and Salaried Workers, Industry millions[b]	Wage Earners and Salaried Workers, All Sectors millions
Actual, 1927–28	35.4	11.6	5.0	1.85	4.25	2.68	103	3.5	11.4
1st FYP goal, 1932–33									
Minimal variant	68	19	17	5.4	8.3	4.36	125	4.4	14.8
Optimal variant	75	22	22	6.2	10.4	4.67	145	4.6	15.8
Actual, 1932	64.4	21.4	13.5	3.48	5.93	2.69	103	6.7	22.6
2nd FYP goal, 1937	152.5	44.3	38.0	7.5	17.0	5.10	125	10.2	28.9
Actual, 1937	128.0	28.5	36.2	5.45	17.73	3.45	182.9	10.1	26.7
3rd FYP goal, 1942	230.0	49.5	75.0	10.00	27.5	4.90	n.a.	11.9	32.0
Actual, 1940[a]	165.9	31.1	48.3	5.68	18.32	3.95	211.0	11.0	31.2
Actual, 1945	149.3	19.4	43.3	1.84	12.25	1.62	63.1	9.5	27.3
4th FYP goal, 1950	250	35.4	82.0	10.5	25.4	4.69	240	(12.0)	33.5
Actual, 1950	261.1	37.9	91.2	10.19	27.33	3.90	203.4	14.1	38.9
5th FYP goal, 1955	373	70	164	22.4	44.3	6.3	315	(16.0)	44.7
Actual, 1955	391.3	70.8	170.2	22.48	45.27	5.91	274.5	17.4	48.4
6th FYP goal, 1960	593	135	320	55	68.3	7.27	455	(19.1)	55
Actual, 1958	496.1	113.2	235.4	33.31	54.92	5.79	335.8	19.7	55.9 (34.3)[c]
Actual, 1960	513	147.9	292.3	45.5	65.3	6.39	419.3	21.1[c]	61.9 (60.6)[c]
7-yr. plan goal, 1965	600–12	230–40	500–20	82	86–91	7.7–8.8	515	(24.0)	66.5
Actual, 1961	510	166	327	50.9	70.7	6.42	442	22.2[c]	64.6[c]
Actual, 1962	517	186	369	57.3	76.3	6.45	456	23.1[c]	67.0[c]

Sources: For goals of the First First Five Year Plan see Gosplan, Piatiletnii plan narodno-khoziaistvennogo stroitel'stva S.S.S.R., 1 (Moscow, 1929), 127, 128, 142–44; 2, Part I (Moscow, 1929), pp. 153, 218, 227; of the Second Five Year Plan, Gosplan, The Second Five Year Plan . . . of the U.S.S.R. (New York, n.d.), pp. 188, 545, 549, 624, 625; of the Third Five Year Plan, Gosplan, Tretii piatiletnii plan . . . Soiuza S.S.R., 1938–42 (Moscow, 1939), pp. 199, 202, 203, 205, 209, 228; of the Fourth Five Year Plan, Zakon o piatiletnem plane . . . na 1946–1950 gg. (Gospolitizdat, 1946), pp. 11, 13, 36, 51; of the Fifth Five Year Plan, Pravda, January 15, 1956; of the Seven Year Plan, Pravda, February 8, 1959, and, for cement, New York Times, October 21, 1958. For industry, goals in parentheses are inferred from goals for output and productivity.

Actual figures for 1927–28 are from the same source cited for the goals of the First Five Year Plan. For cement, steel, cotton cloth, and boots and shoes, see G. Warren Nutter, The Growth of Industrial Production in the Soviet Union (Princeton, 1962), pp. 420, 427, 455. For 1932–60 see Narkhoz, 60, pp. 241, 254, 262, 269, 305, 321, 337, 633, 636. For employment in industry see also TSUNKHU, Trud v SSSR (Moscow, 1936), pp. 10–11; TSU, Narodnoe khoziaistvo SSSR (Moscow, 1956), p. 190; Barney K. Schwalberg, "Industrial Employment in the USSR," U. S. Bureau of the Census, International Population Reports, January 13, 1960, and the sources for goals. For 1961 see Pravda, January 23, 1962, and TSU, SSSR v tsifrakh v 1961 godu (Moscow, 1962), pp. 127, 311. For 1962, see TSU, SSSR v tsifrakh v 1962, pp. 93 ff., 266.

a. Figures are believed to refer essentially to postwar territory.

b. The scope of these data has varied in the course of time and in ways not always clear. For 1932 and earlier years, I believe the figures omit forestry and fishery employees and members of industrial cooperatives. For 1937 and later years, forestry and fishery employees but not members of cooperatives are included.

c. For 1958 and 1960 figures outside parentheses include, and those inside parentheses omit, 1.3 million MTS workers who ceased to be wage earners and salaried workers in 1958. For 1960, 1961, and 1962 all figures exclude cooperative artisans who became wage earners and salaried workers in 1960. In all, 1.4 million artisans were thus transformed; of these, 1.2 million were employed in industry.

from somewhat more illuminating evidence on the fulfillment of the plans for 1957 and later years. Obviously there
must often have been an excessive use of labor, relative to
that called for in the annual plan as initially formulated. It
would be surprising, however, if performance generally had
not been superior to that under the five-year plans.[9]

Regarding economy of costs, particularly labor costs, we
may conclude that the Soviet industrial administrator usually must have been more nearly a "satisficer" than a "maximizer." Where plan targets were taxing, he still must have
behaved very much like a maximizer, but they were not
always very taxing.

MOTIVATION SINCE 1957

Reference thus far has been to postwar years before 1957. Regarding the concern for labor-cost economy,
the war period necessarily was special and can be of little
interest here, but reference should be made to prewar years

9. On plan fulfillment for 1960, see Table 12.1. Since the government did not publish the target for employment, it is difficult to
judge performance in this respect, but its claimed productivity increase
in industry (5 per cent) was somewhat below that initially planned
(5.8 per cent). See *Pravda* (October 28, 1959) and (January 26, 1961).
The claimed increase in industrial labor productivity also fell short
of the previously announced target in 1961 but surpassed it in 1957,
1958, and 1962. See *Pravda:* February 6 and December 20, 1957;
January 27, 1958; January 16, 1959; December 21, 1960; December 7,
1961; January 23, 1962; January 26, 1963. The government's claims
in this sphere, however, cannot be taken at face value. On plan fulfillment, see also Naum Jasny, *Soviet Industrialization, 1928–1952*
(Chicago, 1961), pp. 247 ff. Although not as germane at this point,
reference should also be made to the detailed and thorough study
of Eugène Zaleski, *Planification de la Croissance et Fluctuations en
U.R.S.S., 1, 1918–1932* (Paris, 1962). On tautness of Soviet plans generally, see also Holland Hunter, "Optimum Tautness in Development Planning," *Economic Development and Cultural Change, 9,*
Part I (July 1961), 561–72.

under the plans and to the period since 1957. As to the former, it may suffice to say that pertinent working arrangements were broadly similar to those just described. Especially in the earliest years, however, controls over financial matters affecting labor inputs appear to have been decidedly more permissive than they were in postwar years before 1957. Hence managerial personnel must have shown less interest in economy of costs, particularly labor costs. In formulating plans, however, the government and party hardly were less demanding, but particularly in the earliest years the inflated targets they set could not have had much operational meaning.[10]

As to the period since 1957, in economic affairs this year is notable chiefly for the reorganization of industry. But while this was a wholesale reform, the main effect was to change lines of authority rather than success criteria.[11] The same has been true of reorganizations of industry that have occurred since 1957. For this reason, the concern for economy of costs, including labor costs, should have been little affected. By subordinating the enterprise to regional rather than branch masters, however, the government hoped to foster an industry-wide—in place of the previous "narrow" departmental—outlook among managerial personnel, and in this way to realize diverse gains. In fact, the consequence sometimes has been to replace the narrow departmental attitude by a narrow regional one, and thus to establish new tendencies toward "localism" (*mestnichestvo*). But no doubt a favorable change in outlook often has occurred.

10. In addition to the data in Table 5.2 on fulfillment of the five-year plans, for early years see the data compiled on fulfillment of annual plans in Zaleski.

11. On the industrial reorganization of 1957, see Oleg Hoeffding, "The Soviet Industrial Reorganization of 1957," *American Economic Review*, 49S (1959), 65–67; Michael Kaser, "The Reorganization of Soviet Industry and Its Effects on Decision Making," in Gregory Grossman, ed., *Value and Plan* (Berkeley, 1960).

In any event, the regional economic councils may be more concerned with financial discipline than were the ministries and the *glavki*. Excess use of labor by one industry now may only prejudice possibilities of plan fulfillment by another for which the regional council is equally responsible. The reform also saw in diverse ways the increase in power of Gosplan, an organization with a nation-wide purview; and more recently much authority has been transferred to republican and all-union economic councils, which have, in respect of either the different republics or the country generally, similar broad scope. Possibly these developments have also enhanced the concern for cost economy.

If the reorganizations have not been very consequential in this sphere, another development may prove more so. While before 1957 premiums for managerial personnel in industrial enterprises were based chiefly on performance regarding production, occasional use was made, sometimes in an experimental way, of alternative schemes rewarding cost economy. After 1957 premiums continued as a rule to be paid primarily by reference to output, but by a decree of July 1959, as part of a general reform of premium arrangements in the economy, industrial enterprises were required to institute a new system for payment of premiums to leading personnel.[12] Under the new procedure, the cardinal criterion for the payment of premiums is performance regarding costs. As a rule premiums are to be paid depending on the degree of fulfillment and overfulfillment of the plan target for cost reduction. Typically in industry for fulfillment of the target, leading personnel are to receive a bonus of 10 per cent of their basic pay. For each tenth of a per cent of overfulfillment there is to be a further bonus of 1.5 per

12. *Spravochnik partiinogo rabotnika* (Moscow, 1961), pp. 190 ff.; Dmitrieva, *Rentabel'nost' promyshlennogo predpriiatiia* . . . , pp. 195 ff.; M. A. Bishaev and M. M. Fedorovich, *Organizatsiia upravleniia promyshlennym proizvodstvom* (Moscow, 1961), pp. 108 ff.

cent of the base pay.[13] Premiums are to be paid only within limits of the planned wage bill. If the output target is not fulfilled, premiums are to be reduced. While the foregoing arrangements were to be instituted generally, in certain branches, including coal and ore mining, petroleum, and chemicals, managerial personnel were to be paid additional premiums in the light of their performance regarding output.

These arrangements manifestly represent something of a break with the past, and their application should enhance the concern for economy of costs, including labor costs. Their application on a comprehensive scale, however, apparently has been delayed. Even where applied, the new premium criteria must still leave untouched the problem of the safety factor, for under the new criteria managerial personnel in the enterprise still have every incentive to understate capacities and so to limit plan targets to begin with.

One must read partly in this light the curious fact that now, only a short time after the introduction of a significant reform in premium arrangements, Soviet economists are debating the merits of an even more significant one. Liberman's much publicized proposals regarding industrial planning appear to have been implemented, if at all, only on a limited, experimental basis, and cannot be explored in any detail here. But a cardinal feature is the proposal for a wholesale revision of managerial success criteria. Also, through the proposed reform, which entails relating bonuses to a novel scale of "profitability," it is hoped to repair

13. Reference is to the monthly base pay, but for managerial personnel with plant (as distinct from shop) responsibilities, supposedly the premiums were to be determined in the light of quarterly results. This might mean that premiums of the indicated amounts were to be paid only once a quarter, though this seems unlikely.

diverse deficiencies. Among these not least is the continued tendency to limit tasks. Through introduction of the new criteria it is hoped to provide the enterprise with the "greatest possible moral and material interest in making full use of reserves not only in plan fulfillment but also in the very compilation of plans." [14]

While managerial personnel in industry continue to seek limited targets, Gosplan still seeks taxing ones. It has been suggested, however, that Gosplan has been less demanding lately than it was formerly, and that the targets have tended less often to be excessive. It is difficult to judge to what extent this has been so. In his report on the Seven Year Plan (1959–65) to the party Congress in January 1959, Khrushchev declared that the new program was being formulated "in such a way that it can be carried out without overstrain." [15] Apparently the new program was intended to be more realistic than the abortive Sixth Five Year Plan (1956–60) turned out to be. Judging by the record to date, probably it will be more nearly fulfilled than was the latter. But how it will compare with the Fifth Five Year Plan (1950–55) is still uncertain. Of course, here as elsewhere we must consider that degree of fulfillment does not necessarily measure tautness. As for annual plans, some support of the notion that targets lately have been less taxing can be found in government claims of significant overfulfillment of targets for gross industrial output for several recent years. The import of such claims for tautness, however, is especially difficult to judge. In any case, similar claims were often made in

14. *Current Digest* (October 3, 1962), p. 13. See also Marshall Goldman, "Economic Controversy in the Soviet Union," *Foreign Affairs, 41* (1962–63), 498–512.

15. Herbert S. Levine, "A Study in Economic Planning: The Soviet Industrial Supply System" (dissertation, Harvard University, 1961), pp. 304–05.

the early fifties. Certainly targets lately have been more realistic than those of the earliest years under the five-year plans, but this is not the issue.

AUTHORITY WITHIN THE ENTERPRISE

Within the enterprise, it has been assumed that administrative responsibility falls primarily on managerial personnel consisting of the director and his chief assistants. What of the enterprise party cell, with its own chief, the secretary? And what of the enterprise trade union, with its factory committee? This is not the place to examine in detail the heritage from the famous "triangle" that once prevailed in the Soviet enterprise. Suffice it to say that responsibility for administration of the enterprise generally and for fulfillment of the annual plan particularly has indeed been vested in those formally occupying managerial posts, and first of all in the director. I refer to the principle of one-man direction (*edinonachalie*). A Soviet textbook of 1956 on the economics of the industrial enterprise explains the principle in these terms: "One man direction means the subordination of the collective of workers to the single will of the leader, who is vested with the necessary rights in the administration of the sector of production entrusted to him and bears for the work of this sector full responsibility before the superior agency." [16]

In principle, the party cell has had the task of fulfilling party directives. In economic affairs this means that it has been expected to oversee fulfillment of the plan. By counseling the management, by organizing mass support, and in other ways it has also been expected to contribute to effective use of the enterprise's resources generally. But supposedly it

16. *Ekonomika sotsialisticheskikh promyshlennykh predpriiatii* (Moscow, 1956), p. 36.

should not intervene in administration. In practice, according to many accounts, including those by emigrée former officials, the party cell has engaged in activities of varying scope in different enterprises, but the director usually has been the chief executive officer in fact as well as in theory. In any case, for the party secretary himself plan fulfillment has been a cardinal measure of success, and the attitude of the director toward this task no doubt reflects a similar attitude on the part of the party secretary. Both in implementing and in formulating the plan, the director may possibly have exerted himself more than he would have otherwise, and in a more responsible manner, because of the presence of the party secretary. But it has not been easy for the latter to escape the "web of mutual involvement" that is woven into the enterprise to ensure at least a necessary minimum of harmony.

As a creature of the party, the trade union has long ceased to have any pretensions to executive authority in the enterprise, but it has continued to have diverse tasks there. A cardinal one must seem strange to Western eyes: By organizing workers' production conferences, stimulating "socialist emulation," fostering workers' discipline, and in other ways, the trade union is to "mobilize the masses" in the interest of promoting the growth of output generally and the fulfillment of the plan in particular. The unions also have had other responsibilities, however, one of which has been to ensure the observance of minimum standards of health and safety, although how effectively this has been done is not clear. Also, dismissal of a worker because of incompetence or for certain other reasons has long been subject to determination or review by a Norms and Conflicts Commission (RKK) in which management and the trade unions participate on an equal basis. Trade unions were relatively moribund under Stalin but have lately been somewhat revivified.

91

Thus, in a resolution of December 1957, the party called on the unions, particularly at the level of the enterprise, to take a more active role in economic affairs. Reportedly the resolution has not been without effect.[17]

17. Emily C. Brown, "The Local Union in Soviet Industry," *Industrial and Labor Relations Review, 13* (1959–60), 192–215.

6 INDUSTRIAL LABOR RECRUITMENT AND UTILIZATION

FREEDOM OF CHOICE IN EMPLOYMENT

We must now consider more expressly working arrangements for determining employment in nonfarm pursuits, and the households from which such employment is recruited. A cardinal factor on which such employment must turn is the stocks of "fixed" capital at the disposal of different productive enterprises; but this is a matter for later inquiry, and here such stocks are viewed as data. As a result of current investment they may vary, and while the resultant additions to capacity will be employed chiefly in future periods, to some extent they may be employed currently. But, if so, how this occurs and to what extent are not now of concern.

I also take more or less as a datum the structure of nonfarm output. Or rather, the system's directors are supposed to seek some structure for such output. Presumably the

93

structure sought is related to ends, but how is again a matter not now of concern, although it may vary with the general level of output. Any limitations in capacity to produce one or another good should have been considered in the determination of the desired structure, but otherwise they are understood to be a possible source of divergence from it. Reference is to the structure sought not only for the U.S.S.R. generally but within different market areas.

Although my concern here is with all nonfarm employment, as before circumstances in industry may be taken as illustrative. Unless otherwise indicated, therefore, reference is particularly to the latter sector.

The foregoing does not completely define the limits within which I propose to proceed, but other aspects to be considered as data will become evident as the discussion progresses.

As thus delimited, the sphere of resource use in question has diverse facets, but in part the task is to recruit labor into different pursuits, and here evidently the government has had open to it an option similar to that which confronted it in disposing of consumers' goods. The worker can be recruited through an open market, where at prevailing money wage rates he is free to choose his occupation and place of work. Alternatively, he can be recruited by compulsion, his occupation and place of work being determined in some degree administratively. Which procedure has been employed? As in the case of the disposition of consumers' goods, the government's policy has varied at different times, and here in a particularly complex way.[1]

1. See especially Bergson, *The Structure of Soviet Wages,* pp. 143 ff., 234 ff.; Solomon M. Schwarz, *Labor in the Soviet Union* (New York, 1951), chs. 2 and 3; Vladimir Gsovski, "Elements of Soviet Labor Law," U. S. Bureau of Labor Statistics, *Bulletin,* No. 1026; Jerzy G. Gliksman, "Recent Trends in Soviet Labor Policy," *Monthly Labor Review, 79* (1956), 767–75; Emily C. Brown, "The Soviet Labor Market," *Indus-*

Industrial Labor

During the period from the outset of the five-year plans to 1940, the worker's freedom of choice of occupation and place of work was expressly granted by law, and appears also to have been more or less a fact. Nevertheless, in order to combat the inordinately high labor turnover that developed under the First Five Year Plan (Table 6.1), the govern-

TABLE 6.1.

New Employment and Departures of Wage Earners, Plants of Soviet Large-Scale Industry, in Relation to Average Monthly Number of Wage Earners Employed
(percentages)

	1928	1929	1930	1931	1932	1933	1934	1935
New employment	101	122	176	151	127	125	101	92
Departures	92	115	152	137	135	122	97	86

Source: TSUNKHU, *Sotsialisticheskoe stroitel'stvo v SSSR* (Moscow, 1936), p. 531.

ment adopted a variety of measures that must have restricted freedom of choice of place of work. Most importantly, after rationing had been in effect for some time, ration privileges were placed under the control of the employing establishment. Also, where the worker occupied housing administered by the employing establishment, he was made subject to eviction if he severed his connection with the latter. At the time, however, the demand for labor was intense, and one wonders how effective such measures were. Despite the restrictions, workers did manage to change jobs at a notable rate. As judged from the government's complaints, the turnover was only in part on its own initiative.

The labor flow declined under the Second Five Year Plan, and continued to decline during 1935, after major food products had been derationed. In that year it was only

trial and Labor Relations Review, 10 (1956–57), 179–200; U.S. Bureau of Labor Statistics, *Principal Current Soviet Labor Legislation*, Report No. 210 (January 1962).

slightly below that of 1928, when restrictive measures had not yet been introduced. In good part the decline must have been due simply to the attenuation of the forces which caused it, particularly the food shortage and the extraordinary expansion of employment. As for the latter, the annual increase in working force in large-scale industry, which was 12, 38, and 28 per cent in 1930–32, fell to 1, 0, and 7 per cent during the next three years.

Trends in labor turnover after 1935 are not known, but by a decree of December 1938 the government introduced an additional device to limit mobility: social insurance and vacation benefits were made dependent on length of service in a particular establishment.

There were also restrictions on freedom of choice among particular categories of workers. For example, on the eve of the five-year plans, the graduate of a university or technicum was required to work at his specialty for a limited period. Under decrees of September 1933 and June 1936, this period was fixed first at five, and then at three years, while the place of work was also to be determined administratively. By another decree of September 1933, the graduate of a factory apprentice school was required to serve three years in directly productive work at his specialty.

While the worker's freedom of choice was restricted before 1940, this year should be considered as marking the end of one period and the beginning of another because of measures introduced in June and October 1940: (1) subjecting to criminal prosecution the worker who might leave his place of work without the permission of the director of the employing enterprise or institution, (2) establishing a new system of vocational schools, the "labor reserve" schools, for which students were to be recruited from among youths of fourteen through seventeen by means of a draft by local officials, and whose graduates were to be subject for a period of four years to administrative assignment to jobs, and (3) subjecting diverse specialists, again with criminal prosecution threatened for failure to conform, to administrative transfer from one enterprise or institution to another (although with assurance against material loss). A law enacted in December 1938, requiring a workbook to be maintained for each worker and held by the management in each place where he was employed, assumed special significance after the 1940 laws had been enacted. All these measures preceded the Nazi attack, but after it, additional ones followed, so that employment of virtually all the able-bodied urban population became a matter for administrative determination. Moreover, those violating the law often became liable to prosecution by military tribunals.

After the conclusion of hostilities the wartime legislation for the most part was apparently allowed to lapse. The legislation of 1940, however, continued on the books and remained there until 1955–56, when by decree the diverse compulsory features introduced in 1940 were abandoned.

While such controls were on the books, freedom of choice must have been limited, but the constraints perhaps were not quite so serious as might be supposed. Thus the controls were employed with varying severity in the course of time. Although the evidence is somewhat conflicting, criminal penalties provided for in the 1940 legislation may have ceased to be invoked in any general way by about 1950. In any event, while the legislation of 1940 was on the books, according to many reports shifts of labor from one establishment to another continued on some scale, and while these sometimes may have been made administratively, the worker, too, must have been able to exercise some initiative. Curiously, such turnover occurred even during the war.[2] In 1947

2. *Izvestiia* (October 27, 1944), as cited in Solomon M. Schwarz, p. 126.

departures of workers from plants of the iron and steel industry were 37.3 per cent of average employment.[3] This, of course, is well below rates that prevailed in industry generally during 1928–35; but by 1956, a year during most of which voluntary transfers were legal (the decree abandoning the 1940 prohibition was issued in April), the departure rate had fallen to 20–22 per cent.

According to Soviet authorities, quotas for new recruits to labor reserve schools actually were being met largely or entirely by volunteers long before the legal provision for a draft of such persons was formally annulled. What volunteering might mean for youths of fourteen to seventeen is not explained, but perhaps the labor reserve schools did exercise some attraction—if not for the pupils, at least for their parents—in view of the free tuition and material support provided. It should be recalled that generally tuition was charged for upper grades of secondary schools from 1940 to 1956. No information is at hand on the extent to which the 1940 law providing for administrative transfer of specialists was invoked; but here, too, compulsion probably tended to become less important in the course of time.

Since their abandonment in 1956, neither the controls of 1940 nor any others have been introduced, and the worker again has substantial discretion as to occupation and place of work. As before 1940, however, he is subject to constraints. Indeed, these appear to be essentially those that prevailed in the earlier period, although whether the worker who on his own initiative leaves his employing establishment is still evicted from housing controlled by the latter is not clear.[4]

3. M. Gardner Clark, "Comparative Wage Structure in the Steel Industry of the Soviet Union and Western Countries," in Industrial Relations Research Association, *Proceedings of the Thirteenth Annual Meeting* (December 1960), p. 287.

4. Another constraint is imposed by the internal passport system, in operation since the early 1930s. This system has served in some

In sum, under the five-year plans the industrial worker's freedom of choice was seriously constrained for a decade or so beginning in 1940. Since that interval was occupied largely by war and reconstruction, the concern here is properly with other years, although the draconian controls of 1940 and after are of interest for their own sake. In these other years the constraints do not appear to have been seriously restrictive.

DETERMINATION OF LABOR REQUIREMENTS

So far as freedom of choice of occupation and place of work prevailed, the supply of labor for different industrial pursuits at prevailing wage rates must in effect have been determined. What of the demand? Requirements for labor in different pursuits, that administrators of agencies exercising operational control over industry have sought to meet, manifestly must have depended in part on the volume of output in each branch and market area. But any given output could have been produced with varying amounts of labor in different occupations and enterprises. How have requirements for such labor been determined?

As we have seen, in implementing the plans, particularly annual ones, managerial personnel in industry have been more or less concerned to economize costs, including labor costs. Yet according to familiar reasoning, given this concern, requirements at prevailing wage rates for labor in different occupations and enterprises are correspondingly determined. The administrator's interest in cost economy, it is true, has frequently been mild. For this reason, his labor requirements in some degree must have been arbitrary. But for the rest, they must have been fixed in principle by the concern to limit costs.

---

degree to limit the worker's freedom of choice as to the locality of employment. Particularly, movement into several major cities has been restricted.

99

Or rather, this is the case if the administrators have the authority to act accordingly. In inquiring into the question posed, therefore, the first issue to consider is the extent to which administrators have had such authority.

What is in question is the authority, under the annual plan of managerial personnel, to economize wage costs by determining three aspects: the total volume of employment in any enterprise in relation to the volume of output, the occupational structure of employment in any enterprise, and the relative volume of employment among different enterprises in the same industry and market area. Under the annual plan, managerial personnel in industry have been free throughout to exploit any opportunities to economize on wage costs by limiting the volume of employment in relation to output within the enterprise. This has been true even of managerial personnel within the enterprise itself, for no sanction by superior agencies would have been required.

In seeking to economize costs under the annual plan, the administrator was confronted with separate targets for labor and materials. Hence freedom to substitute one for the other was limited. With due regard to this restriction, authority to limit employment was in hand. However, management, in seeking to curtail staff, has sometimes been hampered by the union factory committee.[5]

As to occupational structure of employment within the enterprise, under the annual plan, as was indicated, during postwar years to 1957 targets were set for both the wage bill and employment. This was also true at other times under the five-year plans. Therefore, freedom to determine the occupational structure in the interests of economy of

5. Emily C. Brown, "A Note on Employment and Unemployment in the Soviet Union in the Light of Technical Progress," *Soviet Studies,* *12* (1960–61), 234 ff.

wage costs by substitution of more low-paid for fewer high-paid workers has been restricted. Under the annual plan for the enterprise there have also long been targets for employment and the wage bill for different categories. Thus, according to recent practice, there have been separate targets for ordinary workers of rank below foreman, engineers and technical and managerial personnel, clerical and other office workers, janitorial and other service personnel, apprentices, and security personnel. This classification has been observed for "industrial productive" personnel. There have also been targets for employment and the wage bill for secondary activities.

Subject to the approval of the *glavk* or ministry (before 1957) or of the *sovnarkhoz* (since then), however, the enterprise has been free to redistribute among these different categories the totals allowed for employment and the wage bill in all categories together. But the *glavk* and the ministry, and now the *sovnarkhoz,* appear to have been similarly limited in some degree. In any event, from recurring complaints of factory directors on this score, one gathers that they have often been somewhat hampered by the separate targets for different occupation categories.[6]

Discretion over the relative volume of employment in different enterprises in the same industry and market area could be vested only in agencies superior to the enterprise. The extent to which such discretion has been so vested under the annual plan is not altogether clear, but among other things the ministry and the *glavk* after 1955 had the authority, subject to concurrence of the Ministry of Finance, even to create, reorganize, or liquidate enterprises. Subject to the approval of the republican Council of Ministers, the regional economic council has inherited this authority. Un-

6. For a recent example, see *Ekonomicheskaia Gazeta* (December 18, 1961), p. 9.

der the circumstances, at least recently, these organizations should have had some discretion to redistribute employment among enterprises.[7]

Not infrequently the plan for the enterprise in its final version was formulated only after the year to which it referred had begun. This was particularly true before the war, but the practice continued thereafter, and as late as the mid-1950s cases are still reported where the plan for the enterprise was not formulated until the end of the year.[8] This does not mean that the enterprise could proceed meanwhile without constraint; rather, it ordinarily was subject to the selected targets that the annual plan was to elaborate. But the enterprise management did have more discretion as to the volume and structure of employment than it otherwise would have had.

In implementing the plan, then, industrial administrators have had substantial discretion to economize wage costs, and requirements for labor in different pursuits should have been determined to a corresponding degree by such a concern.

Nevertheless, the discretion was not complete; and where it was not, we must consider a further question: where opportunities for wage-cost economy could not be exploited under the plan, to what extent might they have been in the formulation of the plan?

While the industrial administrators have had reasons to seek economy of costs, including labor costs, under the plan, they have not been concerned to do so in formulating it. What is in question now, however, is not the targets for employment and the wage bill generally, but the separate targets for different categories of workers; for it has been

7. The *sovnarkhoz*, however, was at first granted and then in January 1959 denied authority to redistribute materials, fuel, machinery, and equipment among enterprises in different branches.

8. *Den'gi i kredit*, No. 10 (1955), 4.

chiefly here that the concern for wage-cost economy has been hampered. Also, while seeking to limit the task regarding cost economy, the administrators should have had no reason to seek an uneconomic division of the labor and wage bill quotas allowed them. On the contrary, the task regarding cost economy would be less arduous if this division were economic.

Of course, the party leaders, the Council of Ministers, and Gosplan have also participated in the formulation of the plan, and these authorities should have been concerned to assure an economic division of labor and wage bill quotas in any event; but the industrial administrators have been more intimately acquainted with opportunities for cost economy at this point, and it is important that interests be harmonious.

While participating in formulation of the plan generally, the administrators have had much to do with the division of labor and wage bill quotas by categories. At least recently, this has been so even at the level of the enterprise. Thus, under a decree of August 1955, the director of the enterprise was for the first time given the authority to approve the tekhpromfinplan for the enterprise in its final version.[9] While the approved plan had to include many targets already approved by superior agencies, these have often been less detailed than the final plan, especially for labor and wages. However, some restrictions as to occupational structure—for example, between ordinary workers and others— probably have still been imposed.

Under the circumstances, it might be supposed that the enterprise director has had a corresponding authority to revise the plan after he has formulated it, and hence that the plan could not have been very restrictive regarding occupational structure after all. The plan in its final version, however, is filed with the enterprise's superior agency

9. *Zakonodatel'nye akty*, 1, 185 ff.

103

The Economics of Soviet Planning

and still serves there as a control over the enterprise's activities. But revisions may have been easier to arrange since 1955 than they were before.

Of course, whatever the authority of the enterprise in this regard, the plan has been subject to revision. It is not easy to generalize, but changes have been frequent, and this must be considered in judging the extent to which the structure of employment could be adapted to the requirements of cost minimization.

DETERMINATION OF EMPLOYMENT GENERALLY

Three efficiency rules are pertinent to the sphere of resource use in question. Reference is to an economy where labor in nonfarm pursuits generally works for hire and is compensated at a money wage and where freedom of choice prevails as to occupation and place of work. The first rule is: In each employing establishment in nonfarm sectors, any given output is produced ideally, so that at prevailing wage rates the total wage bill is a minimum. Within any market area, this must also be so for all establishments in the same industry taken together.

So far as the concern is to observe this rule, requirements for labor in different nonfarm occupations and enterprises are in effect determined in relation to the level of output in the industry and market area and to prevailing wage rates. At the same time, given freedom of choice, some supplies will also be forthcoming. The second and third rules assure that these two aspects should correspond. Thus rule two stipulates that the total output of all nonfarm goods taken together should be so determined that requirements for labor generally are just sufficient to absorb available supplies. Hence there must be no over-all excess or deficiency of labor relative to demand. Under the third rule, a correspondence of requirements and supplies is also estab-

104

lished in each nonfarm pursuit, for supposedly relative wages are adjusted to assure this result.

These rules are supposed to be observed whatever the structure of nonfarm output.

So far as these rules presuppose freedom of choice for the worker and an impelling and effective concern for wage-cost economy for the manager, we have already seen that in the U.S.S.R. they have in some measure been violated. As illustrated by circumstances in industry, this has been so even in peacetime periods. But in inquiring further into working arrangements for determination of labor services employed in nonfarm pursuits and households from which they have been recruited, we may still usefully consider how nonfarm output and relative wages for different nonfarm pursuits are dealt with. Thus, granting that neither requirements nor supplies have been determined fully as stipulated, to what extent have nonfarm output and relative wages been determined so as to make supplies and requirements correspond generally and in individual pursuits?

In determining nonfarm output the government has indeed sought to assure a correspondence of requirements for, and supplies of, nonfarm labor. (I consider now nonfarm sectors generally, and not merely industry.) Thus an account of nonfarm labor requirements and supplies has for many years been still another of the balances struck in the formulation of long-term and annual plans, and to reconcile the two aspects on this basis necessarily has been important.

Furthermore, in this endeavor the government has met with some success. Thus, on the average during the fiscal year 1927–28, 1.29 million persons, or about 8.3 per cent of the nonfarm labor force, were registered as unemployed with the labor exchanges that functioned at that time. Subsequently, as employment increased under the First Five Year Plan, the number of registered unemployed declined. Toward the end of the plan employment exchanges were abandoned, and publication of data on unemployment was suspended and has not been resumed since. In the U.S.S.R. it is often claimed that "unemployment has been liquidated," and the implication sometimes is that there is not even any "frictional" unemployment. Obviously this is not so, and we know that young people especially have had difficulty in finding a suitable job.[10] But no doubt unemployment of a persistent sort has not been sizable for many years.

With the nonfarm workers it has employed, however, the government often has been unable to fulfill the output targets established. Hence, in a sense, requirements have been not only sufficient but more than sufficient to assure full employment. But more germane here would be a general excess of wage appropriations to enterprises over the amounts they could actually spend, and of this there is little evidence. There often have been reports, however, of difficulties encountered by individual enterprises in meeting labor quotas, and these may have been pervasive, especially immediately prior to the enactment of the 1940 labor controls. Since in the 1930s, particularly in the early years, financial controls were notably lax, the degree to which wage appropriations could be spent can serve at such times only as a rather elastic criterion for gauging the satisfaction of enterprise requirements for labor.

RELATIVE WAGE DETERMINATION AND EMPLOYMENT STRUCTURE

As for relative wages,[11] within any industrial branch the degree of correspondence of supplies and re-

10. Brown, *Soviet Studies, 12* (1960–61).
11. I rely here chiefly on Bergson, *The Structure of Soviet Wages;* Brown, in *Industrial and Labor Relations Review* (January 1957);

quirements achieved in different pursuits theoretically depends on the extent to which differentials conform to relative "marginal productivities" and, for workers on the margin of choice between pursuits, to "supply prices." Where, in any pursuit, extra effort is required to yield extra output, the relation of differentials to the supply price for such extra effort is also in question. Or, rather, this is so where labor supplies reflect freedom of choice and requirements reflect an impelling and effective concern for wage-cost economy. To repeat, these conditions have not been fully met in the U.S.S.R. With due regard to this fact, however, we may perceive a very broad though fluctuating tendency of wage differentials to be related to productivity and supply prices. The tendency is seen in these circumstances:

Under the five-year plans, the earnings of the industrial worker have turned first of all on his occupation, for in each industrial branch a cardinal feature in the determination of wages has been the occupational wage scale. This is a scale of coefficients relating the wage of any category to that in the first category (Table 6.2). For purposes of determining the rates to be paid, different occupations are distributed

A. E. Grigor'ev, *Ekonomika truda* (Moscow, 1959); Aganbegian and Maier, *Zarabotnaia plata;* Murray Yanowitch, "Trends in Occupational Wage Differentials," *Industrial and Labor Relations Review, 13* (1959–60), 166–91; Murray Yanowitch, "Trends in Differentials between Salaried Personnel and Wage Workers in Soviet Industry," *Soviet Studies, 11* (1959–60), 229–52; Walter Galenson, "The Soviet Wage Reform," and M. Gardner Clark, "Comparative Wage Structures in the Steel Industry of the Soviet Union and Western Countries," in Industrial Relations Research Association, *Papers Presented at the Thirteenth Annual Meeting* (December 1960); and E. I. Kapustin, ed., *Zarabotnaia plata v promyshlennosti SSSR i ee sovershentstvovanie* (Moscow, 1961). With his kind permission, use was also made of an unpublished essay of Leonard Kirsch, "Recent Changes in Soviet Wage Policy."

TABLE 6.2.

Wage Scales in Chemical and Rubber Enterprises and in
Related Mining Works, U.S.S.R., 1958

	I	II	III	IV	V	VI	VII	VIII
				Wage Category				
				Wage coefficient				
Chemical and rubber	1.0	1.14	1.30	1.49	1.71	1.96	2.26	2.60
Extraction and ore enrichment	1.0	1.16	1.35	1.58	1.85	2.17	2.55	3.00
				Basic wage rate[a]				
Chemical and rubber time workers:								
In normal working conditions	13.67	15.58	17.77	20.37	23.38	26.79	30.89	35.54
In dangerous and heavy work	15.63	17.82	20.32	23.29	26.73	30.63	35.32	40.64
In especially dangerous work	18.75	21.38	24.38	27.94	32.06	36.75	42.38	40.75
Chemical and rubber piece workers:								
In normal working conditions	15.63	17.82	20.32	23.29	26.73	30.63	35.32	40.64
In dangerous and heavy work	17.58	20.84	22.85	26.19	30.06	34.46	39.73	45.71
In especially dangerous work	20.70	23.60	26.91	30.84	35.40	40.57	46.78	53.82
Workers engaged in extraction and enriching ores:								
Underground piece-workers	19.53	22.65	26.37	30.86	36.13	42.38	49.80	58.59
Pieceworker in surface mines	17.58	20.39	23.73	27.78	32.52	38.15	44.83	52.74
Time workers in surface mines, etc.	15.63	18.13	21.10	24.70	28.92	33.92	39.86	46.89

Source: Sotsialisticheskii trud, No. 2 (1958), 140.

a. In pre-1961 rubles, for a seven-hour day.

among the different wage-scale categories. The precise basis
for distribution has varied, but essentially consideration
has been given to the complexity and exactness of the task
and to the degree of responsibility associated with it. Although the training required is also taken into account,
this is usually taken to be an aspect of the other criteria. The
treatment accorded arduousness of the work and unfavorable working conditions has also varied, but for some time
these have often been the basis, not for classifying the
occupation in a higher category, but for the establishment
of a separate wage scale with higher absolute rates of pay,
although possibly the same coefficients. Consequently, the
worker performing more skilled or more arduous work or
performing such work under less pleasant conditions has
tended to be systematically paid at a higher rate.

For any occupation, however, the wage scale has been a
device for determining only the basic wage rate. The individual worker's actual earnings have also varied with his
own performance. Thus workers have been remunerated
either on a piecework or a time basis. In the former case,
actual earnings have varied with a worker's output in relation to an established norm. In the latter case, such variation has been precluded; but practically all time workers
have long been compensated by premiums for superior
performance. The criteria for determining such performance have been diverse, but often workers in a section, shop,
or department have received premiums for fulfillment of
the output target for that division. In addition to these
arrangements, others have been used to reward both piece
and time workers for special achievements. For example,
bonuses have been paid workers generally out of the enterprise fund.

Interestingly, of the two forms of remuneration, that
based on piecework has long been predominant, although
recently it has been on the decline:

Wage Earners in Industry
Remunerated on a Piecework
Basis, per cent of Total

1928	57.5
1936	76.1
1953	77.0
1956	72.0
1961 (circa)	60.0

Piecework has been of various sorts, and has changed over time. Thus "straight" piecework, which was initially universal, to a significant extent gave way in the 1930s to "progressive" piecework. But recently the latter has largely been supplanted by a piecework-premium system. In the piecework-premium system, workers in one or another section, shop, or department are paid individually on a straight piecework basis, but as a group also receive premiums for fulfillment of the plan for output.[12]

Under these procedures, the inequality of actual earnings among wage earners in different industries in the U.S.S.R., as measured by the "quartile ratio" of the frequency distribution of such earnings, was somewhat less in 1928 than it had been for wage earners in the same industries in Tsarist Russia in 1914, and close to that for wage earners in the same industries in the United States in 1904. As a result of a wholesale reform in wage scales initiated in December 1926, the degree of inequality in the U.S.S.R. in 1928 was somewhat less than that which had prevailed previously, and this trend toward declining differentials continued after 1928. But beginning in 1931, under a further widespread change in wage scales, differentials were again

12. See Bergson, *The Structure of Soviet Wages,* pp. 158 ff.; Aganbegian and Maier, *Zarabotnaia plata,* pp. 153 ff.; Kapustin, pp. 48, 96 ff.; S. Shkurko, "Material'noe stimulirovanie i formy oplaty truda v promyshlennosti," *Voprosy ekonomiki,* No. 5 (1962).

widened, with the result that toward the end of 1934 inequality in different industries exceeded that of 1928.[13]

Because of the government curtailment of releases of systematic data on earnings differentials, more recent trends in inequality are difficult to gauge. The inequality must have tended to increase after 1934, but to decline beginning in 1946. Since 1956, industrial wage scales have been undergoing still another extensive reform. While the spread in basic wage rates has sometimes been reduced, the effect on actual earnings is not clear. In iron and steel, the reform had only a limited impact on differentials, while on its eve the variation in actual earnings in an integrated Soviet steel plant was distinctly greater than that in a comparable American plant. As late as 1959, the inequality of actual earnings in industry in general probably still exceeded that of 1934.[14]

In all the foregoing Soviet policies and procedures, the concern avowedly has been to see that wages correspond to the quantity and quality of work, as is held to be appropriate under socialism. Nevertheless, the wage-scale changes of December 1926 and later were undertaken for the declared purpose of reducing an inequality of earnings considered under a "dictatorship of the proletariat" to be "incongruous," and seemingly this course continued to be pursued for a time without regard to the extraordinary increase in requirements for skilled labor that resulted from the initiation of the First Five Year Plan. But with the reversal of 1931, such "left equalitarianism" was cast aside, and higher differentials were expressly called for in the in-

13. Bergson, *The Structure of Soviet Wages,* particularly chs. V–VII.
14. Yanowitch, *Industrial and Labor Relations Review, 13* (1959–60); Galenson, pp. 4 ff.; Clark, "Comparative Wage Structures"; M. Mozhina, "Izmeneniia v raspredelenii promyshlennykh rabochikh SSSR po razmeram zarabotnoi platy," *Trud i zarabotnaia plata,* No. 10 (1961).

terest of heightening incentives. If, as seems likcly, differentials were reduced in 1946 and later, this was due chiefly to an increase in 1946 in wages of low-paid workers to compensate them for boosts in ration prices that preceded the restoration of the open market. The wage-scale revision initiated in 1956 purportedly has had as one aim the narrowing of differentials. This has been held to be in order in view of the increase in the supply of qualified labor under the five-year plans, and the concern in the long run to achieve a more equalitarian distribution.

The changes in arrangements as to incentive systems, particularly the recent shift from piece to time work, have occurred to a considerable extent since 1956 as a part of a general wage reform embracing the revision of wage scales just referred to. It has been said to be in order, however, partly because piecework previously had often been introduced where it was inappropriate and partly because, with changes in technology, it often ceased to be appropriate where it once had been.

Reference has been to "wage earners," consisting chiefly of ordinary workers of rank below foremen. For "salaried workers," comprising engineers, technicians, managerial personnel, and office workers, basic rates initially were determined like those for wage earners by use of wage scales. But since the early 1930s a somewhat different procedure, involving the compilation of a list of "occupational rates" (*dolzhnostnye oklady*), has been used: essentially absolute rates established specifically for different occupations, as distinct from coefficients referring to wage-scale categories. As for wage earners, however, the concern has been to differentiate tasks according to the qualifications and nature of the work. At least in recent years this has also involved for many responsible posts systematic differentiation of rates among enterprises, depending on their volume of output, labor force, complexity of work, etc. (Table 6.3). Whether

TABLE 6.3.

Monthly Occupational Rates for Selected Occupations,
Asbestos and Graphite Enterprises, U.S.S.R., 1959 (circa)

OCCUPATIONAL RATE, PRE-1961 RUBLES

	Enterprises of Category I	Enterprises of Category II	Enterprises of Category III
Director	2,500–2,800	2,200–2,500	1,900–2,200
Chief specialists and directors of departments	1,800–2,000	1,600–1,800	1,400–1,600
Chiefs of basic shops	1,800–2,000	1,600–1,800	1,400–1,600
Chiefs of other shops	1,400–1,600	1,200–1,400	1,100–1,300
Mining foremen; production foremen	1,300–1,500	1,200–1,300	1,100–1,300
Other foremen	1,100–1,300	1,000–1,200	900–1,000
Engineers	1,000–1,200	900–1,000	900–1,100
Technicians	700– 900	700– 900	700– 800

Source: Aganbegian and Maier, Zarabotnaia plata, p. 142.

differentiated by category of enterprise or not, rates for any
occupation usually have been established initially in the
form of a range, the rate for an individual worker being
determined within the specified limits. While salaried workers have all been time workers, those in managerial posts
have been able to earn sizable premiums, depending on
the performance of their enterprises. Where feasible, premium systems have also been established for other salaried
workers.

Under the five-year plans, differentials between salaried
workers and wage earners increased from 1928 to the mid-
1930s, but have tended to decline since then (Table 6.4).
These trends must be read in relation to changes in differentials among wage earners discussed above, and changes
in supplies and requirements for salaried workers, which of
course paralleled those for skilled wage earners.

Attention has been focused on wage differentials within

113

TABLE 6.4.

Relative Earnings of Wage Earners and Salaried Workers
in Industry, U.S.S.R.
(percentages)

	Selected Industries			*All Industries*			
	1928	*1934*	*1935*	*1940*	*1950*	*1955*	*1962* (circa)
Wage earners	100	100	100	100	100	100	100
Engineers and technicians, including managerial personnel	238[a]	292[a]	236	210	175	165	150
Clerical and other office workers	122[a]	137[a]	126	109	93	88	n.a.

Source: For selected industries, Yanowitch, *Soviet Studies*, *11* (1959–60), 233–34; for all industries for 1935–55, Aganbegian and Maier, p. 202; for all industries for 1962, V. F. Maier, *Zarabotnaia plata v period perekhoda k kommunizmu* (Moscow, 1963), p. 98.

different industries. Regarding differentials between industries, which are also of concern, what is in question is the extent to which these assure a correspondence between requirements to meet given outputs, and supplies. So far as freedom of choice prevails, the latter reflect workers' supply prices. Obviously differentials must in fact have been determined broadly in this way. Thus, according to a recent text,[15] such differentials are determined from a consideration of such aspects of work in different branches as the arduousness and complexity of typical activities and the social importance of the different branches. These factors are considered within a region, but location too is taken into account. At least recently different branches apparently have been graded systematically in the light of scores imputed to the different factors.

If read in the light of familiar facts on comparative

15. Aganbegian and Maier, *Zarabotnaia plata,* pp. 183 ff.

trends in requirements, particularly between "heavy" and "consumers' goods" industries, changes in the ranking of different industries regarding earnings (Table 6.5) are also illuminating. At many points the changes also raise further questions, which we cannot pursue here.

TABLE 6.5.

Rank of Industries According to Average Wage, U.S.S.R.

	1924	1928	1935	1940	1950	1956
Coal	10	14	4	1	1	1
Iron ore	15	12	6	5	2	2
Iron and steel	13	9	5	2	3	3
Petroleum	11	8	1	3	4	4
Paper	7	11	13	14–15	6	5
Machinery and metal processing	4	1	3	4	5	6
Electric power	n.a.	3	2	7	7	7
Chemicals	5	6	7	6	8	8
Wool	12	13	14	14–15	9	9
Leather and fur	3	5	10	11	12	10
Wood products	9	15	11	12	13	11
Cotton	14	16	12	10	11	12
Printing	1	2	8	8	10	13
Shoe	2	4	9	9	15	14
Linen	16	17	17	16–17	14	15
Food processing	6	10	16	16–17	16	16
Clothing	8	7	15	13	17	17

Source: Aganbegian and Maier, p. 190.

It was said that within any industry where relative wages assure a correspondence of supply and demand, they must also be proportional to marginal productivities. Theoretically, this can be so only where, in seeking to economize costs, those employing labor take wage rates as "data" or "parameters"; for otherwise such persons may limit their requirements for one or another kind of labor, and so depress wages in such pursuits in relation to marginal productivities. In other words, the employer is supposed to behave like a competitor rather than a monopolist at this point. Has this been so in the U.S.S.R.?

From what has been said, it should have been so, at least broadly, and wage rates have been the more apt to be treated as data because, while administrative practice regarding wage determination has varied in the course of time, this task, almost throughout, has been performed in a relatively centralized way. Thus broad policies have been established by the party, while in the work of implementation the Council of Ministers has played a cardinal role, though with the support of Gosplan. At different times, use has also been made of one or another committee. For example, the Committee on Labor and Wages, formed in 1955, has borne much of the responsibility for the reconstruction of wage scales and incentive arrangements under the wage reform initiated in the following year.

Nevertheless, subordinate agencies exercising operational control have also played a role. At all levels, as for plan targets generally, those for average wages must have been subject to negotiation. Within any agency, the administrators also have contributed in various ways to the task of determining the wage structure. Thus the enterprise management necessarily has had the primary responsibility for details of norm setting, and it has long participated in other ways, e.g. determination within established limits of individual salaries, awarding of premiums, and the like. And superior agencies have had a larger role. Ministries—when they functioned—sometimes even promulgated the scales of basic wage coefficients applicable to their industries. Even where authority has been decentralized, however, monopoly power must have been more or less limited, since the agencies concerned have had to compete for industrial labor generally and often for labor in particular occupations as well. Not surprisingly, therefore, the authority has generally been used not to limit wages of different workers, but to raise them.

The efficiency rules presuppose the absence of monopoly power not only from the side of employers but from that of workers. Obviously trade unions in the U.S.S.R. have had no power to restrict entry into different pursuits or to limit the effort of any worker who wishes to exert it. At one time, however, they played a major role in determination of wages, particularly of the intrabranch structure, and apparently they were chiefly responsible for the equalitarian turn in wage policy initiated in December 1926. But the reversal in 1931 was instigated by Stalin. Since that time the union organizations have continued to participate in wage fixing, but there is no evidence of their ever having endeavored to pursue an independent course. In its resolution of December 1957 on union affairs, the party called on the unions to participate more actively in aspects of wage determination such as norm fixing. Reportedly the unions are now doing so.[16]

While neither industrial administrators nor unions appear to have engaged in monopolistic practices as to wage fixing, under the administrative arrangements that have prevailed there have often been anomalies. Sometimes—as when, because of a failure to revise production norms, piece-work earnings soared far above basic rates—there may not have been any consequential departure from principles discussed here. But often there must have been such departures, as when—because of the ministerial approach that prevailed before 1957—there were wide variations in wages of workers engaged in the same type of work and in the same locality. For example, in 1956 in a given area a cashier in nonferrous metals might earn 718 pre-1961 rubles a month, but if he were in meat processing his salary was 379 pre-1961 rubles. Before 1956 such variations were more

16. Brown, in *Industrial and Labor Relations Review, 13* (1959–60).

the rule than the exception; thus there were some two thousand different basic pay rates for workers in the first grade of a wage scale. More generally, the wage system in the course of time had become extraordinarily complex. To simplify it and to do away with anomalous features were major aims of the wage reform initiated in 1956.[17]

WAGES AND TAXES

I have been discussing, with special reference to industry, working arrangements for nonfarm labor recruitment and allocation from the standpoint of three relevant efficiency rules. There is also a fourth rule: in disposing of his earnings, the worker must be subject to no tax that varies with their amount. In other words, both income taxes and sales taxes are precluded. In principle, however, there is no bar to a lump-sum tax—which might vary with aspects other than income, including need or even native talent, so far as they may be discerned without reference to income. But while this rule is familiar in theory, it is hardly so in practice, and needless to say it has not been observed in the U.S.S.R. The nature of the budgetary charges that have been levied directly or indirectly on the Soviet industrial worker might be discussed at length,[18] but it suffices to observe here that of the various charges in question, by far the most important has been the turnover tax. Collected in a variety of ways (as a lump-sum per unit, as a percentage of selling price, and the like), the tax is essentially a sales tax. Under Soviet circumstances, however, the line between sales taxes and charges for factors cannot be very clear. Possibly the turnover tax is in part something of an offset

17. Galenson; Margaret Dewar, "Labor and Wage Reforms in the USSR," in H. G. Shaffer, ed., *The Soviet Economy* (New York, 1963).
18. For further details and citations, see below, Appendix A.

Industrial Labor

to deficiencies in such charges,[19] but for the rest it necessarily represents a violation of our efficiency rule.

Since its introduction in 1930 to unify diverse taxes levied previously, the turnover tax has been collected predominantly on consumers' goods and on materials used in their fabrication, and for such goods it has been a major constituent in selling price. For example, in 1950 taxes levied directly or indirectly on goods sold to households in government and cooperative retail shops totaled some two hundred billion rubles, or 61 per cent of such sales at retail prices, including taxes. In 1958, the corresponding figures were 250 billion rubles and 42 per cent.[20]

In addition to the turnover tax, the government has derived revenues from an income tax, which for industrial workers has been mildly progressive. Currently, the maximum rate is 13.0 per cent. Under a decree of May 1960 the government committed itself progressively to limit this tax and to abandon it altogether by 1965. Subsequently, persons with very low incomes had their levies reduced or were exempted, but in September 1962 it was announced that further reductions and exemptions were to be postponed. For workers earning more than 100 rubles a month (post-January 1, 1961 rubles), earnings in part were to have been subject to an offsetting reduction anyhow.

For many years, the government also obtained funds from the industrial worker through semicompulsory bond sales, but in 1957 it announced the discontinuance of such issues. At the same time it declared a twenty-year moratorium on the servicing of the outstanding debt.

As the magnitude of the turnover tax revenue indicates, the government's budgetary requirements under the five-

19. For example, see below, p. 168, n. 10.
20. See *Real SNIP*, p. 150, n. 22, and p. 307; Nancy Nimitz, *Soviet National Income and Product, 1956–1958*, RAND RM-3112 PR (June 1962), p. 141.

119

year plans have been notably large. This testifies to the special nature of Soviet behavior in a crucial sphere, choices between present and future, and to the resulting magnitude of investment. But this is a subject for later discussion.[21]

CONCLUSIONS

What may we conclude as to ends sought regarding nonfarm labor recruitment and utilization? Soviet working arrangements have conformed, if only very broadly, to three efficiency rules that are corollaries of a concern for consumers' welfare. Therefore, the system's directors can be said to have behaved more or less consistently with the latter end. But in respect of labor use the concern for consumers' welfare means only that the social cost of shifting a worker from one use to another is measured by his own price for making the change. Similarly, the social cost of having him exert an extra effort is the price that must be paid him to do so. Under Soviet-type socialism, even if they should not

21. Under the five-year plans, the government has supported in its budget a variety of activities, some conventional (education, health care, and defense) and others not so conventional (investment). But through all alike it has released purchasing power to households without making consumers' goods available to them in the retail market. Thus finance has been but one side of a two-sided problem with which the government has had to deal, the other being the absorption of excess purchasing power. Such absorption has been necessary in order to limit demand to available supplies of consumers' goods in the retail market. It follows, too, that the levies described in the text may be viewed as devices for absorbing excess purchasing power as well as for providing finance. The government has financed its budgetary needs in part through other levies, particularly by charges on profits of government and other enterprise, and so far as such levies have meant higher prices for consumers' goods they too might be considered means of absorbing excess purchasing power. But for the rest, finance has been raised and excess purchasing power absorbed by the levies described, at least so far as industrial workers are concerned. However, the resulting correspondence between demand and available supplies of consumers' goods has at best only been approximate.

120

be particularly concerned with consumers' welfare, the system's directors might find it expedient to calculate social costs in this way. And in that case, our rules generally should be appealing. Thus, with costs determined in the prescribed manner, conformity with the three rules assures ideally that the total nonfarm output produced at any total cost is a maximum. Alternatively, the costs of producing any given output are a minimum.

Payment to the worker ultimately entails provision to him of consumers' goods. Conformity to the rules, therefore, ultimately assures also the economy of consumption relative to the volume of nonfarm output.[22]

Yet resource use has diverged in some measure from our efficiency rules. Sometimes the divergencies must have been due simply to administrative deficiencies, but not always. Thus costs must often have differed from any reflecting household preferences because of the government's own actions, particularly the restraints imposed on freedom of choice of employment. Even as an expedient, therefore, is it not evident that the system's directors were not really con-

22. Assume provisionally that supplies of workers in different occupations and labor effort are given. Conformity to our efficiency rules would then assure that there are no unexploited opportunities to increase the volume of nonfarm output produced at a given total cost by more effective use of labor in any enterprise or by redistribution of labor in different occupations between enterprises and industries. Similarly the cost of producing a given nonfarm output could not be further reduced in these ways. With supplies of labor in different occupations variable, opportunities to cut costs without reducing output by cutting wage differentials for more arduous, skilled, or responsible work would also have been exploited. At this point, when effort is variable the supposition is only that workers should be able to adjust freely to uniform differentials for extra output resulting from extra effort. But, given this, opportunities to cut costs or increase output through a redistribution of effort among different workers in the same occupation generally should also have been exhausted. However, on the relation of our three efficiency rules to cost economy and also to economy of consumption relative to the volume of nonfarm output, see also below, n. 26.

cerned to calculate costs in the prescribed manner? Obviously they cannot have been meticulously so, but the restrictions on freedom of choice were most severe during the decade or so after 1940. During much of this time, circumstances were rather special. While some constraints prevailed at other times, even where consumers' welfare is the standard, account must be taken of extra-private costs, like those entailed by an inordinately high labor turnover.

In trying to understand Soviet labor recruitment and allocation, we must also consider that here again the labor value theory is not incisive. An adherent to this theory can readily find grounds for observing principles akin to our efficiency rules. Thus, in both the labor value theory and the marginal value theory, wage cost economy is in order. However, the labor value theory provides no very logical basis to value labor itself, as exerted in different pursuits. But here reference is properly made to the famous analysis of Marx concerning the lower and higher phases of social development, after the proletarian revolution. Thus the expected variation in over-all capacity to produce goods in different phases after the Revolution was for Marx but the basis for a further supposition regarding income distribution: after it achieved full abundance, society might properly "inscribe on its banners: from each according to his ability, to each according to his need." [23] But meantime "bourgeois right" must still prevail in this sphere, and such right recognizes "unequal individual endowment and thus productive capacity as natural privileges."

It is along these lines that Soviet economists reason in expounding principles of labor recruitment and allocation; and if working arrangements have conformed at all to our efficiency rules, this fact must be viewed accordingly. Among other things, following Marx, the concern avowedly is to pay labor according to "quantity and quality of work." In

23. *Critique of the Gotha Programme,* pp. 8 ff.

122

practice, this hardly has precluded fixing relative wages in accord with supply and demand. One still wonders, however, whether conformity with the latter features would not have been closer if marginal rather than labor value theory had been taken as a point of departure.

But Soviet working arrangements regarding labor use are entirely in conflict with our fourth efficiency rule concerning taxation. Since the lump-sum tax that is called for is not in consequential use in any modern society, this hardly calls for explanation, but we should observe that in principle this tax might commend itself from the standpoint of diverse ends. Thus, where the concern is with consumers' welfare, alternative taxes are taboo because they impair the incentive value of wage differentials. This is true not only of a progressive income tax but also of a proportional income tax, or even of a sales tax on consumers. All such taxes limit unduly the incentive of the worker to produce more by the exertion of greater effort or by entering more arduous, more exacting, and more responsible pursuits. Only by use of the lump-sum tax are such consequences avoided. But one also might wish to avoid them even if consumers' welfare were not especially the concern.

At any rate, any use that has been made of other forms of revenue in the U.S.S.R. must have been a source of inefficiency even from the standpoint of the system's directors. Even if they had been inclined to discount household preferences generally, they hardly can have felt the worker to be excessively zealous, and hence have sought expressly through the levies employed to overrule household preferences in this regard. Yet the alternative lump-sum tax probably has never been contemplated. If it has been, the Soviet government presumably has been led, as others have, to reject it on administrative and political grounds.[24]

24. I assume that sales taxes and income taxes alike unduly limit the incentive of the worker to produce more by the exertion of greater

Instead of the lump-sum tax, the government has used diverse levies, chiefly a sales tax. In this way, the system's directors have violated the labor theory, but this must be a case where the government as the master of economic law has felt other considerations to be overriding. The considerations presumably have been much the same as those urged in support of the sales tax elsewhere. I refer particularly to the familiar arguments concerning the relatively limited political impact and adverse effect on incentives of a sales tax compared with an income tax yielding the same revenue. In respect of the effect on incentives, of course, the difference between the two levies becomes particularly material if the income tax is progressive. Supposedly sales taxes are also administratively easier to levy than income taxes. In the U.S.S.R., because the latter levy is withheld this could not have been much of a consideration in industry, but it must have been of concern in the case of agriculture, which we have yet to consider. Evidently similar arguments must apply where the alternative to the sales tax is semicompulsory loans.

Reasons for reliance on sales taxes in the U.S.S.R. are

---

effort or by entering more arduous, more exacting, and more responsible pursuits. But so far as sales taxes and income taxes in substance reduce "real" wage rates, might not the workers exert additional effort or enter more arduous, more exacting, and more responsible pursuits in larger numbers? In other words, may not the "income" effect of the taxes in inducing greater effort and the like more than offset the "price" effect in inhibiting such activities? So theory teaches; but here the choice is not between some taxes and no taxes but between sales and income taxes on the one hand and theoretical lump-sum taxes on the other, and it is essentially the "price" effect alone that matters. This necessarily is adverse to effort where sales and income taxes are employed in place of lump-sum taxes. In other words, workers may exert themselves more at low than at high real wage rates, but they should do so still more at high real wage rates where they have also to pay a lump-sum tax leaving real income no higher than it would be, say, at low real wage rates.

124

somewhat speculative because, while Soviet economists admit that the heavy turnover tax on consumers' goods represents a departure from the labor theory of value, they nowhere explain the basis for its use. In fact, the turnover tax is held to be not a sales tax to begin with but a transfer to the government budget of income created by the government's own enterprises. By the same reasoning, the projected elimination of the income tax on households avowedly meant that the government would pay all, and the citizen none, of its expenses! [25]

While taxes are a source of revenue, they are often employed to rectify inequities in income distribution. This must also have been a concern in the U.S.S.R., but, one surmises, not an impelling one. Thus the sales tax has borne especially heavily on bread. While there have also been heavy exactions on luxuries, the burden of all levies on industrial workers on the average probably has been little, if at all, heavier on those with high than on those with low incomes.[26]

25. See above, p. 119.

26. F. D. Holzman, *Soviet Taxation* (Cambridge, Mass., 1955), p. 290. While application of our efficiency rules means inequality in earnings, as is not always clearly understood, such inequality may not be inequitable. This is so even where equity is seen in terms of consumers' welfare. At least, equity so viewed should admit of differentials compensating for differences in disutility, and so far as the differentials correspond to transfer prices they do just that. On the other hand, such correspondence occurs only for workers on the margin of choice between occupations. For other intramarginal workers, there necessarily are "rents" which are unrelated to transfer prices and hence to disutilities. By implication, equity could still be realized through a discriminatory wage policy, but this is hardly practicable. Then, too, where entry into any pursuit is dependent on natural talent, differentials that correspond to transfer prices and hence to disutilities of marginal workers may still not reflect disutilities in any meaningful sense for workers generally. In the interest of equity the lump-sum tax would indeed have to vary with native talent, but this is hardly practicable either.

The wage reform initiated in 1956 was scheduled to be completed in 1962. But in establishing new wage scales the government has sought to assure that earnings in the lowest category at any time conform to a legal minimum wage that it has also fixed.[27] Moreover, the minimum has been increased since 1956, and seemingly the government is now committed to increase it further during 1963–65. How wage scales generally will be revised concomitantly is not clear.

Throughout this chapter I have taken as a datum the supply of labor available for nonfarm pursuits. However, this has been a variable, and one over which the government might be expected to try to exercise some control. On the eve of the five-year plans, the U.S.S.R. was still predominantly an agricultural country, with some three-fourths of the population supported by farm pursuits. So far as the supply of labor available for nonfarm pursuits has been a variable subject to control, the source of variation of chief interest has been recruitment of the rural population for urban work. This aspect is considered when we come to discuss agriculture (Chapter 10) and technology (Chapter 11). In doing so, we may gain insight into an interesting feature which is already evident, the fact that under the plans nonfarm employment has tended systematically to exceed the government's own projections.

Where an open market prevails, it was said above that by observing the efficiency rules a community maximizes the total output obtained from any volume of consumers' goods made available to workers. So far as there are rents, of course, the government conceivably could, through a discriminatory wage policy, produce the same volume of output with a smaller volume of consumers' goods, or alternatively produce still more with the same volume of consumers' goods.

27. A scale of legal minimum wages was promulgated periodically in the 1920s, but it was not revised after 1927, and as money wages spiraled it lost its meaning. The government published a new scale of minimum wages in 1956, however, and has been raising the level since that time.

7 INDUSTRIAL MATERIALS SUPPLY

In a modern economy, goods produced by any sector ordinarily are allotted to two broad uses: those within the sector where goods are wholly consumed currently in the production of more goods; and diverse others either within or outside the sector. As for the latter uses, output may be allotted to other sectors to be used up currently there in the production of more goods. It may be allotted to investment, where it becomes part of the community's stock of fixed capital or inventories, and as such is employed either within the sector or elsewhere. Or it may become part of consumption, private or collective. For convenience I refer to goods that are used up currently to produce more goods as "materials," and those that are used within the division that produces them as "materials for own use." Goods disposed of otherwise will be referred to as "end products" of the division.

The two categories thus distinguished evidently are closely related to, but not quite the same as, two more familiar ones: "intermediate products" and "final products." Thus, intermediate products usually correspond to materials as understood here, and hence unlike materials for own use include all such goods, regardless of where they are employed. Similarly, final products consist only of supplies going to consumption and investment, and unlike end products of a particular sector omit all materials. The two classifications tend to converge as fewer and fewer sectors are distinguished; and finally coincide where reference is to the entire economy.

We have already become involved with working arrangements prevailing in the production and disposition of nonfarm goods. I propose now to probe further into this area. More specifically, attention is directed to procedures for determining the supply of nonfarm goods which become materials for own use within nonfarm sectors, taken together, and their disposition among different productive users. Reference is made particularly to industrial products used within industry alone. The procedures regarding these products are not altogether representative of those prevailing in respect of all nonfarm goods, including the services of transport and trade. But in the U.S.S.R. industrial goods that are materials for own use within industry constitute the bulk of nonfarm goods that are materials for own use within nonfarm sectors. Also, it is about procedures for determining the former that there is most information.

As before, I take as a point of departure the stocks of fixed capital at the disposal of different productive enterprises. For obvious reasons, I can no longer do likewise for the structure sought for outputs generally, but it is still best to avoid becoming involved with the related question of the structure sought for the bill of end products made available. As before, the desired structure presumably is determined in the light of limitations of capacity to produce one or another good, but where this is not done it is understood that a divergence from the desired structure may occur. Also, reference again is to the structure sought not only in the U.S.S.R. generally but in different market areas. Other aspects to be taken as data will become evident as I proceed.

We are thus led to inquire how the Russians deal with the problem of "inter-industry relations," which in the West has lately been the subject of searching examination in theory. In input-output analysis, however, the supposition is often made that in any industry the volume of each material needed per unit of output is constant. This famous postulate of fixed coefficients is at best only an approximation, and in inquiring into working arrangements employed regarding supplies and allocations of materials for own use in the U.S.S.R., so far as the material input coefficients are variable, we must consider how they are determined.

But the inquiry will be facilitated if initially we proceed as if these coefficients were indeed quasi-fixed, in this sense: at any time, depending on the working arrangements, more or less of any material may be employed to produce any given volume of product, but the amount required is not affected by the amounts of other materials used at the same time. In other words, the coefficients are variable, but the variation occurs without there being any substitutions among materials.[1]

Quasi-fixed coefficients are still not fixed coefficients, but I believe the two come to much the same thing.[2] In any event, we may usefully consider in the light of input-output

1. I propose also to bypass completely the possibility of substitution between materials and labor, but the general nature of the working arrangements bearing on this aspect should become fairly clear.
2. See below, n. 3.

analysis the nature of the problem of resource use confronting the system's directors at this point. It is extraordinarily intricate. Thus the immediate concern must be to determine the supply of each product to be made available as materials for own use and its disposition among productive consumers. But both the materials needed for the production of any good and the supplies that can be made available for use as materials in producing other goods depend on the volume of output of that good. Hence, supplies and allocations of materials for own use have to be settled in a larger context, where output too is a variable. Furthermore, since materials for each good are ordinarily drawn from supplies of many others, outputs of different products tend at once to become interrelated, and must somehow be determined together. Also, material requirements depend on material input coefficients, and if the latter are variable at all, they too must be determined.

Nevertheless, from input-output analysis we see that the problem at least in principle can be solved. Particularly, depending on material input coefficients and the bill of end products, outputs are fully determined by an almost endless series of simultaneous mathematical equations. The equations are familiar, relating for each product output to the uses made of it; that is, they are of the form

$$X_i = a_{i1}X_1 + a_{i2}X_2 + \cdots a_{ii}X_i + \cdots a_{ij}X_j \cdots + a_{in}X_n + d_i.$$

Here X_i is the total output of the ith industry, a_{ij} is the material input coefficient relating to the use of the ith good in the production of the jth, and d_i is the amount of the ith good allotted to use as an end product of the sector considered. With outputs determined, supplies and allocations of materials for own use can also be calculated.

What of the material input coefficients and the bill of end products? These, too, are determined, at least in principle, so far as the system's directors seek to observe two efficiency

Industrial Materials Supply

rules. First, within any market area money outlays on materials in the production of a given product must be limited
as much as possible at prevailing prices. If material input
coefficients are quasi-fixed, this means only that the amount
of each material employed in the production of a given output must be a minimum, but if the rule is observed, the corresponding coefficient is determined. As was explained, I
take as a datum here the bill of end products sought. Hence,
the second efficiency rule is that the bill of end products
realized must correspond to the one sought. If this rule is
observed, the bill of end products too is settled, at least as
far as it can be at this stage.

Actually, we took as a datum not the bill of goods sought
but its structure, and where the latter alone is specified, the
structures of outputs and supplies and allocations of materials for own use, not their absolute magnitudes, are determined. However, if the efficiency rules are read together
with those set forth for nonfarm labor, not only structures
but absolute magnitudes are settled. Thus, for any given
supply of nonfarm labor, the volume as well as structure of
output and of supplies and allocations of materials for own
use are determined.

These are the consequences of the application of the
efficiency rules to all nonfarm sectors, but the results are essentially the same if, as is more appropriate here, we consider them applicable to industry alone. It must be understood, however, that the structure sought for the bill of industrial end products is now a datum, and that it is the
structure of outputs of industrial goods and the structure of
supplies and uses of industrial materials for own use that are
determined. If the labor supply available to industry is
given, absolute magnitudes are also determined.[3]

3. In input-output analysis, principles regarding the relation of outputs, supplies, allocations of materials for own use, and end products
usually are derived for an entire economy, and moreover a self-con-

In inquiring into working arrangements for determining supplies and allocations of industrial materials for own use, therefore, we must consider to what extent these procedures may assure conformity to the two foregoing rules. The first, of course, presupposes that employment of materials involves the use of money. At least, the employing enterprise must be charged for such inputs at some established prices, and records must be kept of costs incurred. Under the *khozraschet* system, however, such procedures are employed in industrial enterprises in the U.S.S.R. Realization of the

---

tained one. Attention is directed here to a division of an economy, either nonfarm sectors generally or industry alone, and one where the economy is to some extent open. But evidently this can give rise to no new principle. For a division of an open economy as for an entire closed one, where the bill of end products is given, the corresponding outputs are determined, and so too are supplies and allocations of materials for own use.

Strictly speaking, however, in reference to a sector of an open economy we must also consider as among the determined variables materials procured from other sectors or from abroad, although the results would be subject to review along with the associated bill of end products. I refer to materials supplies of which are obtained solely from other sectors or abroad. Where supplies in part originate in nonfarm sectors or industry, amounts obtained elsewhere might simply be viewed here as data. Since we do not wish to become involved in questions of location, we must proceed similarly regarding exchanges between market areas, although if these are taken as data probably they are best understood not to be constants but to vary in some way—for example, so as to assure an unchanging interregional structure.

As was stated, in input-output analysis materials input coefficients are taken as fixed. Conceivably, such coefficients might vary in diverse ways, and, as is not always made clear in theoretical writings, not all such variation need be excluded. Changes in coefficients associated with substitutions between different material inputs or with changes in output have to be ruled out, but not necessarily variations which, depending on the degree of economy exercised, might occur in one material input where other materials and also output are given. In other words, the fixed coefficients come to essentially the same thing as the quasi-fixed ones considered here. In the case of the latter, however, I also do not rule out variations associated with changes in output.

132

first rule must also turn on the concern of administering agencies exercising operational control in industry to economize money costs, and this, too, has already been discussed. However, the concern for cost economy was examined previously with particular reference to labor, and it remains to consider it in respect of materials.

As to the bill of end products, we have yet to examine how the structure sought is determined. But any decision made initially is presumably subject to continual review in the light of results obtained. Consequently, in the last analysis, is not whatever is sought in this regard necessarily also realized? This at best could only be so in a superficial sense. In any event, working arrangements for determining supplies and allocations for industrial materials for own use might conceivably either implement choices as to end products or, by progressively limiting alternatives, inhibit such choices, and this may be a matter of some consequence for resource use. Conformity of what is realized to what is sought—in the deeper sense to which this distinction points —is what is of particular interest here, although admittedly it is an elusive matter.

PLAN FORMULATION BEFORE 1957

For facets of the Soviet economy considered thus far the diverse working arrangements employed have one common feature. Resource use has been determined only to a relatively limited extent in plans. Much has been left to be settled in the implementation of such programs, and indeed by decision makers at the lowest level, including the household and the enterprise. I refer especially to the autonomy enjoyed by the household (never complete and sometimes severely restricted) as to its purchases of consumers' goods and occupation and place of work, and the discretion permitted the enterprise regarding employment of workers in different pursuits. In the sphere of industrial materials supply, working arrangements are different. Almost inevitably, the government has still had to leave many questions of detail to be determined in the implementation of plans. Hence it has allowed some latitude to the individual enterprise. But, to a much greater extent than in regard to employment of labor and disposition of consumers' goods, it has sought to determine in the plans themselves the supply of industrial materials for own use and their disposition. For this reason, the process by which the plans are formulated now requires more attention.

If I may turn first to this matter,[4] the Soviet government draws up plans for periods of different length, but, as before, that for the year is of chief interest. Furthermore, working arrangements employed in the formulation of the annual plan for supplies and allocations of industrial materials for own use have evolved in the course of time. It may suffice here if I describe the procedures followed in the postwar years preceding 1957, the year of wholesale industrial reorganization, and then refer to changes that have occurred since then.

In postwar years before 1957, as we have seen, for different agencies exercising operational control over industry the annual plan established corresponding targets for output. Any output, however, requires among other things material

4. In this section and the next I often do little more than summarize Herbert S. Levine, "The Centralized Planning of Supply in Soviet Industry," in *Comparisons*, Part I (Washington, D.C., 1959), and Levine, *A Study in Economic Planning*. I am indebted to Professor Levine also for advice on a number of points. See also E. Iu. Lokshin, *Planirovanie material'no-tekhnicheskogo snabzheniia narodnogo khoziaistva SSSR* (Gospolitizdat, 1952); M. Z. Bor, *Planovyi balans narodnogo khoziaistva SSSR* (Moscow, 1959); Iu. I. Koldomasov, *Metod material'nykh balansov v planirovanii narodnogo khoziaistva* (Moscow, 1959); Alec Nove, *The Soviet Economy* (New York, 1961), chs. 2, 7; and H. S. Levine, "Recent Developments in Soviet Planning," in *Dimensions*.

inputs, and necessarily targets were also established for such inputs. Furthermore, the input targets were fixed in physical terms and in some detail. At the ministerial level, for example, such targets were established in 1946 for 70 different kinds of ferrous rolled metal products. While practice varied subsequently, targets for materials were still formulated in some detail on the eve of industrial reorganization.

In formulating these related targets for output and material inputs, the government in effect determined in corresponding detail goals for supplies and allocations of materials. At least this was so to the extent that it necessarily also established targets bearing on the volume of supplies to be disposed of alternatively as end products. Given the projected allocations of supplies to end products, how were the targets for outputs and material inputs determined? The question can best be answered if I first describe the steps through which the targets were formulated and then elaborate the procedures employed in dealing with certain cardinal aspects.

Targets were formulated essentially in four steps. First, in the first half of the year preceding the plan year (let us call it the base year), data were compiled and analyzed on pre-plan performance at all levels. Reference was made to the performance during the year preceding the base year and the first half of the base year. Also, performance during the second half of the base year was estimated. Second, Gosplan[5] prepared so-called "control figures," or tentative targets for different strategic aspects, including the output of a limited number, say a dozen, significant commodities. An attempt was made to assure that projected supplies of such commodities corresponded to requirements, including those implicit in the output targets. The control figures supposedly were formulated with due regard for targets set in the long-term plan then in effect and for general directives issued by

5. See above, p. 36.

the Council of Ministers on behalf of or jointly with the highest party organs. Usually formulated by June or July, the control figures were subject to the approval of the Council of Ministers.

Third, even before the publication of control figures, agencies exercising operational control—the ministries, *glavki*, and enterprises—began to work on their programs for the plan year. Among other things, tentative agency targets were formulated for output and material requirements. The latter most often were calculated by the "direct method": assumed input norms were applied to the tentative output targets. But once the control figures were released, all the agencies concerned were expected to review their initial projections. At each level, control figures were, on the one hand, elaborated into more detailed targets for inferior agencies, and, on the other, taken into account in the negotiations with inferior agencies that inevitably followed. In aggregative terms, targets for output and inputs thus formulated were supposed finally to find their way up to Gosplan by September 1–15. Gosplan then undertook again to ensure a correspondence of output and requirements, though now on a much grander scale than before. Where necessary, it also negotiated with different ministries to rectify imbalances.

Fourth and last, as thus reformulated and after its approval by the party and government, the plan, including output and material input targets, was again submitted to the ministries as an operational directive. More detailed programs were also worked out for inferior agencies, in part by the agencies concerned. Although not formally part of the plan, the final stage may properly be considered the determination for user agencies of the specific sources of their supply, and arrangement with them regarding specifications, delivery dates, prices, and the like.[6] The formula-

6. See below, Ch. 8.

tion of the plan was thus ordinarily concluded with the signing of procurement contracts between users and suppliers. Contracts usually were signed at all levels, although in less detailed form at higher levels than at lower. At all levels the agencies concerned employed specialized departments for this work, including at the level of the ministry separate *glavki* for procurement and sales.

The foregoing represents a more or less typical sequence that prevailed in the formulation of output and material input targets. Almost inevitably, however, Soviet practice varied over time and between industries.

To come to the cardinal aspects, the first is the determination of input norms. In principle, the norms were supposed to be fixed at a minimum level. This was to be achieved through application of the "analytical-computational" method, involving compilation of data on past performance and systematic analysis of possibilities for improvement. In practice, the same conflicting forces were at work here as prevailed in the determination of plan targets generally. On the one hand, management of the enterprise generally sought to limit the task, and make its fulfillment easier. The *glavk* in its dealing with the ministry seemed to have the same attitude, as did the ministry in its dealings with Gosplan. On the other hand, reflecting demands of the highest organs of the party and government, Gosplan was concerned to uncover "concealed reserves" and ensure more demanding assignments; and the ministry had often to take this position in dealing with the *glavk,* and the *glavk* in dealing with the enterprise.

In order to limit material outlays, Gosplan concerned itself not only with aggregative norms applying to the ministry, but often with more detailed ones applying to the *glavk* and in some cases even to the enterprise. Moreover, the ministry often approved norms applicable to the enterprise as well as to the *glavk,* although many enterprise norms remained to be approved by the *glavk*. However, the task of all superior agencies in dealing with the enterprise was often made difficult because of their lesser knowledge of pertinent factual details, although they could compensate in some measure for this disadvantage by comparing the performance of different enterprises.

I posed earlier the question whether material inputs tend to be minimal in relation to any given output. So far as such inputs were determined in the plan, they must have been more than minimal wherever the enterprise succeeded in padding its norms. If only because of the nature of the production process, one might suppose that the opportunities for padding must have been limited, but careful students of the Soviet economy agree that the inflation of norms was a phenomenon of some importance.[7] However, complaints have also been voiced in the U.S.S.R. as to the unrealistically low norms fixed, and one is led to believe that this phenomenon too was not unusual. This conclusion is confirmed as one explores further the procedures for formulation of the plan, particularly those regarding a second cardinal aspect, reconciliation of targets for output and requirements.

We come then to a feature on which Soviet economists are most articulate when they discuss their economic system: the "method of balanced estimates." Designed to ensure conformity to "the law of planned, proportional development," this famous method is applied in the formulation of the plan generally, but nowhere more systematically than for industrial materials. In postwar years before 1957, as was implied, the method was employed in regard to industrial materials at two stages: initially in formulating preliminary control figures and later on a much larger scale in formulating final targets. If I describe the method in the latter

7. Berliner, *Factory and Manager,* ch. VII; Levine, *A Study in Economic Planning,* pp. 105 ff.; Granick, *Management of the Industrial Firm,* ch. VII.

phase, the manner of its use in the former will also be evident.

The method employed to determine final targets involved for each industrial product used in whole or in part as a material compilation of an account for the plan year of sources of supply and requirements (Table 7.1). The princi-

TABLE 7.1.

Categories of Supply and Requirements in Material Balance
for an Industrial Product

Source of Supply	Disposition
1. Output, by producing ministry or other major producing agency	1. For production and other operational needs, by user ministry or other major user agency
2. Imports	2. For construction by major agency
3. Other current sources	3. For "market" funds
4. Initial stocks of producers, by ministry or other major agency	4. Exports
	5. Increase in "state reserves"
	6. Increase in reserves of Council of Ministers
	7. Final stocks of producers, by ministry or other major agency

pal source of supply ordinarily was current output. In compiling the account, entries were made under this heading for different major producers in accord with the provisional output targets already established. Supplies to be obtained from imports or other sources, e.g. scrap, were also recorded in the light of the plan thus far formulated. The account of supplies was completed with the inclusion of an estimate of stocks that producers would have on hand on January 1 of the plan year.

The requirements of chief interest here are those of industrial users, and for these the appropriate entries were found simply by applying to the provisional output targets of *these* agencies norms for use of the material in question, as thus far determined. For the rest, supplies might go to productive users outside industry; construction; "market funds," representing current consumption, including collective sorts (although, contrary to the table, which is based on a Soviet source, current military uses probably were represented by a separate heading); exports; "state reserves," maintained for defense and other large purposes; and reserves of the Council of Ministers, maintained for current operating purposes. For all these uses, entries were made in the light of the plan generally, as it then stood, before reconciliation of targets for output and requirements. On the same basis, an allowance was made for stocks that would have to be available to producers on December 31 of the plan year.

As thus determined, almost inevitably supplies and requirements often diverged. What then? Necessarily Gosplan had to revise the provisional targets, and in the process it had to grapple with the awkward problem concerning "secondary effects": The revisions in targets pertaining to the balance for one product might call for further revisions in those pertaining to another, and these for still further ones pertaining to still others, and so on in an almost endless chain. How were the necessary revisions made? While Soviet economists have written much about their method of balanced estimates, they are not very illuminating on this crucial aspect. But a cardinal concern throughout was simply to limit secondary effects as far as possible. This might be done in diverse ways. For one thing, an appropriate adjustment might be made in requirements for industrial end products, particularly those not related to current productive uses elsewhere. For another, requirements for materials within industry or for industrial end products used as materials elsewhere might be altered by changing input norms of users. Production targets for industrial suppliers might also be altered, and where possible without changing *their* material allocations. In other words, changes might be made in input norms for suppliers.

We may now consider in this light a further question of particular interest here: To what extent are supplies and allocations of industrial materials for own use determined so as to generate supplies of end products of a desired structure? Under the method of balanced estimates, Gosplan did seek to ensure that goals for outputs, material supplies, and allocations were consistent with those for end products. By the same token, it in effect sought a solution for the pertinent "simultaneous equations." So far as the accounts for different products finally were balanced, such a solution was achieved, and with it the desired consistency in targets. But the solution and the resultant consistency evidently must have been more or less arbitrary. Emerging from a process of negotiation, input norms must have been rather artificial in any event, but when adjusted to avoid secondary effects they must often have become more so, and the solution necessarily reflected this circumstance. Furthermore, to ensure a balance, goals for end products were also often revised, and while Gosplan could appeal to the same ends as had been considered to begin with, in the interests of avoiding secondary effects the system's directors were probably often compelled to accept a solution that even from their own standpoint was inferior. If it had not been excluded by the procedures employed, perhaps some other mix of end products would have been preferred. For example, if supplies of coal initially diverged from requirements, no doubt a necessary balance could have been established without any secondary effects by adjusting allocations to home heating, but the system's directors themselves might have preferred that allocations also be adjusted to electric power, even if only in order that home electric power should bear part of the burden.

The attempt to avoid secondary effects must have resulted

in arbitrariness even if the initial imbalance that was corrected involved an excess of supplies over requirements, but apparently the more usual situation was the reverse, and the adjustments must be viewed in this light. Even so, the resultant difficulty perhaps was somewhat mitigated so far as the shortfall in supplies arose from the padding of input norms by enterprises, *glavki,* and ministries. But since it was not so easy to tell just where the padding occurred, downward revisions in a particular norm might or might not be warranted even though some norms were inflated.

As has been explained,[8] output targets for industrial products frequently were ambitious relative to the available labor supply. There are reasons to think they often were also ambitious relative to stocks of fixed capital. While the result was that the plan for material supplies and allocations was even more difficult to implement than it might have been, there need have been no further tendency on this account for projected requirements to exceed projected supplies. On the contrary, the inflation in output targets relative to labor and capital should have affected targets for both requirements and supplies alike. One wonders, however, whether the tendency for requirements to be in excess may not have originated in part in a more basic tendency to establish targets for supplies of industrial end products that were ambitious in relation to those established for total output. If so, especially where the industrial end products went to current productive uses in other sectors, the disproportion was apt to be deeply embedded in the plan, as initially formulated. Here, too, therefore, adjustments that avoided secondary effects might not have done much to repair the initial distortion.[9]

8. See above, pp. 81 ff., 89.

9. As Professor Levine has pointed out (*Comparisons,* p. 165), a procedure like the method of balanced estimates might be applied so as to assure consistency of outputs and material supplies and alloca-

In applying the method of balanced estimates, Gosplan was limited regarding the fineness of commodity breakdown considered. The aggregative targets that emerged from its labors, therefore, had still to be elaborated into highly detailed ones appropriate to individual enterprises. This was an enormous task, as may be judged from the fact that every year the chief administration for ferrous metal sales had finally to issue some half-million production and delivery orders to subordinate enterprises.[10] Not surprisingly, therefore, further imbalances appeared at this point: between delivery assignments for supplying firms and their projected output, between specifications of materials that might become available and specifications of materials that would be required, and so on. To what extent such incongruities in targets were finally dispelled is not known, but the need to grapple with them must have markedly compounded the arbitrariness of supplies and allocations.

Before 1957, for purposes of economic administration, industrial goods used as materials in the U.S.S.R. were classified into a number of categories. The chief was that comprising "funded" goods, an allotment of which to an enterprise was known as a "fund" (fond). This category included products that were considered especially important or that were in particularly short supply, including ferrous and nonferrous metals, chemicals, construction materials, fuels, and the like. Two other important categories were "centrally planned" goods, and "decentrally planned" goods. In the

tions with end products without arbitrary adjustment of input coefficients or end products. Thus, starting with any provisional solution for outputs and material supplies and allocations, by successive "iterations" one may approach a final one where the desired consistency of input coefficients and end products is realized. But to carry out the required iterations would be a forbidding task; in any case, Gosplan failed to accomplish it so far as it limited secondary effects under the method of balanced estimates.

10. Ibid., p. 169.

former were classified the more, and in the latter the less, significant products not considered as funded goods, although here too differences in availability were considered.

In all that has been said thus far I have been referring particularly to funded goods. Although the procedures employed for other categories were broadly similar to those used for funded goods, they did vary. In respect of funded goods, Gosplan played a major role, particularly the all-union office, Gosplan U.S.S.R. For other categories, substantial responsibilities were delegated to other agencies: for centrally planned goods to supplying ministries, including their sales departments, and republican offices of Gosplan; for decentrally planned goods to organs of local governments and to local agencies of supplying ministries.

How such differences in the responsible agencies might have affected determination of input norms it is difficult to say. Where, as often was the case, requirements were balanced with supplies by a single supplying ministry, secondary effects must have been given even less attention than in the case of funded goods. Also, in producing goods in any one product category, presumably it was often necessary to use as materials goods produced in others. How in the circumstances the coordination of actions of different agencies was achieved is not known, but difficulties must have been encountered. If only for these reasons, supplies and allocations of all industrial materials for own use probably were often even more arbitrary than for funded goods alone.

The classification of goods that has been described, of course, reflected in part the prevailing priorities, and these necessarily were considered at other points. Most importantly here as for labor, in negotiations on input coefficients, demands on higher priority agencies tended to be less taxing than those on lower priority ones. In this way, targets presumably were made less arbitrary than they might have been otherwise.

144

Industrial Materials Supply

Like the administrative structure in industry, working arrangements for the formulation of the plan for supplies and allocations of industrial materials for own use were substantially altered in 1957 and have continued in flux since. As of mid-1962, the principal changes from the pre-1957 procedures were as follows.

Among agencies exercising operational control over industry, the replacement of all-union and union-republican ministries by regional economic councils has meant a corresponding change in agencies concerned with the formulation of targets for supplies and allocations of materials. Thus, whereas formerly directives from the all-union Council of Ministers and proposals from the enterprise typically flowed through a branch ministry at the all-union level and a sub-branch *glavk*, or these together with a republican branch ministry, now they flow typically through a republican ministerial council, and a regional and perhaps also republican economic council, together with their branch *glavki*.

While in this way the authority over operational matters has been in principle transferred to the republican ministerial councils and the new regional and republican economic councils, in the formulation of the plan for supplies and allocations of materials, Gosplan has come to play an even larger role than before. Thus, Gosplan has taken over from the industrial ministries much of the work of formulating targets on a national scale for an entire industry. Moreover, the sales departments of the ministries have been transferred to Gosplan, and with them many of their responsibilities, including those for plan formulation. Reference is to Gosplan U.S.S.R., but the status of republican offices of this organization has also been enhanced.

Reflecting the change in agencies and their general re-

145

sponsibilities, there has been a change in the classification of industrial commodities. Thus in place of the categories considered previously, there are these three: commodities which are particularly important for the national economy, or in especially short supply, or produced and used in several republics; commodities of less importance, not in short supply, and produced largely or entirely within a single republic; and commodities of least importance and produced wholly within the territory of one regional council. The first category covers practically all products formerly classified as funded goods, and many others formerly classified as centrally planned. The second and third categories cover the balance of products.

Plans bearing on supplies and allocations of the first sort of products are now formulated in a manner broadly similar to that which prevailed before for funded goods, but at the center Gosplan now deals with republican rather than ministerial suppliers and users, and formulates targets for the former in place of the latter. By the same token, republican have replaced ministerial suppliers and users in the accounts compiled in the application of the method of balanced estimates. Within each republic, apparently the corresponding office of Gosplan deals similarly with the regional economic councils. However, the division of authority between the Gosplan office and the republican economic council (where there is one) is not clear. Moreover, Gosplan U.S.S.R. still concerns itself with allocations and delivery assignments not only between but within republics, and even among enterprises. After some experimentation, such activities have come to be among the principal tasks assigned to the reorganized sales administrations of the old ministries, although supposedly this work is to be performed "together with" republican agencies.

Procedures now employed for the second and third categories of goods are more or less similar to those employed for the first, but for the second, republican agencies, and for the third, regional economic councils assume primary responsibility in place of Gosplan U.S.S.R.

Working arrangements for formulation of the plan for supplies and allocations of industrial materials for own use were complex before 1957. As the foregoing brief description may suggest, they have now become more so. For this reason and because of the continuing changes, it is not easy to ascertain the precise nature of the new procedures. Not surprisingly, these appear frequently to have been obscure to Soviet administrators themselves.

Nevertheless, in introducing changes the government hoped among other things to improve the practice of determining material input norms. Particularly, by shifting responsibilities for administration to some extent from Moscow to republican and regional economic councils, it was felt that the padding of norms might be more effectively restricted. Since the republican and regional agencies concerned must often produce materials which they themselves use, they may have a greater incentive than the old ministries to limit input norms of enterprises. However, each area must obtain materials from other areas, and here as elsewhere departmentalism must often have given way to localism, with the republican and regional agencies still acquiescing in padding where substantial supplies must be drawn from other localities. In any event, complaints are still voiced about inflation of norms.[11]

If such inflation has been curtailed at all, imbalances that must be dealt with by Gosplan U.S.S.R. through the method of balanced estimates should be less significant than formerly. If there has also been a trend toward greater realism in planning generally,[12] this might have contributed further to a decline in imbalances. However, Gosplan, in order to

11. Levine, *A Study in Economic Planning,* p. 305.
12. See above, p. 89.

discover and repair the imbalances that do exist, continues to employ the method of balanced estimates, and moreover in a way to limit secondary effects. For this reason, the resulting mix of end products must still be more or less arbitrary. Indeed, while imbalances may be less consequential than before, Gosplan U.S.S.R. now must adjust accounts where users are classified regionally rather than industrially. Hence it must sometimes be more difficult than it was before to assure that revisions are made with due regard to the mix of end products sought.

The elaboration of aggregative targets by Gosplan U.S.S.R. into detailed targets relevant to the individual enterprise now goes hand in hand with the application of the method of balanced estimates within republics and regions, and as a result there may have been some improvement over previous procedures at this point. But here, too, old complaints are still heard; as where the enterprise targets for output have been reported to be in conflict with those for both material inputs and delivery assignments. Probably it is especially to such anomalies that a Soviet authority on the materials supply system refers when he informs us that:

> The supplying of industry is sharply affected by shortcomings in the planning of material and technical supply. The chief shortcoming is that the material and technical resources necessary for the established production and construction assignments are not ensured in planning. This type of discrepancy is a direct violation of the requirements of socialist planning: scientific soundness of plans and coordination of individual sections of the plan . . . Voluntarism and arbitrariness are especially inadmissible in planning, and particularly in the planning of material and technical supply.[13]

13. E. Lokshin, in *Current Digest* (May 3, 1961), p. 20.

148

But "voluntarism" and "arbitrariness" must be due in turn to other, more basic causes. Thus, while a central aim of the reorganization avowedly was to transfer decision making from the center, Gosplan still actively intervenes in the determination of supplies and allocations within republics and regions. Indeed, through the reorganized ministerial sales administrations, it exercises major responsibilities in this regard. Understandably, therefore, the cumbersomeness of administration remains a major target for criticism in the U.S.S.R., while overlapping of function, always a subject of complaint, seems to be of increased concern. A single example may suggest the nature of the difficulties:

> The union main sales administrations and in particular the Union Main Sales Administration for Heavy Machinery [think they have] the exclusive right to give assignments to factories. They send their orders directly to the producing enterprise. In view of this, the directors of enterprises began more and more frequently to turn to the union main sales administrations for decisions on current problems of production and delivery of equipment. . . . It developed that the orders of the union main sales administrations have become some sort of fetish which has fettered the initiative and operational possibilities of republican organs.[14]

Under the new organizational arrangements, the extraordinary amount of detail that must be handled must also still be a central source of difficulty. Thus it is to this aspect as well as to the continuing centralization that we must look for much of the explanation of, for example, the "absence of order and accurate accounting in the distribution and use of ball bearings," and resultant widespread shortages and surpluses of this material. In all some 9,000 varieties of ball

14. V. Goltvianskii, quoted in Levine, *Dimensions*, p. 179.

bearings are in production. Requisitions for this material alone by one auto factory from the First Government Ball-Bearing Factory were processed by fourteen agencies. In the circumstances, some 430 pounds of documents were generated.[15]

In commenting on the post-1957 procedures from the standpoint of determination of input norms and realization of the mix of end products sought, I have referred primarily to the first category of goods, but what has been said applies broadly to other categories. Reference has been to arrangements prevailing in mid-1962, and these are by no means the last word. Since then, the government has consolidated in a wholesale way the localities administered by the regional economic councils. It has also established a Council of the National Economy of the U.S.S.R. and a Supreme Economic Council of the U.S.S.R. Inevitably there has been still another redistribution of responsibilities for formulation of the plan for supplies and allocations of industrial materials for own use. Among other things, Gosplan U.S.S.R. must have lost some authority to the two new all-union agencies. How the new arrangements will work it is too early to say, although one wonders again at the costs incurred simply because of continuing reorganization.

PLAN FULFILLMENT

I have focused thus far on formulation of the plan. As we turn to implementation, attention is directed, as before, to postwar years. From the standpoint of our two efficiency rules we saw that the process of establishing pertinent targets during this period has been subject to diverse deficiencies. Thus, before 1957, material input norms must often have been either too high or too low, while relative to

15. *Ekonomicheskaia gazeta* (March 30, 1963), p. 7; (May 4, 1963), p. 17; *Pravda* (July 6, 1963); *Plenum Tsentral'nogo Komiteta KPSS, 13–16 Iiulia 1960* (Moscow, 1960), p. 189.

each other targets for end products tended to be dubious even from the government's standpoint. More recently, such deficiencies have persisted, although they may no longer be quite so consequential as they once were. In inquiring into implementation, therefore, we are led to ask how at this stage such deficiencies have been dealt with. Specifically, to what extent has implementation magnified, repaired, or left unchanged limitations of the plan itself?

As for the plan generally, for targets bearing on supplies and allocations of materials, responsibility for implementation has fallen on agencies exercising operational control over industry, and particularly on their managerial staffs. Such personnel as a rule should have sought to use materials at least as economically as the plan required. Of course, where the norms have been unrealistically low, the administrators have been unable to realize them, but so far as feasible the administrators probably have sought to conform to or possibly surpass the plan in this respect.

To refer first to circumstances before 1957, as was explained, the management of the enterprise aimed at this time to fulfill and overfulfill the plan for output, but partly for its own sake and partly on financial grounds a target for costs also had to be considered. To this extent, therefore, there was also an inducement to economize on materials. As finally formulated, targets for materials were expressed not as norms relating inputs to outputs but in absolute terms. Nevertheless, where the enterprise could thereby overfulfill its output target it might still be allotted additional materials, but that this would be done was uncertain, for apparently such supplementary allotments were made only on an ad hoc basis. Given the concern to fulfill and overfulfill the output target, any uncertainty at this point should have tended in some measure to compound the inducement to economize material inputs.

But any uncertainty as to supplementary allotments must

only have mirrored a more basic uncertainty, and moreover one where in consequence the concern for economy could only have been enhanced. I refer to the uncertainty over availability of supplies to cover allotments, including those made under the plan as well as any possible supplements to these quotas. As was foreordained by the manner in which the plan was formulated, supplies of materials tended not only to diverge from, but often to fall short of, requirements. Both under the Council of Ministers and within individual ministries, reserves might be available to meet such contingencies. But even after being allotted materials under the plan—indeed even after having contracted for their supply—the management of the enterprise was by no means assured of obtaining them, and still less of obtaining them on time. Hence arose the notorious *tolkach* or pusher, who was employed almost everywhere, apparently illicitly, to visit suppliers and see that contracts for deliveries were met. If in the process the *tolkach* formed personal connections, he could become more effective, and he might also seek to enhance his influence with material means. In a word, he might exercise what came to be called *blat*. An account of circumstances of prewar years based on interviews with emigrées applies, I believe, also to the period now of concern:

> Various officials of the enterprise may play the part of the *tolkach*. . . . But such people are only amateur *tolkachi*. Larger enterprises can afford to retain full-time *tolkachi*, who have no functions other than to "push for the interests of the enterprise" . . . They [the *tolkachi*] literally live on wheels, apparently spending most of their time out in the "market," frequenting the supply depots, purchasing organizations and supplying enterprises, seeking to expedite the shipment of commodities to their enterprises and coping with emergency needs for materials as they arise. . . . They

152

are used not only when trouble arises, but "in order to see that the materials will come through without any trouble. When we expect trouble in the future the *tolkach* will be sent out earlier." [16]

Despite such exertions, the management might be disappointed. The market for materials was a sellers' market; at least it was a hazardous one for buyers. Consequently, buyers might be expected to be fairly frugal in the expenditure of supplies procured.

Management of the ministry and the *glavk* should have been no less concerned than that of the enterprise to economize materials. Hence what has been said of the latter should apply to industrial administrators generally.

As to circumstances since 1957, the impact of the changes in administrative structure on the concern for economy of materials is difficult to judge. While norms may sometimes be less inflated than before, it is not easy to see why as a result of the change in structure the enterprise management would be any more or less concerned than before to fulfill them. However, the change in bonus arrangements of 1959 may have led to a heightened interest in fulfillment and overfulfillment of targets for costs, and it may also have increased concern for economy of materials. On the other hand, because of an assumed trend toward more realistic planning, it has been suggested that the market for materials is less a sellers' market than before. It is no easier to get at the facts on the latter than on the trend in planning itself, but a change in the market for materials, such as is supposed, itself might have weakened the concern for economy of materials.

It is interesting to contrast the attitude toward economy of materials, as determined, with that toward economy of labor. To the extent that both stemmed from an interest in

16. Berliner, *Factory and Manager,* pp. 210 ff. Italics added.

satisfactory performance in respect of the target for costs, the concern for economy should have been no greater in the case of one input than in that of the other. On the other hand, while targets for both inputs have been expressed in absolute terms, additional allotments to permit overfulfillment of the output target have been provided for under an established procedure in the case of labor but may or may not have been forthcoming in the case of materials. More basically, administrators have often encountered difficulties in meeting their quotas for employment of labor, but there hardly can have been any parallel here to the continuing and pervasive sellers' market for materials. By implication, the concern to economize materials should have been greater than that to economize labor, and surely this has been so.

What of the structure of end products? Particularly, how in the implementation of the plan are available supplies allocated if they are insufficient to meet requirements? This is not easy to appraise. In choosing between conflicting claims to their output, suppliers at all levels should consider the prevailing priorities revealed in the plan itself and in other official pronouncements. But the allocations also depend on such activities as those of the *tolkach,* and these persons pursue priorities of their own. Not surprisingly, therefore, supplies are often misallocated. Materials appear frequently to find their way into the hands of users who are not only of inferior status but also not lawfully entitled to them at all.[17] Here as elsewhere the reorganization must have had some positive effect, but the new tendency toward localism has been a source of difficulty. Of this we may judge from the need to introduce the decree of April 1958, which provided that a failure to meet requirements of extraregional users made the responsible official subject to disciplinary action and possibly legal prosecution. Despite this decree, complaints continue to be aired regarding localism:

17. Ibid., pp. 218 ff.

With the direct knowledge of the economic councils, individual plants (and sometimes even the economic councils . . . themselves) display unhealthy tendencies. Thus it was noted at a plenary session of the Leningrad Province Party Committee that the Kirov plant, while regularly failing to meet the plan for deliveries of ferrous metal for all-union purposes, overexpended more than 4,000 tons of rolled metal on its own needs. In the first nine months of 1960 the metallurgical plants of the Ukraine Republic delivered to consumers in their own republic 132,000 tons of ferrous metals and 21,000 tons of steel pipe over and above the plan, yet fell short in deliveries to enterprises of other republics, ministries and agencies by 82,000 tons of rolled metal and 18,000 tons of steel pipe.[18]

Our concern here is not so much with the regional allocation of end products as with the structure of such goods within a region; the localism must often also affect the latter, however, as well as the former.

In fulfilling its target for output, the enterprise supposedly has had to observe established quality standards. Nevertheless, as will be explained later,[19] in seeking to control quality in this way the government has encountered major difficulties. Moreover, these have only been compounded where, as is usually the case, the enterprise produces not one product but a variety of products, so that control has also to be exercised over the assortment. In discussing working arrangements as to quality and assortment, I shall focus primarily on enterprises producing articles used chiefly as consumers' goods, but similar difficulties have been encountered in other enterprises, including those producing goods used substantially as industrial materials. And

18. Lokshin, in *Current Digest* (May 3, 1961), p. 21.
19. See below, Ch. 12.

such difficulties have further complicated the task of determining industrial materials supplies and allocations in a manner to ensure end products of a desired structure.

This must be so if the goods are themselves used as end products, but for a modern industrial enterprise the need for material inputs of precise kinds and specifications is frequently compelling. The limitations in control over quality and assortment, therefore, have been peculiarly troublesome where the goods are used as material inputs, as witness the experience described in a recent Soviet survey already cited:

> There are also irregularities in deliveries and incomplete deliveries; the grades, types and sizes of materials ordered are frequently replaced by other less economical ones. For example, the Ukraine Chief Supply and Marketing Administration sent the Novo-Kakhova Electrical Machinery Plant a large amount of 750 × 1500 mm. sheet steel for dynamos instead of 860 × 1720 mm. sheet; as a result the coefficient of use of the metal dropped by 23 per cent.
>
> Shortcomings in supply affect the economics of enterprises . . . At the Rostov Farm Machinery Plant, for example, there were approximately 11,000 substitutions of rolled metal shapes and dimensions in five years— that is, an average of seven substitutions a day; this resulted in an overexpenditure of more than 22,000 tons of metal. Frequently there are also huge losses from the low quality of the products supplied, in particular cast parts.[20]

Limitations in control over quality and assortment of output probably have been one of the major sources of divergence in the U.S.S.R. between the mix of end products realized and that sought.

Since the plan has often been completed late, industrial

20. Lokshin, p. 19.

156

administrators have enjoyed somewhat greater discretion in determining supplies and allocations of materials than they would have otherwise. But there probably has been little gain in consequence regarding the economy of material inputs, while so far as different administrators have acted independently of each other, realization of the mix of end products sought can only have been made more difficult. Then, too, the plan has been subject to revision, and in the case of materials the revisions have been especially numerous—so much so that one wonders whether in the process the plan has not tended to lose its identity. The resulting flexibility must have its merits, but as Soviet writers point out, it often creates new incongruities. During 1958, for example, the RSFSR Council of Ministers issued 140 operational orders to secure additional supplies for the Moscow *sovnarkhoz,* although it did not always allot further supplies to other *sovnarkhozy* from which such materials were to be drawn. During 1959, because of supply difficulties, the Kazakh republican office of Gosplan changed allocations of rolled steel 538 times.[21]

21. Nove, *The Soviet Economy*, p. 203.

8 INDUSTRIAL MATERIALS PRICE FORMATION

In the preceding chapter, in exploring working arrangements regarding the supply of industrial materials for own use, material input coefficients were taken to be quasi-fixed, i.e. more or less of a material may be employed to obtain a given volume of output, but the amount required is not dependent on the amounts of other materials used at the same time. In other words, substitutions among materials were excluded. We now consider the case of substitutions. Also, in discussing procedures where substitutions are excluded, I did not comment on the rationale of the working arrangements. Therefore, after we examine the procedures that are pertinent where there are substitutions, we shall consider the rationale of all procedures.

158

Industrial Materials Price Formation

SUBSTITUTION AMONG MATERIALS

Where substitutions are possible, the two efficiency rules set forth[1] still apply, but that concerning economy of money outlays on materials previously required only
that a minimum volume of any materials be employed to
produce a given output. Now this condition still holds; or
rather it holds if both output and input of other materials
are understood as given. But the rule now requires also that
any substitutions between materials at prevailing prices that
might reduce money outlays should be made wherever available supplies permit.

Moreover, with this additional requirement, input coefficients now depend, as they previously did not, on prices.
Hence, in order that the coefficients be determined, a third
rule of a two-sided sort must be satisfied. On the one hand,
prices charged enterprises for all products employed as materials must assure that requirements correspond to amounts
available for use as materials. In other words, prices must be
at clearing levels.[2] On the other hand, the price charged enterprises for each product used as a material must correspond to its marginal cost. Since stocks of fixed capital available to different enterprises are taken as given, reference is
to marginal cost of a short-run sort, representing the additional outlays on labor and materials required per unit of
output to produce an increment of such output. For an enterprise producing a good used as materials, marginal costs
of materials which it employs must be calculated in terms of
prices which reflect in turn their marginal cost, and this

1. See p. 130.
2. For any level of output, of course, an enterprise's requirements
here represent the amounts it might wish to employ at prevailing
prices from a concern for cost economy and without regard to the availability of supplies at such prices.

159

might seem circular. But this means only that, here as elsewhere, determination of supplies and allocations of materials is an intricate matter and in principle one entailing the solution of simultaneous equations.

Prices at clearing levels may not correspond to marginal costs and, conversely, prices corresponding to marginal costs may not be at clearing levels. But with supplies appropriately determined, the two conditions can be met at the same time, and this is what the third rule requires. Reference is to a correspondence of requirements to supplies and of prices to marginal cost within any market area. Also, the latter relation is supposed to hold for individual enterprises as well as for an entire branch.[3]

In inquiring into procedures where substitutions are possible, therefore, we wish to know to what extent cost economizing substitutions that are permitted by available supplies are apt to be exploited, and also to what extent prices may tend to approach clearing levels and marginal cost. In regard to the former aspect, the pertinent facts are not clear, but apparently decisions on materials used by any enterprise have been made jointly by administrators in the enter-

3. It has been said that prices must be equal to marginal cost. Would it not suffice for prices to be merely proportional to marginal cost? This view is not heard as often as it once was, but it may be well to be explicit that in the sphere of industrial materials supply proportionality has its merit. Nevertheless, without equality there may ultimately be adverse effects on the worker's incentive to exert effort or to enter more arduous, more responsible, and more exacting pursuits (see above, pp. 122 ff.). Then, too, for any material that passes through a varying number of stages of fabrication, choices among fabricated products may also be distorted.

While reference is to short-run marginal costs, in the case of extractive industries an appropriate charge for depletion should be included. However, no further allowance for rent on natural resources could properly be included in marginal cost. If prices correspond to marginal cost, any excess over average cost necessarily constitutes such an additional rental charge.

prise and superior agencies. With the aid of specialized "technologists" and "designers," however, the superior agencies have tended to play the decisive role, especially where choices have been particularly consequential.

As to how the choices have been made, the delimitation of what is feasible technologically has been a cardinal preoccupation; and with prices fixed in a manner that is explained below, the need to avoid use of "deficit" and increase use of "surplus" materials has also been a continuing concern. But within limits thus defined economy of money outlays has also been sought, as the third efficiency rule requires.[4]

Nevertheless, in the determination of materials used, the concern for such economy must have been chiefly a reflection of, hence no more potent than, that for economy in money outlays generally. At least, this should have been so for the enterprises, and probably before 1957 the *glavk* and the ministry also viewed matters in this way. Since then, the regional council may have been impelled to give greater weight to economy of money outlays on materials which its own enterprises must supply. Then, too, especially at the enterprise level norms established for different material inputs often have been expressed simply in physical terms. In advocating particular qualities and specifications, therefore, the enterprise management must frequently have found it expedient, within limits of the physical volume allowed, to seek expensive varieties even though their contribution to output might not be commensurate with their higher price. If it has so behaved, the enterprise management would only have been conforming to a pattern that it has pursued systematically in the determination of the assortment of goods produced.[5]

4. Levine, *A Study in Economic Planning,* pp. 167 ff.
5. See below, Ch. 12.

FORMATION OF MATERIALS PRICES

In considering administrative attitudes toward cost economizing substitutions, I have focused on postwar years, and shall continue with this emphasis in regard to prices.[6] In fixing prices the government has taken it as a norm that the price of an industrial good used as a material should cover average cost and allow producing enterprises to earn a limited planned profit. Apparently the planned profit has been intended chiefly to permit the enterprise to meet certain financial requirements, particularly additional working capital needs, without recourse to the government budget. In the mid-fifties, a markup of 4–5 per cent above costs ordinarily was deemed sufficient for such purposes.

Average cost has been that for an entire branch, either for the U.S.S.R. generally or for a region. In either case, the fixing of prices in relation to branchwide costs has meant that different enterprises earn different profits. But where such variation has been consequential, profits have been redistributed appropriately by a producing or selling *glavk* or similar agency, the redistribution being effected through the use of differential accounting prices for individual firms. Alternatively, recourse has been had to compensatory transactions with the government budget, including if necessary the granting of "subsidies" to firms suffering losses.

6. Among the more useful studies are Maizenberg, *Tsenoobrazovanie v narodnom khoziaistve SSSR*, ch. III; Kondrashev, *Tsenoobrazovanie v promyshlennosti SSSR*, ch. III; Turetskii, *Ocherki planovogo tsenoobrazovaniia v SSSR*, ch. III; Gregory Grossman, "Industrial Prices in the USSR," *American Economic Review*, 49S (1959), 50–64; Morris Bornstein, "The Soviet Price System," *American Economic Review*, 52 (1962), 64–103; L. Maizenberg, "Peresmotr optovykh tsen i problemy tsenoobrazovaniia v SSSR," *Voprosy ekonomiki*, No. 11 (1961); Morris Bornstein, "The Soviet Price Reform Discussion" (processed).

Industrial Materials Price Formation

Average cost pricing has been the norm but by no means an inviolate one. Indeed, for a few years after the war it hardly was the norm at all, for, continuing a policy initiated during the war, the government then held prices of most industrial materials constant. Since costs meantime had risen sharply, this policy necessarily meant widespread losses and correspondingly widespread subsidies. This policy was pursued under the exceptional circumstances of the time, but was abandoned with the introduction of an extensive price reform in January 1949.[7]

But, while average cost pricing did become the rule with the latter reform, the government again and again has departed from it. This it has done in diverse ways, but not least is one concerning relative prices of different varieties of the same good. In determining such prices the government has often sought with varying emphasis to consider, in addition to costs, values to users, as manifest in qualitative features and availability. For example, in fixing the relative prices of different grades of coal from the same basin, the government has apparently subordinated costs to calorific value and related characteristics, although the "presence of resources and the expressed demand" have also been considered.[8] Similarly, for different iron ores from one mining area, relative prices have been fixed to take account of ore content and other qualities. Again, because of the relative scarcity of quality steels, their prices have been set at levels disproportionately high in relation to costs.

7. Under the five-year plans, however, the policy was not unprecedented. The government had held prices of most industrial materials constant for a protracted period in the face of sharp cost increases beginning early in the period of the First Five Year Plan, with resultant wholesale losses and subsidies. This experience ended with the introduction of an extensive price reform in the spring of 1936.

8. Turetskii, p. 123.

The government has often found it desirable to consider user values and availability not only in fixing prices of different varieties of the same good but also in fixing prices of different goods that are still close substitutes. Thus, in relation to that of other major fuels, the average cost of oil is notably low, but even if priced in proportion to its calorific value it would be in relatively short supply. At any rate this appears to be the Soviet view, and it is chiefly for this reason that the price of oil has been set disproportionately high in relation not only to cost but to calorific value (Table 8.1). On similar grounds, the price of natural gas

TABLE 8.1.

Calorific Value, Costs, and Prices of Different Fuels
in Relation to Coal, U.S.S.R., 1955
(percentages)

		COST PER CALORIFIC UNIT		WHOLESALE PRICE PER CALORIFIC UNIT	
	Calorific Value	Extraction	Extraction + Marketing	Excluding Transport	Including Transport
Coal	100	100	100	100	100
Coal, Donets only	118	113	99	110	97
Fuel oil	179	35.3	60	131	127
Natural gas	150	8.3[a]	27.2[a]	n.a.	87[b]
Peat	44	111	116	119	121
Fuel wood	35	183	178	180	174

Source: Turetskii, *Ocherki planovogo tsenoobrazovaniia v SSSR*, p. 110.

a. 1957.

b. 1958.

has also been raised well above cost, although in relation to coal not disproportionately to calorific value. Again, because of the "well-known insufficiency of non-ferrous metals," prices of these products have been fixed at disproportionately high levels relative to costs in order to induce increased use of ferrous metals as substitutes.[9] Where price markups above cost have varied in the foregoing ways, prices in an entire branch may have exceeded or fallen short of the amounts required for internal financing of working capital and the like, but such incongruities have been dealt with by use of a device sometimes employed in similar circumstances for individual enterprises: compensatory transactions with the government budget. Where, as has sometimes happened, prices have been fixed below cost even for an entire branch, the compensatory transaction has again involved the granting of a subsidy to cover losses. Because of the extraordinarily high markups established for oil products, only a limited part of the resulting revenues has been allowed to accrue as profits. A large part has been taken into the budget at once by means of the turnover tax. Among industrial goods used as materials, the turnover tax is also levied on electric power, although in somewhat different circumstances.

Under average cost pricing reference is supposed to be made to branchwide costs, but here again there have been variants. For some items, e.g. basic steel products, prices have been related primarily to costs of advanced plants. Curiously, reference sometimes may be made to costs of less advanced ones; at least, the markup over average branch costs may be increased somewhat to assure that their costs are covered.

In all the foregoing cases the government has departed from average cost pricing as a matter of principle. Among remaining divergencies from this standard, it may suffice to refer to one which originates in a rather different cause, the infrequency of price change. Thus, since the price reform of January 1949, the government has revised prices of industrial goods used as materials on a more or less extensive scale on four occasions, January 1, 1950; July 1,

9. Ibid., p. 150.

1950; January 1, 1952; and July 1, 1955. Another large-scale revision was initiated during 1961 and was to have been completed during 1962, but work on it was still in progress in early 1963. Except for the changes at these times, prices of different products have been altered only infrequently or not at all. In appraising the effect of this practice on relations of prices to average cost, we must consider that money wages in industry rose moderately over the decade 1950–60 (during 1950–58 they increased some 22 per cent) and that costs have tended to decline. However, cost trends must have varied widely in different branches.

MATERIALS PRICES VERSUS CLEARING LEVELS AND MARGINAL COSTS

How have Soviet prices for industrial materials been related to clearing levels and marginal costs? To refer first to the relation to marginal costs, in Soviet accounting practice the industrial enterprise is charged systematically for labor, materials, and depreciation on fixed capital, but not for rent for natural resources, or for interest on fixed capital. Essentially, therefore, costs consist of charges for labor, materials, and depreciation. By the same token, depreciation aside, average cost corresponds to average "variable cost," as understood in contemporary Western theory. It follows, too, that prices fixed in accordance with the government's norm may in some measure have corresponded to marginal cost, at least to the short-run sort of concern here. Indeed, since the markup for planned profits is small and depreciation tends to be relatively limited, the two must have come to much the same thing whenever variable cost per unit has not differed markedly among different enterprises and has tended to be constant as output varies. But in Soviet circumstances, where the introduction of new enterprises alongside old ones has been an outstanding feature, the first condition can rarely have been met. This must be so even if we consider only conformity of price to marginal cost within a market area, so that where prices have varied regionally it is only differences in costs within any price region that matter.

Moreover, while industrial enterprises are often held to be subject to a constant average variable cost over a considerable range of output, no one would contend that this is so when capacity is approached, and in the U.S.S.R. this has been a usual state. Also, variable cost per unit can be constant only in manufacturing. But in the U.S.S.R. average cost pricing has been practiced in extractive branches as well. By implication prices fixed to conform to the government's norm must have diverged from marginal cost after all, and often widely. Application of the government's price fixing norm has required that prices be related to planned cost, and this probably has tended to fall short of actual cost, while with capacity operations marginal cost must ordinarily have exceeded average variable cost. Hence divergencies from marginal cost may have been even greater than they would have been if reference had been to actual cost, although they must have been affected differently for different commodities.

As for the departures of prices from the norm of average cost, obviously these must have affected the relation of prices to marginal costs differently in different cases. Perhaps they have nevertheless had some systematic impact, but this is difficult to perceive.

Our third efficiency rule implicitly requires that within any market area marginal cost be the same for different enterprises. In the U.S.S.R., with a concern for cost economy on the part of administrators not only of individual enterprises but of superior agencies directing groups of enterprises, there should have been a tendency toward uniformity in marginal costs among different enterprises in the same region, but how much of one is conjectural. On the other hand, to the extent that marginal cost has varied among enterprises, the relation of prices to such costs for a branch as a whole must be understood as an average one for enterprises generally. References to this relation in the above discussion must be construed accordingly.[10]

In scheduling the output of an industrial material for succeeding periods, the government necessarily has considered any surplus or deficit currently prevailing. Hence, with average cost pricing, prices must have tended to approach clearing levels, but since both requirements and supplies alike have been continually in flux, this tendency should have been weak. Yet in departing from average cost pricing the government has sometimes considered availability, and to the extent that it has, the tendency should have been

10. It was said that the industrial enterprise in the U.S.S.R. is not subject to a rental charge for the use of natural resources. Although this is so generally, since 1949 timber extraction has paid certain "stumpage fees," which vary systematically by major regions, depending on the availability of forest reserves, and within regions depending on qualitative features, such as specie and thickness, and on length of haul to the floating point or rail head. How the fees are fixed is unknown, but evidently they are in some degree like rent. Also, while prices for lumber vary zonally, under average cost pricing the inclusion of such stumpage fees in costs should tend to make prices in each zone conform more to marginal costs. Actually, this must be so where, as in the case of the length of haul to the floating point or rail head, the fee is meant to compensate for cost differences. But in timber extraction, where marginal cost might be expected to exceed average cost, the inclusion of the fee should bring prices closer to marginal cost generally. The fees might also be viewed as in part a charge for depletion, but to the extent that the inclusion of such a charge is in order, it still makes for a greater conformity of prices to marginal cost, inclusive of depletion.

Reference has been made to the levying of turnover taxes on oil products. It sometimes is suggested that here, too, the government is in effect introducing a rental charge. Although there is some basis for this view, I believe the analogy to rental charges is limited.

reinforced, and the presumption must be that this has also been so where user values have been considered. But such departures have not always been commensurate with their intended purpose.[11] Furthermore, departures from the norm for other reasons must have affected the relation of prices to clearing levels in diverse ways. In sum, divergencies from clearing levels were probably pervasive, and all that is known about the Soviet market for industrial materials is to this effect.

Properly understood, our third efficiency rule presupposes that users of industrial materials have no monopoly power over the prices they pay for such goods, and hence that they take such prices as data in determining their purchases. How far has this been so in the U.S.S.R.? As already implied, here as elsewhere in the U.S.S.R. the fixing of prices has been accomplished in a relatively centralized way. Prices for industrial materials for the most part have been fixed by or subject to the approval of the Council of Ministers of the U.S.S.R. In exercising this responsibility, the Council has been aided at different times by diverse agencies. The chief one most recently has been Gosplan. Inferior agencies, and for some goods even the users, have also played a role. Moreover, even where price fixing is administratively centralized, large users through an appropriate determination of the volume of their purchases might still influence the outcome. But I think we may safely consider that monopoly power is not a consequential source of divergencies from our third rule.

The efficiency rule also presupposes that the money wages

11. According to calculations of M. A. Pavlov, in order to compensate for additional costs that its use imposes on producers of pig iron, the price of Krivorog ore of 55 per cent iron content must be less than one-third of that of Krivorog ore of 65 per cent iron content, but in 1955 the price of the former was as much as 70 per cent of that of the latter. See Turetskii, pp. 143–44.

included in marginal costs conform to other rules previously stated, but the degree of such conformity in the U.S.S.R. has already been discussed.

Thus far I have focused on the prices of industrial materials which are of industrial origin and which therefore are not themselves fabricated in any consequential way of agricultural materials. What of the prices of industrial materials that are so fabricated? Such products characteristically seem ultimately to be processed into consumers' goods which are more or less identified with the materials from which they are fabricated. By the same token, their use relatively often must occur in a meaningful sense under conditions of fixed, or at least quasi-fixed, coefficients. It also follows that pricing of such materials probably is more consequential for the bill of end products than for the structure of material inputs into any product. The little I can say about materials pricing even from the latter standpoint is best said later.[12]

CONCLUSIONS

In exploring Soviet working arrangements for determination of supplies and allocations of industrial materials for own use, we have considered particularly the extent to which these procedures conform to three pertinent efficiency rules, and the conclusion must be that while there is some degree of conformity, there are also marked divergencies. The three rules are supposed to assure an economically rational use of resources from the standpoint of consumers' welfare, but according to familiar reasoning their observance means that at any level of industrial employment the volume of end products of a desired structure is a maximum. For this reason it is not easy to imagine alternative ends according to which the principles would

12. See below, Ch. 12.

170

no longer be imperatives.[13] Why, then, the divergencies in the U.S.S.R.?

Where consumers' welfare is the end, supplies and allocations of industrial materials for own use are supposed to be determined exclusively from a concern for the supplies of the end products that result, and the suggestion is sometimes made that from the standpoint of the system's directors in the U.S.S.R., not only supplies of end products but total outputs are of interest. If this is true, resource use probably is no more rational economically than it was before. Thus for each bill of end products there is a corresponding bill of total outputs, and conversely; hence the system's directors cannot decide on each independently. But even if they were concerned primarily with total out-

13. What, however, if a bottleneck is encountered in the production of one or another end product? Might this not limit the volume of output of end products of a given mix below the maximum defined by the efficiency rules? By the same token, might not observance of the efficiency rules beyond a certain point be footless? A partial answer to these questions was given at the outset of this chapter: The system's directors presumably try to determine the structure of end products to be sought in the light of limitations in capacity to produce one or another good; where they err in this regard, there may be a divergence from the desired structure. But perhaps I should now explain that the volume of end products of a given structure that can be produced may well be limited by bottlenecks in the production of an end product, but the system's directors presumably would still wish to bar the possibility that there are unexploited opportunities to produce more of some things without the output of any others being any the less. With the mix sought viewed accordingly, the rules should be no less impelling than before.

In referring at the outset to capacity limitations, I considered those associated with limitations in capital stocks, but all that has been said here still applies if bottlenecks arise on other accounts, particularly the need to employ in the production of one or another end product specialized labor that is in short supply, or specialized materials that are produced with such specialized labor.

puts, it is not easy to see why the working arrangements should be any more favorable than they were before to realization of a desired structure. And as for the other two efficiency rules in question, their observance ensures a maximum volume of total outputs of any desired structure at the same time that it ensures a maximum volume of end products of any desired structure. Hence they should be just as applicable as they were before.

Whether the system's directors are primarily concerned with end products or total outputs, the fact that a desired structure is not realized does not mean that it is not being pursued. Similarly, avoidance of an absolute excess of any material input is also expressly taken as a desideratum in the U.S.S.R. But our remaining efficiency rule has diverse facets; and in respect of some of these, divergencies often occur in part simply because the rule is not considered a desideratum. Thus prices fail to conform to marginal cost partly because those responsible for fixing prices do not accept that as an objective to begin with. While to some extent availability of supplies is considered, to fix prices systematically at clearing levels is also not attempted. But the reason for these practices may be found in a feature now familiar: the commitment to the labor theory of value. As understood in the U.S.S.R., this precludes marginal cost pricing. Clearing prices are not considered as precluded ideologically, but from the standpoint of the labor theory there is little basis to exert oneself especially to realize them.

For the rest, divergencies from our rules presumably reflect administrative deficiencies, but these in turn must often be due to the highly centralized decision making. For the system's directors may not this type of decision making be an end in itself, to be pursued even at the expense of economic efficiency? As yet we have explored the Soviet economic system only in part, but we may consider here that, while centralization varies in different spheres, it prevails

Industrial Materials Price Formation

to a notable degree for resource use generally. Indeed, in the U.S.S.R. this is an outstanding feature. Moreover, the system's directors opted for working arrangements where decision making generally is highly centralized almost at once after they come to power. While the circumstances of the Revolution and Civil War were special, so too were those of the period of the New Economic Policy when the system's directors found it expedient to disperse some responsibility. And with the initiation of the five-year plans and wholesale collectivization, decision making again became notably centralized, and so it has remained ever since.

As to why the system's directors have chosen to rely on working arrangements of this sort, Soviet sources are not very informative, but when Lenin and his associates came to power, they had studied and apparently were impressed by the Germans' experience in organizing their economy in World War I.[14] Whether under the influence of this experience or otherwise, the system's directors must have assumed their centralized working arrangements to be economically efficacious. To what extent the procedures have been so compared with others that might have been employed is another question, and one on which this inquiry may shed some light. In any event, nonmaterial aspects must also have been of concern, though these may have been more complex than the question posed above suggests. Thus it would be surprising if centralization of decision making were not gratifying in itself for the system's directors, but they have also had to consider that decentralization in economic affairs might have unwanted political consequences. Also, in view of familiar Marxian tenets about the "anarchy" of market processes under capitalism, one wonders

14. V. I. Lenin, *Collected Works, 21,* Book I (New York, 1932), 197, 200, 210–12; Lenin, *Selected Works, 7* (New York, n.d.), 364–65; L. Kritsman, *Geroicheskii period velikoi russkoi revoliutsii* (Moscow, 1926), pp. 72, 77.

173

whether the government has ever seriously contemplated any real alternative, at least one where decentralization would be far reaching.

While under the five-year plans decision making has always been highly centralized, the degree of centralization has varied, particularly in recent years. Shifts in the distribution of authority under Khrushchev have been complex, and initial developments in this regard already seem to be in the process of being reversed, but no doubt there has been some retreat on balance from the extremes of centralization reached under Stalin. Also, to a novel degree economists lately have been allowed at least to debate further reforms, where decentralization might be more far-reaching.[15] The system's directors may not be quite as committed as they once were to their highly centralized system; and if so, their attitude toward nonmaterial aspects may also have been evolving; but the directors may also wish to limit centralization for other reasons, particularly the ever-growing complexity of the economy.

I have referred previously to the reluctance of the government to commit itself to economic principles. This reluctance must be seen in relation to the attachment of the system's directors to centralized decision making generally. To have sanctified economic principles would have diminished the role and perhaps also the authority of the system's directors. Here too, however, their attitude may be evolving to some extent. This is suggested by, among other things, very recent developments regarding materials supply, which remain to be considered.

Of the working arrangements employed, an outstanding feature is the method of balanced estimates. Even with centralized decision making, an alternative procedure for coor-

15. A leading advocate of decentralization has been Dr. Liberman. For him, decentralization is to go hand-in-hand with a change in success criteria for enterprise management. See above, p. 88.

dinating targets, and one that might be more effective, is the familiar mathematical one associated with input-output analysis: the formulation and solution of explicit mathematical equations regarding supplies and allocations.[16] The Russians have not yet applied this alternative approach, at least not until very recently.[17] They have lately been exploring systematically the possibility of doing so, however, and have already compiled and in part published a detailed input-output table for 1959. Reportedly they have also compiled a corresponding table with projected magnitudes for 1962, although the targets of the plan for that year were formulated at least primarily by the method of balanced estimates. Serious investigation of the input-output approach could only be undertaken if the basic analysis could be distinguished doctrinally from other branches of contemporary Western theory. Seemingly this has been possible, although not without the assertion of curious claims to Soviet priority in the development of the discipline. Another reason for the Russian lag in use of input-output analysis no doubt has been the lack until recently of needed

16. See above, p. 130.

17. On recent developments in the U.S.S.R. regarding the application to planning of input-output analysis and also of the related methodology of linear programming referred to below, see Levine, *A Study in Economic Planning*, ch. IX; Levine in *Comparisons*, pp. 170 ff.; "A Note on the Introduction of Mathematical Techniques into Soviet Planning," United Nations, *Economic Bulletin for Europe* (June 1960); Benjamin Ward, "Kantorovich on Economic Calculation," *Journal of Political Economy, 68* (1960), 545–56; V. S. Nemchinov, "Application of Statistical and Mathematical Methods in Soviet Planning" (processed), a paper contributed to International Conference on Input-Output Techniques, Geneva, September 11–15, 1961; Robert W. Campbell, "Marx, Kantorovich and Novozhilov: Stoimost' versus Reality," *Slavic Review, 20* (1961), 402–18; H. S. Levine, "Input-Output Analysis and Soviet Planning," *American Economic Review, 52S* (1962), 127–37; also Abraham Becker, *Input-Output Analysis and Soviet Planning*, RAND RM-3532-PR (March 1963).

175

computers. The merit of the input-output approach in determining on a nation-wide scale supplies and allocations of industrial materials for own use, however, still remains to be tested. The Russians will probably find it of use as either an alternative or a complement to the method of balanced estimates.

Closely related to input-output analysis is linear programming, and in principle it, too, might be applied in the determination of supplies and allocations of industrial materials for own use. Soviet economists have put forward claims to Russian priority in respect of linear programming, also, and not without basis. Exploration of this technique has lately been permitted, but to date it reportedly has been applied only experimentally and in limited contexts.

I referred above[18] to a reform in the prices of industrial goods that is now in progress. Under this reform prices of industrial materials are currently being changed extensively, but chiefly in order to take into account changes in circumstances since July 1955, the time of the last major revision. The current revision thus represents an application of essentially the same principles. However, some allowance apparently is now being made for differential rent in extractive industries: Prices in extractive industries are being established by reference to average costs, not for entire branches but for such branches exclusive of the most favorably situated enterprises.[19]

18. See p. 166.
19. Maizenberg, *Voprosy ekonomiki*, No. 11 (1961), 53. In principle, input-output analysis might be used as an alternative to the method of balanced estimates and as a device to facilitate coordination of decisions on materials prices. Although there is no evidence, the Russians may be employing input-output analysis in connection with the current price reform. Linear programming, too, has applications going beyond the realm of coordination of targets, and indeed in respect of prices they are of a deeper sort than those of input-output analysis, but this technique hardly can have been employed in the work on the current price reform.

Industrial Materials Price Formation

In exploring working arrangements for determination of supplies and allocations of industrial materials for own use I have throughout taken as a point of departure the desired structure of the bill of end products. Among these end products are inventories held within industry. Since I shall have little to say about inventories when I discuss the desired structure of the bill of end products, it should be observed here that even on a theoretic plane determination of appropriate inventories for an industrial enterprise is a complex task. Understandably, therefore, the scheduling of such inventories has been particularly troublesome in the U.S.S.R.[20] Understandably, too, among different participants in the process of plan formulation, attitudes vary regarding norms for inventories no less than regarding norms for inputs. Thus, especially at the level of the enterprise, the concern is to inflate requirements, while Gosplan seeks systematically to deflate them. In this sphere the former probably enjoy the greater success. Relative to output, industrial inventories have been incongruously high.[21] While this high ratio may reflect various causes, an important one must be the concern of the Soviet manager to establish a safety factor.

20. Berliner, *Factory and Manager,* chs. VI and VII; Levine, *A Study in Economic Planning,* pp. 105 ff., 197 ff.
21. R. W. Campbell, "Soviet and American Inventory-Output Ratios," *American Economic Review, 48* (1958), 549–65. The comparative inventory data in Appendix B are very crude but seem to corroborate Campbell.

9 COLLECTIVE FARM INCENTIVES

Is the Soviet collective farmer interested in productivity? To what extent? In economics interest in the productive use of resources usually is supposed to turn on material incentives. If this is true of the collective farmer in the U.S.S.R. (and no one urges otherwise), his concern for productivity can hardly have been very intense. Recently, however, it should have been greater than it was under Stalin. Thus material incentives for the Soviet collective farmer are seen here in a broadly familiar way. But I turn to resource use in Soviet agriculture, and here collective farm incentives are basic. It is well to begin with a review of this theme.

The pertinent working arrangements have been complex. Probably this is one reason why they have not been especially effective. A further consequence, however, is that the procedures must be examined in some detail.

Collective Farm Incentives

DISTRIBUTION OF DIVIDEND

Collective farmers in the U.S.S.R. receive as a material reward for their work a sum of produce and money that is expressly made available for their use.[1] If material incentives are as stated, this is the net result of more or less divergent currents established by two sorts of procedures concerning this allotment, or (as we may properly call it) "dividend." On the one hand, there are the procedures for determining the shares of different members in the dividend. Usually these should have fostered a concern for productivity. On the other, there are those for determining the magnitude of the dividend itself. These have had a contrary effect. However, it is due primarily to changes in procedures regarding the magnitude of the dividend that material incentives may be more impelling now than formerly.

To turn first to the procedures for determining the distribution of the dividend, reference here is primarily to the famous "labor day" (*trudoden'*) system.[2] Essentially, in ac-

1. For certain industrial crops, of which cotton and sugar beet are the most important, the allotment to the membership is exclusively or almost exclusively in money. In inquiring into material incentives, I shall focus on nonindustrial crops, but it should be noted that in the case of some industrial crops, particularly cotton, circumstances, at least until recently, have been more favorable to a concern for productivity than in the case of farm produce generally.

2. On the arrangements for distribution of the dividend among collective farmers, see *Kniga kolkhoznika po planirovaniiu i organizatsii truda* (Moscow, 1953); John J. Vogel, "Labor Day Remuneration on the Collective Farm" (typescript) (New York, 1955); *Spravochnik predsedatelia kolkhoza* (Moscow, 1956); N. I. Nizhnii et al., *Denezhnaia oplata truda v kolkhozakh* (Moscow, 1961); I. I. Dmitrashko, *Oplata truda v sel'skom khoziaistve SSSR* (Moscow, 1962); Nove, *The Soviet Economy*, pp. 45 ff., 121 ff.; Alec Nove, "Incentives for Peasants and Administrators," in Roy D. Laird, ed., *Soviet Agricultural and Peasant Affairs* (Lawrence, Kansas, 1963).

cord with a model charter issued initially in 1935 and revised from time to time by the government and the party,[3] the different members share in the dividend in proportion to the number of labor days each has earned. To determine such earnings an appropriate norm for every kind of task that must be performed is established for a day's work. At the same time, in the light of the skill required, the effort exerted, and similar aspects, the worker performing any given task is credited with a corresponding number of labor days for fulfilling the norm. The number of labor days credited per calendar day also varies commensurately with the degree of fulfillment of the norm.

In determining work norms and labor day credits the collective farm is supposed to take as a guide illustrative labor day scales formulated for this purpose. Thus since 1948 reference is supposed to have been made to a scale issued in that year by the Council of Ministers of the U.S.S.R., according to which the different tasks are classified into nine categories, with labor day credits for fulfilling the daily norm varying from 0.5 in the lowest to 2.5 in the highest. For some time, further guidance has been provided the collective farm in the form of published tables of norms for different tasks and corresponding credits. At least in recent years, the latter tables have been extraordinarily detailed. For example, in a list in effect in the mid-fifties, separate norms and credits are shown not only for a major task like the sowing of a specific crop, but also for different types of sowing, the latter being distinguished by equipment used, the nature of the area, and so on.

3. The initial charter nominally was adopted by a conference of collective farmers and then approved by the Council of Ministers (then Commissars) of the U.S.S.R. and the party Central Committee. In revising the charter after 1935, the latter agencies have not always troubled to observe the formality of having the revisions first accepted by a conference of collective farmers.

Collective Farm Incentives

As so determined, labor day credits for work at any one task simply represent the result of the application of a form of piece work, particularly the "straight" variety. But there have been variations from this formula. Thus, in carrying out their assigned tasks, collective farm members work in "brigades" and often also constituent "squads," each of which is responsible for a particular section of the farm's fields or herds. Depending on the fulfillment of the plan for output for the group to which he is attached, the individual farmer has often been credited with a number of labor days varying from that called for by the straight piecework formula. Apparently in order to allow for harvest fluctuations, the performance of any one group might be gauged by reference not only to its output plan but to the performance of other groups engaged in similar work. Application of such bonus arrangements, however, has varied in the course of time. While their use was fostered by the decree of the Council of Ministers of 1948, they have been applied less frequently since 1956. Since then, the collective farm has been allowed to determine for itself the nature of the bonus arrangements it should employ, and seemingly the decision often has been to employ none.[4]

There is, of course, a plan for the collective farm—indeed, as everywhere else, a complex of plans—but the annual plan is of chief interest here. A detailed program, this supposedly is formulated with the participation of the collective farm. However, targets frequently have been determined primarily by central and local government and party agencies, although this has been less true since than it was before 1955.[5] In any event, because of official secrecy it is not easy to judge just how ambitious the output targets have been, although

4. At present, however, the government is endeavoring to revive the use of bonuses.
5. See below, pp. 204–06, 214 ff.

they surely have been ambitious. Indeed, in the longer-range plans targets for agriculture have tended to approach the absurd. The annual plans probably have been more realistic, but these too have often been far beyond reach. Where employed, the bonus arrangements for collective farmers have to be read accordingly. Because the targets have been unrealistic, the rewards offered presumably have not been very impelling. Where different groups of farmers have been judged relative to each other, however, the lack of realism may not have been consequential.

In any case, the foregoing procedures generally should have fostered a concern for productivity. Under these procedures, shares in the dividend are determined in essentially the same way as industrial wage differentials. Nevertheless, the farmer's concern must have been qualified. Thus a farmer's share of the dividend often depended primarily not on output but on the volume of work performed. While in a sense this only means that here as elsewhere in the use of piecework quality control becomes important, such control has been difficult to perfect where the "product" to which rewards are related is frequently an intangible service rendered over a large area. Of course, under the bonus systems described, the farmer's share has also depended on the output of his brigade. But any one farmer might still have earned a larger share by performing more inferior work rather than less work of better quality.

I have been describing the manner in which shares are determined where the collective farm conforms to authorized practice, but such conformity has been far from universal. Moreover, where the authorized procedures have been violated, circumstances must often have impaired material incentives—for example, where, as reportedly has occurred, farmers who have not fulfilled the harvest plan have been credited by their brigade leader with the same number of labor days as those who have; or farmers have worked "in a crowd" and each one has been credited with the same number of labor days; and so on.[6]

While the relation of shares to productivity would not thereby be affected, how impelling the relation might be for the membership must also have depended on the time when their shares were actually paid. For a long time much if not all of the dividend was distributed at the end of the year, but recently the practice of making "advances" on the final money dividend at intervals throughout the year has been increasing. This practice has become widespread since March 1956, when the government and party "recommended" it to collective farms generally, and also arranged for the collective farms to receive advances on their sales of produce so that they might have the necessary funds. At present a majority of the collective farms make several advances in the course of a year, although less than one-fourth are able to pay their members 10 or more times annually.[7]

Some farms have also guaranteed their members regular payments of specified amounts per labor day. In some instances, the guarantee has been expressed simply in relation to output and without reference to the labor day at all. Nevertheless, the attempt to extend such practices has encountered difficulties, chiefly because of insufficient resources.

DETERMINATION OF THE DIVIDEND UNDER STALIN

The procedures for determining the magnitude of the dividend have evolved in the course of time. Although there is no need to inquire into the earliest formative years,

6. Vogel, pp. 60 ff.; H. S. Dinerstein and Leon Goure, *Communism and the Russian Peasant* (Glencoe, Ill., 1955), pp. 42 ff.

7. Nizhnii et al., pp. 51 ff.; Dmitrashko, pp. 22 ff.; *Direktivy, 4* (Moscow, 1958), pp. 603–05; E. Lazutkin, in *Current Digest* (June 7, 1961); Nove, "Incentives for Peasants and Administrators."

it is advisable to consider subsequent years under Stalin, particularly in peacetime, as well as the period since his passing.[8] To begin with the former period, as under the plans generally, the dividend was partly in money and partly in kind. The part in kind represented essentially the current output remaining after production requirements were met

TABLE 9.1.

Grain Output and Disposition, U.S.S.R.
(millions of tons)

	1928	1937	1952	1958
Gross output	73.3	97.4	91.8	132 (141.2)[a]
Less: production expenses; losses	32.5	34.5	34.0	52
Net output	40.8	62.9	57.8	80 (89.2)
Marketings				
MTS payments	n.a.	11.2	18.0	
Compulsory deliveries	n.a.	10.9	10.0	31.2
Government purchases	n.a.	3.3	.5	
State farm deliveries	n.a.	3.9	5.0	21.9
Other deliveries to government and cooperative procurement agencies, including return of seed loans, milling tax, etc.	n.a.	3.6	3.2	5.3
Collective farm market sales	n.a.	2.5	3.7	2.2
Unaccounted for	n.a.	2.6	...	1.8
Total	12.0	38.0	40.4	62.4
Residual	28.8	24.9	17.4	17.6 (26.8)

Sources: Real SNIP, pp. 321 ff.; Karcz, pp. 198, 445; Nimitz, *Soviet National Income and Product, 1956–1958*, p. 40. For marketings in 1928, I cite an unpublished estimate by Karcz, which is more comparable in scope with corresponding figures for later years than the figure given in *Real SNIP*, p. 327—namely 8.3.

a. I show in parentheses the official gross harvest; outside parentheses, the same net of cleaning and drying losses.

8. For useful surveys see Jerzy F. Karcz, *Soviet Agricultural Marketings and Prices, 1928–1954*, RAND RM-1930 (July 2, 1957); Nancy Nimitz, "Soviet Agricultural Prices and Costs," in *Comparisons*, Part I.

and after marketings. As is proper here, we disregard production requirements. Hence, in order to grasp how the magnitude of the dividend in kind was determined, we must simply know how the volume of marketings was fixed.

One outstanding feature, of course, is the notorious government exactions, but under Stalin the procedures for determining these and marketings generally were complex. Moreover, the latter comprised diverse sorts of deliveries (Table 9.1). Thus, as a rule, some produce was sold on the collective farm market, the amount being determined by the collective farm itself. Before it could make such sales, however, or indeed any other dispositions, the collective farm had to make several kinds of deliveries to the government, including chiefly two. It had to turn over an appropriate part of its produce in payment for services rendered it by the machine-tractor station (MTS). It had also to make deliveries to the government at established norms. The latter "compulsory deliveries" were not made free of charge, but compared with the prices prevailing in the collective farm market those paid by the government were nominal (Table 9.2).

In addition to payments in kind for MTS services and

TABLE 9.2.

Realized Farm Prices for Grain, by Type of Marketing, U.S.S.R.
(rubles per ton)

	1928	1937	1952	1958
Average, all marketing	70	150	n.a.	650
Average, all marketing other than collective farm market sales	n.a.	85	125	n.a.
Compulsory deliveries	n.a.	80	90 ⎫	
Government purchases	n.a.	115	125 ⎬	630
Collective farm market sales	n.a.	1,000	n.a.	2,160

Sources: Real SNIP, p. 324; Karcz, pp. 33, 34, 229, 354, 363; Nimitz, Soviet National Income and Product, 1956–1958, p. 40.

compulsory deliveries to the government, the collective farm normally delivered some supplies to the government, or to cooperative agencies acting on its behalf, at "state purchase" prices. Supposedly the collective farm was free to determine the amount of such sales. While the state purchase prices too were notably low, they were above those paid for compulsory deliveries, and collective farms located far from a collective farm market may well have found it to their interest to deliver supplies to the government at the former prices. Moreover, the government often made available, in return, supplies of scarce manufactured goods as an added inducement to collective farms to market produce at state purchase prices. But such sales must frequently have been made under duress. For this reason the distinction between compulsory deliveries and sales at state purchase prices cannot always have been clear, at least to the collective farmers.

The foregoing represent the most important forms of marketings, though not all forms. For grain their comparative importance may be gauged roughly from Table 9.1, showing marketings not only for collective farms but for others. For products other than grain, the structure of marketings under Stalin was broadly similar to that for grain, but there were some outstanding differences. Among other things, no MTS services were rendered and no payments were made for such services in the case of products like meat and milk. Also, collective farm market sales were generally more important for other products than for grain. The data on prices received for grain in different forms of marketings (Table 9.2) are illustrative of price relations prevailing for farm products generally. In relation to compulsory delivery prices, however, those paid for state purchases usually were markedly higher for other products than for grain.

The collective farm money dividend was derived from the sales of produce, just described, and from other activities, chiefly small-scale industrial production, that the collective farm engaged in. Before any money distribution could be made among members, however, funds had to be allocated to meet money production and similar expenses (Table 9.3). Moreover, the government claimed a share in the form of a money income tax, and also required that further allocations be made to the so-called "indivisible fund," representing sums for capital investment. Funds had to be allocated, too, for repayment of outstanding loans, and customarily the collective farm made some limited additional allocations

TABLE 9.3.

Money Income of Collective Farms by Use, U.S.S.R.
(billions of rubles)

	1938	1952	1958
Money income, all[a]	16.60	42.8	132.0
Taxes	1.50	4.2	10.3
Repayment of loans[b]	0.08	2.0	n.a.
Allocations to "indivisible fund"[c]	2.32	7.4	34.4
Cultural fund	0.50	0.9	2.0
Money production expense[d]	3.25	15.0	34.0
Administration	0.25	0.5	1.5
Payments to members[e]	8.70	13.0	49.8

Sources: Jasny, *The Socialized Agriculture of the USSR*, p. 687; Nimitz, *Soviet National Income and Product, 1956–1958*, p. 98; *Narkhoz, 1960*, p. 496.

a. Minor discrepancies between indicated totals and sums of items unexplained.

b. For 1958, included in allocations to indivisible fund.

c. For 1958, includes allocations to working capital.

d. For 1952 and 1958, includes insurance and fees.

e. Includes, at least in 1952 and 1958, some limited payments other than on a labor day basis. For 1958, about 2.1 billion rubles of labor day payments from funds allocated to investment are included in allocations to indivisible fund.

for special purposes, particularly the maintenance of a "cultural fund."

In short, whether in kind or in money the dividend represented a residual claim, and in view of the prior ones, procedures for determining the dividend must have tempered any concern for productivity that procedures for determining individual shares in it stimulated. Nevertheless, prior claims even if burdensome might affect material incentives variously depending on the manner in which they are determined in relation to productivity. Thus, depending on the share of the residual claimant in fruits of *increased* productivity, he might still be more or less interested to achieve it.

It should be observed, therefore, that norms for compulsory deliveries in principle were fixed in absolute terms: until 1940, depending on the planned sown area in the case of crops and on the number of animals in the case of livestock products; and after 1940, for products of both sorts, depending essentially on the arable land. This is to say that the compulsory deliveries for any collective farm supposedly did not vary with the harvest. By the same token, they should not have impaired interest in *increased* productivity. In practice, however, the norms frequently turned out to be elastic, with the result that a varying amount of additional output went to the government. By all accounts, the experience of a former collective farm chairman in the late 1940s was by no means unique:

> By the end of August we had completed our compulsory grain deliveries and I promised the kolkhoz members that they would receive two kilograms of grain per labor day. Then I was ordered to make supplementary deliveries and my hopes evaporated. The supplementary delivery plans that were given out were not supposed to be divulged to the kolkhoz members or even to the Party organization. Although these plans were

188

given out later, they were to be camouflaged as part of the original plan.[9]

By implication, compulsory deliveries must often have affected material incentives adversely, and sometimes markedly so.

As explained, the line between sales at state purchase prices and compulsory deliveries was not always clear, and one wonders whether in instances where compulsory delivery norms are reported to have varied, the government sometimes may not have simply expanded its procurements at state purchase prices instead. In any event, the presumption must be that the government did sometimes expand such procurements as an alternative to exacting larger compulsory deliveries, but the effect on material incentives, especially in the case of grain, must have been similar.

As for other dispositions of produce and money income, the more consequential were determined in diverse ways, though as a rule not so as to preclude the peasants from sharing in the fruits of higher productivity. The dispositions must have been adverse to material incentives, however, and should have compounded the effect of the obligatory deliveries and government purchases. Thus, payments in kind to the MTS were sizable. They were also levied at varying rates depending on the yield. While from 1939 reference for many operations was to the yield not in any one farm but in a whole district,[10] the yield was of the elastic "bio-

9. Fedor Belov, *The History of a Soviet Collective Farm* (New York, 1955), p. 137. See also Jasny, *The Socialized Agriculture of the USSR*, pp. 363 ff.; Karcz, pp. 62 ff.; Nancy Nimitz, *The New Soviet Agricultural Decrees*, RAND RM-1178 (January 13, 1954); Dinerstein and Goure, p. 55.

10. L. E. Hubbard, *Economics of Soviet Agriculture* (London, 1939), pp. 148 ff.; Jasny, *The Socialized Agriculture of the USSR*, pp. 280 ff.; Nancy Nimitz, *Soviet Agriculture since the September 1953 Reforms*, RAND RM-1552 (September 15, 1955), pp. 14 ff.

logical" or on-the-root sort, and at least after 1947, when
responsibility for estimating it was transferred from the
Central Statistical Administration to procurement agencies,
who in turn relied partly on MTS materials, it might be
overstated in order to inflate payments in kind. Hence the
latter must have been adverse to incentives, though for the
individual collective farm the total burden often may not
have increased markedly with superior performance.

The basis for levying the money income tax changed in
the course of time; but throughout, the amount varied pro-
portionately with the amounts of different kinds of income
or output; for example, as of 1948–51 a tax of 6 per cent was
levied on the value at compulsory delivery prices of produce
used for seed, fodder, welfare funds, and the like; one of 6
per cent was placed on receipts from sales at state purchase
prices; one of 12 per cent on the value at state purchase
prices of the dividend in kind; and one of 13 per cent on
receipts from collective farm market sales, industrial activities, etc.[11] The percentage of money income allocated to the
indivisible fund also varied in the course of time. Before
1952 it ranged from 12 to 15 per cent in grain regions and
from 15 to 20 per cent in other regions.

In considering how determination of the dividend might
affect material incentives, a distinction must be made between the variation of the dividend at one time and its
variation over a period of time. Depending on the concomitant variation in the dividend, collective farmers might
have a greater or lesser concern for higher productivity at
any one time. But even if the dividend tended to increase
markedly with higher productivity at any one time, such a
concern might still be impaired if successes were to be followed by heavier exactions, so that the same dividend could

11. Alec Nove, "Rural Taxation in the USSR," *Soviet Studies,* 5
(1953–54), 159–68.

be earned only through still higher productivity. Thus far I have focused on the variation of the dividend in relation to productivity at one time. As for the relation over time, what is in question essentially is the manner in which the collective farmers' real reward has varied in the course of time in relation to his output, and, regrettably, on this the trends are still not very clear. But if we may judge from uncertain knowledge of corresponding trends for Soviet farmers generally, the collective farmers can hardly have found their experience at this point very encouraging. Thus in the late 1930s farm output per man-year employed had recovered fully, while farm household "real" income per man-year employed had recovered appreciably less from the low levels to which they had descended under the First Five Year Plan under the joint impact of wholesale collectivization and government exactions.[12] Subsequently, up to the time of the German attack, output per man-year increased little if at all and real income per man-year may well have declined. From the time of the German attack to Stalin's death, output and real income per man-year both experienced another cycle of decline and recovery, but at the close of the period output per man-year was appreciably above, while real income per man-year probably was still below, the pre-five-year-plan level. Year-to-year changes within the different intervals are entirely conjectural. In appraising in the foregoing light the effect of the variation of the dividend over time on material incentives, the reader should remember that under the plans the government made sizable investments in agriculture, and might have been able to exact an increasing share of output in compensation without seriously weakening material incentives. For several years, however, the investments

12. See D. Gale Johnson and Arcadius Kahan, "Soviet Agriculture: Structure and Growth," in *Comparisons;* D. Gale Johnson, "Agricultural Production," in Bergson and Kuznets, eds., *Economic Trends in the Soviet Union; Real SNIP,* pp. 249 ff., 442 ff.

merely made good the losses of capital, particularly livestock and draft animals, that had occurred under wholesale collectivization.

In principle the variation of the dividend in relation to productivity at one time and over time should alone have mattered, so far as the dividend affected material incentives. But in practice in judging rewards for higher productivity the membership of any one collective farm no doubt also considered how the dividend varied in still another way: among farms.

Differences in productivity among collective farms must be due to differences in several factors: effectiveness of the members in utilizing available inputs, quality of land, and the available capital stock. Of particular interest here is the extent to which differences in productivity due to differences in the first factor accrued to the members, but on the eve of the plans much of the "differential rent" to land must also have accrued to the peasants. For this reason, even if the government thereafter should have sought to appropriate only such rent, and should have allowed differences in production originating in factors other than differences in the quality of land to accrue fully to the collective farmers, the exactions might well have affected adversely material incentives, at least for a time. Moreover, if a collective farm had a large capital stock, this was due to its own investments. Hence, in seeking to use available inputs effectively the members would also have been discouraged if the government should have systematically appropriated the return to this capital.

Seen in this light, the manner in which the dividend varied among farms, at least in Stalin's last years, can only be viewed as a further factor adverse to material incentives. Thus before 1947 the government differentiated in regard to compulsory delivery norms and MTS fees between major regions and even provinces (*oblast'*) and districts (*raion*), and partly in this way appears to have taken for itself some of the excess output obtained in more productive regions. Nevertheless, it did not capture all the excess. Hence the dividend per man-year must have varied markedly between regions. Furthermore, since the norms were uniform within any district, variations in productivity within a district resulted in a more or less corresponding variation in the dividend. Broadly speaking, these arrangements also prevailed after 1947, but by a party decree of February of that year local government agencies were allowed to differentiate compulsory delivery norms even within a single district. Although MTS fees apparently continued to be uniform, under the pressures of the time the local government agencies reportedly often used the new authority regarding compulsory delivery norms to extract much if not all the excess output of the more productive farms.[13]

DETERMINATION OF THE DIVIDEND SINCE STALIN

The changes in arrangements for determination of the dividend since Stalin have been many and diverse. In saying above that procedures for determining the dividend have become more favorable to material incentives I had in mind particularly the measures of 1953–56 initiating revisions in the prices paid procurement agencies for farm produce, a party decree of February 1958, providing for the liquidation of the MTS, and a measure of July 1958 purportedly abolishing obligatory deliveries of farm produce and revising once more the prices paid by procurement

13. I. P. Altaiskii et al., *Dokhody, nakoplenie i finansovoe khoziaistvo v kolkhozakh* (Moscow, 1937), pp. 134 ff.; Hubbard, pp. 180 ff.; Harry Schwartz, *Russia's Soviet Economy* (2d ed. New York, 1954), pp. 317 ff.; Nimitz, *The New Soviet Agricultural Decrees,* p. 10; Karcz, pp. 62 ff.

agencies.[14] The upshot has been that the collective farm has been relieved only nominally from obligatory deliveries, for it is still expected to meet a quota established for supply of produce to the government. But in place of the diverse deliveries that prevailed previously there is now only one: sale at a price. Moreover, for any farm there is now only one price in place of the former multiplicity of prices, and the new price is far higher than the average of the multiple prices was previously. The change for grain is shown above (Table 9.2). For farm produce generally, procurement prices in 1958 were some four times the 1950 level. The collective farm must now provide or pay in money for services formerly rendered by the MTS, but the government is now paying for the deliveries which formerly compensated for these services, and at the new high prices.

Chiefly as a result of these measures the money dividend paid collective farm households in 1958 was 3.8 times that of 1952 (Table 9.3). While material incentives have been fostered thereby, the measures are complex, and the favorable impact may not have been as great as it seems at first sight. Thus, while government procurement prices have been sharply increased, they are still below collective farm market prices. The difference is reduced, however, if account is taken of the high marketing costs incurred on collective farm market sales. Also, the new prices avowedly may be adjusted upward or downward "depending on conditions in a given year and on the harvest . . . ," which is to say that while "they should not change given normal yields," they must be "revised upwards or downwards depending on conditions in the given year." [15] While the government's efforts to grapple

14. *Current Digest* (April 9, 1958); Nimitz, in *Comparisons*, Part I; Lazar Volin, "Agricultural Policy of the Soviet Union," in *Comparisons*, Part I.

15. *Current Digest* (August 6, 1958), pp. 3–4.

with inevitable harvest fluctuations are understandable, the policies pursued might penalize improved performance.

Since 1958 the money income tax has been levied at a single rate, 14 per cent, and the tax base has been changed.[16] But material incentives probably have not been affected consequentially. Quotas for allocations to the indivisible fund were increased somewhat in 1952, and after the liquidation of the MTS the collective farms had to increase these allocations still further in order to finance machinery purchases (Table 9.3). Moreover, collective farms lately have been encouraged even to exceed their quotas in this respect, though such a practice can only have had an adverse effect on material incentives.

As a result of the foregoing measures, the collective farm members should be receiving a larger dividend than they did under Stalin for higher productivity achieved at one time. What, however, of the variation of the dividend in relation to productivity over time and in relation to productivity among different collective farms? From the time of Stalin's death to 1958 both collective farm output and household real income per man-year probably increased markedly. Since 1958 output per man-year has tended to increase little, and household real income per man-year not at all. Rather, in the case of the latter there probably has been a marked decline. In 1958 agricultural weather was exceptionally favorable. The more recent experience as to output and real income has been less favorable than that of 1953–58 partly for this reason. Household real income per man-year, however, probably had already declined both in relation to output and absolutely even before 1963, when the weather was exceptionally adverse.[17]

16. Nove, *The Soviet Economy*, p. 51.
17. See *Real SNIP*, pp. 249 ff., 445 ff.; Nimitz, in *Comparisons*, Part I, pp. 272 ff.; *Narkhoz, 1960*, pp. 492, 493, 521; Rachel E. Golden,

The question concerning the variation of the dividend over time must be judged in this light. As for the variation of the dividend among farms, Stalin's death brought a significant change in procedure. Party actions taken soon after that event proscribed the practice of differentiating per hectare norms for obligatory deliveries for collective farms within any one district, and uniformity of such norms became the accepted rule for all products other than vegetables.[18] By implication, collective farms within a district were again permitted to retain the differential returns which often had been expropriated during Stalin's last years. According to the decree of July 1958 the per hectare quotas for the government purchases that have replaced all former deliveries to the government are also supposed to be uniform within a district, though account is to be taken of differences in specialization of different farms. If official data on money income are at all indicative (Table 9.4), the dividend now varies widely among collective farms.

While obligatory deliveries were abolished in 1958, the collective farms are still required to make produce available to the government in accord with established quotas. In 1961 this requirement was emphasized by the initiation of the practice of having the collective farms enter into contracts obligating them to make such deliveries.[19]

"Recent Trends in Soviet Personal Income and Consumption," and Joseph E. Willett, "The Recent Record in Soviet Economic Growth: Agriculture," in *Dimensions*; Nove, "Incentives for Peasants and Administrators;" U.S. Department of Agriculture, "USSR Farm Production in 1963," *Foreign Agricultural Economics* (January 1964).

18. Karcz, p. 64.

19. This is not a novelty in the U.S.S.R. For industrial materials like cotton and sugar beet, in respect of which material incentives have here been passed by, procurements have long been made on a contract basis. In 1961, however, the practice of contracting for collective farm deliveries was extended to farm products generally. See *Current Digest* (March 22, 1961), p. 7.

Collective Farm Incentives

TABLE 9.4.

Collective Farms of the U.S.S.R. Classified by Money Income
per 100 Hectares of Arable Land, 1960

Money Income per 100 Hectares of Arable Land (rubles)	Number of Farms (per cent)
Less than 1,000	2.5
1,000–2,000	6.2
2,000–3,000	10.2
3,000–5,000	23.9
5,000–10,000	34.6
10,000–20,000	17.9
More than 20,000	4.7

Source: Narkhoz, 1960, p. 47. Money income is in terms of post-January 1, 1961 rubles.

Under the labor day system of determining shares in the dividend, the individual collective farmer could sometimes have earned a larger portion than otherwise by performing inferior work where possible. From the procedures for determining the dividend, we now see that the inferior work might have tended to reduce the dividend, and hence the worth of shares generally, but the resultant loss to any one member would have been small. Hence, inferior work could still have been profitable.

EFFORT VERSUS PRODUCTIVITY

Under the procedures that have been described, the relation between the dividend and productivity must often have seemed tenuous to the collective farmer, though probably less so recently than under Stalin. But we are concerned ultimately with the farmer's interest in exerting himself to assure an effective use of resources, and from this standpoint the adverse effect of the arrangements must have been compounded by another feature: the farmer must

197

sometimes have doubted whether his exertion would be especially favorable to productivity itself.

At any rate, I alluded above to the role of government and party in the formulation of the collective farm's plan. More generally, the determination of collective farm output will be discussed below, but we must consider here that in the U.S.S.R. the farmer faces more hazards than the weather. Because of pervasive governmental and party intervention, there are additional hazards. I refer not to intervention bearing on the relation of the dividend to productivity, but to intervention bearing on productivity itself, for needless to say it does exist, and has by no means always been beneficent. According to both Soviet and non-Soviet accounts, the resulting demoralization, with its attendant impairment of effort and initiative, was a familiar feature under Stalin. It has remained so under Khrushchev, as the tale of the "New Life" collective farm so vividly testifies.[20]

MANAGERIAL INCENTIVES

Up to this point I have been considering the interest of the membership generally in the productive use of inputs. In accord with the model charter, the collective farm is administered by a managerial board, whose chairman is also the chief executive officer of the collective farm as a whole. With responsibility for day-to-day operations, the chairman is assisted by other officials, including brigadiers who supervise the diverse brigades. In the course of time the collective farm has typically become a large and complex undertaking (in 1960, the average farm embraced 383 households and 6,299 hectares of arable land). From the standpoint of resource use, therefore, the motivation of these officials must be of special import.

Like the collective farm members generally, the chairman

20. Fyodor Abramov, *One Day in the "New Life"* (New York, 1963).

198

shares in the dividend on a labor day basis, the number of labor days credited to him being appropriate to his responsibilities.[21] Thus, according to an official scale introduced in 1948 and still widely in effect in the late 50s, the chairman is to be credited with from 2.7 to 5.4 labor days a month per hectare of sown area, an additional 5 to 18 labor days for each kind of livestock holdings (cows, sows, sheep), the precise credit depending on the size of the herd, and still more credits for horse and poultry holdings. This constitutes only the basic income of the chairman, for in addition he is to receive from 25 to 400 rubles monthly depending on the amount of the collective farm's money income. For overfulfilling the targets for crop yields and livestock productivity, the chairman is to receive a bonus amounting to 15 to 40 per cent of his labor day earnings and additional money income taken together. On the other hand, for underfulfillment of targets he may be penalized by the deduction of up to 25 per cent of the labor day income credited to him.

In short, the chairman can gain materially from the productive use of the collective farm's resources. Nevertheless, he apparently can be penalized for crop fluctuations for which he is not responsible. Also, like those for members generally, his material incentives must be affected adversely by procedures for determining the dividend.

While nominally elected by a general assembly of collective farm members, the chairman in fact is often designated by and in any case is dependent for his tenure upon the benevolent opinion of local government and party officials. If only for this reason, fulfillment of the plan must be a major concern. But from the standpoint of the government and party, the paramount test for success is not so much productivity as deliveries to the government. That this was so under Stalin is self-evident; it is still so under Khrushchev,

21. *Spravochnik predsedatelia kolkhoza,* pp. 156 ff.; Dmitrashko, pp. 107 ff.

although not in the same degree.[22] In order to be esteemed by the party and government, therefore, the chairman must first of all fulfill the plan for deliveries to the government. From this standpoint productivity must also be of concern, but where deliveries exceed quotas at the expense of material incentives for collective farmers generally this must often be with the acquiescence if not the active support of the chairman. Inevitably the chairman must also support other actions of the party and government that may not be favorable to productivity.

The brigadiers (in addition to the chairman, it may suffice to refer to no more than these officials) for some time have usually been compensated on a labor day basis, with their number of labor day credits corresponding to their responsibilities. For overfulfillment of the target for yields, the brigadier supposedly receives additional credits 1.5 times those received on the average by members of his brigade. Hence, the brigadier's material rewards are determined in essentially the same way as those for collective farm members generally. His interest in productivity must be judged in this light.

22. The continued priority of deliveries over production is seen in diverse circumstances, but perhaps most clearly in a 1955 reform in planning procedure. Under this reform the collective farm has gained a larger role in the formulation of targets for output and related aspects, but targets for deliveries to the government continue to be determined by the government and party. Since 1955, however, responsibility is not as centralized as formerly. See below, p. 220.

10 MANAGEMENT OF AGRICULTURE

COLLECTIVE FARM PRODUCTION

Having explored the motivation of collective farmers, we may turn more expressly to resource use in agriculture. In doing so, I shall for the present consider diverse facets, of which the first is rather basic: Given the resources of all kinds that are to be employed, including labor of different skills, machinery of different kinds, and so forth, how is the output of the individual farm determined?

While employment of labor is among the resources given, the effort exerted may vary, because of, say, variation in the length of the working day. But even if the working day is viewed, as here, essentially as a datum, effort may vary with the nature of the task. Also, for any one task there may be differences in the intensity of work. In the theoretical analysis of resource use such variations are often neglected, but I have already alluded to them in respect to the worker in

Soviet industry. They are no less deserving of attention for the Soviet farmer.

Hence resource use here is subject to two efficiency rules. First, at any level of effort exerted by different workers, and in the light of available agronomic knowledge, output of any desired structure should be a maximum. Second, for each worker, ideally, additional output resulting from more intensive work should be just sufficient to compensate him for the exertion. In exploring working arrangements for determination of output in the individual enterprise, we wish to gauge conformity with these rules.

The collective farm is the predominant type of farm enterprise in the U.S.S.R., although it must account today for markedly less of Soviet farm output than the 63 per cent of 1937.[1] I shall begin with this organization, and refer initially to procedures bearing on the first rule. Not least among them are the ones concerning material incentives. Even if effort should be the same, depending on the material rewards, collective farmers presumably still might not be especially concerned to see that their skills and exertions are effectively used. Hence it is pertinent here that collective farmers, including members and officials, have been able to gain from the productive use of available resources, including their own skills and exertions. The gains must often have seemed meager and uncertain, however, although less so after Stalin than before. Also, members have been rewarded chiefly for the volume of work performed, which need not mean a corresponding volume of output.

While attention here is on resource use in the collective farm, until 1958 crucial inputs, including services of machinery, were administered by the MTS. For this reason in gauging collective farm productivity before 1958, we must consider that, when the MTS functioned, it employed both

1. Nimitz, *Statistics of Soviet Agriculture*.

collective farm members and a permanent staff.[2] In either case arrangements for compensation varied among different groups of workers and at different times, but they were broadly similar to procedures used to compensate industrial workers, or some combination of these with procedures used to compensate collective farm members. Among other things, where collective farm members were employed, they were compensated by their collective farms on a labor day basis, but the value of the labor day was subject to a guaranteed minimum. After 1953, many such persons were formally attached to the MTS staff, but their compensation continued to be more or less on a labor day basis. The money value of the labor day, however, was more definitely fixed.

Under the circumstances, one might suppose that persons either employed by the MTS or operating machines in its behalf would have been concerned with productivity. But for the MTS a cardinal test of success for the enterprise generally and for managerial personnel, including the director, in particular, was fulfillment of the plan for machine operations in terms of "standard plowing units." This represents the total volume of machine work where different operations are converted into plowing by use of standard equivalents. As might be expected, therefore, the sacrifice of quality for quantity of work was a subject of complaint regarding the MTS hardly less than regarding collective farm members themselves. Because the conversion coefficients were frequently incongruous, the MTS might also find it expedient to favor "soft" over "hard" operations in meeting the needs of the collective farm. In this way arose the curious practice of "chasing hectares," whereby in order to fulfill its target the MTS did even more "soft" work than was planned. Interest in the vital matter of appropriate sched-

2. Jasny, *The Socialized Agriculture of the USSR*, pp. 283 ff.; Yaroslav Bilinsky, "Machine Tractor Stations" (typescript) (Cambridge, Mass., June 1957).

uling of operations also suffered. With due allowance for the excesses of Soviet "self-criticism," complaints regarding the work of the MTS, like this one, are too numerous not to have a basis:

> . . . Our machine-tractor stations are little interested in improvement of yields, in good cultivation, in timely seeding and harvesting. The existing system of evaluation of the work of the MTS in terms of hectares converted to soft plowing equivalent, and the system of incentives for MTS personnel cause many MTS to strive to complete as many light operations as possible instead of heavy plowing work. . . . One must ask what good do the state and kolkhozy derive from such a fulfillment of their plan by the MTS if it results in a low harvest.[3]

After A. A. Andreev addressed the Central Committee in February 1947, the party took steps to correct these abuses, and it was to take further ones to the same end. But complaints continued. In part because it was a budget-supported (as distinct from *khozraschet*) organization, the exercise of effective control over the inputs employed by the MTS itself, in order to achieve a given output, also proved difficult.

For any economic entity, productivity depends not only on material incentives but on the general nature of the organizational arrangements. How the one might affect the other is an intricate topic not readily susceptible to generalization, but it is almost axiomatic that overlapping responsibility, while it may have some virtues, can easily become a vice. In the case of the collective farm, therefore, conformity to the first efficiency rule could hardly have been enhanced by the extraordinary number of authorities in ad-

3. Andreev's talk was published in *Pravda* (March 7, 1947), after the Central Committee had acted on it. Their action had been reported in *Pravda* (February 28, 1947).

Management of Agriculture

dition to its own staff involved in its administration, seemingly often in a detailed and ad hoc way.[4] The chief outside authority was the MTS during the time it existed. While supplying machinery services to the collective farm, the MTS served as a major instrument of control over the latter. Practically if not legally, the MTS concerned itself with almost all activities of the collective farm, including those involved in the formulation and implementation of plans. The MTS, however, was subordinate to a complex of government organs, and these too might intervene directly in the affairs of the collective farm, while the party acted through the MTS and directly. Moreover, after the demise of the MTS other authorities often became more active. In liquidating the MTS, therefore, the party and government no doubt dispelled, as they hoped, the "negative consequences of a situation in which two socialist enterprises . . . manage matters on one and the same land." But referring to agricultural administration as it had evolved by 1961, a careful account could still conclude that "everyone was to some extent responsible, therefore no one was."[5] And in 1962 the government established a quite new hierarchy of agricultural agencies, elaborate even by Soviet standards. Among the new agencies, at the lowest level, is the interdistrict territorial production administration (TPU). This is supposed to advise rather than administer the collective farm, but in setting up the new apparatus obviously a cardinal concern of the government was to reconcentrate authority that had become diffuse after the liquidation of the MTS. Khrushchev himself made clear from the outset

4. Dinerstein and Goure, chs. 3 and 4; Fainsod, *How Russia Is Ruled*, pp. 526 ff.; *Current Digest* (April 9, 1958, March 21, 28, 1962); Alec Nove, "Soviet Agriculture Marks Time," *Foreign Affairs, 40* (1961–62), 576–94; Howard Swearer, "Agricultural Administration under Khrushchev," in Laird, ed., *Soviet Agricultural and Peasant Affairs*.
5. Nove, *Foreign Affairs, 40* (1961–62), 588.

that the advice offered by the TPU would be more than hortatory.[6]

Excessive overlapping of responsibility might have affected productivity adversely in any case, but in the U.S.S.R. the consequences can only have been more deleterious, since many of the persons intervening have not always been aware of the consequences of intervention. At lower levels, even where they have been, the need to conform to less enlightened imperatives received from above might still be overriding. Moreover, party and government officials have been primarily concerned with marketings, not productivity. According to both Soviet and non-Soviet literature, the experience of the chairman of the "New Life" collective farm must seem familiar to his colleagues everywhere:

> He turned over a sodden layer of hay with his boot and released the heavy, fermented smell of manure, and he looked up at the sky. Yes, another couple of days, and it would be goodbye to the hay. . . . No, he had not been right. It was he, after all, who had given orders for people to be taken off the haymaking when the weather was still dry. But he ought to have stuck to his guns. He should have gone into town to the interdistrict office and fought for what he thought was right. After all, there wasn't just *one* district committee above him.[7]

It is almost axiomatic, too, that arrangements regarding responsibility take time to perfect, and that if frequently changed even the best of them may prove dubious. Yet especially since Stalin such procedures for collective farm affairs have been notably in flux. Thus, the MTS was an instrument of control throughout its existence, but only a few years before its liquidation its powers were so enlarged that it was viewed as bearing "full responsibility for the organiza-

6. *Current Digest* (March 28, 1962), pp. 6–7.
7. Abramov, *One Day in the "New Life,"* p. 26.

tion of collective production in all its branches." [8] The union-republican Ministry of Agriculture, through which the government had formerly administered the MTS and overseen the collective farms, necessarily suffered a loss in responsibility when the MTS was liquidated, but its activities were further curtailed by the transfer of functions to other agencies, including Gosplan. By 1961 it was little more than the administrator of an agricultural extension service. After the liquidation of the MTS, responsibility for the supply of machinery to the collective farms and the provision of repair service was at first vested in the newly organized Repair-Technical Station (RTS), but the former function was then shifted to Gosplan. Still later, together with the RTS, it was shifted to a new supply organization. Partly in association with these measures, the responsibilities of other organs of government and party agencies changed. Then in March 1962 came the establishment of an entirely new complex of agencies to administer the affairs of the collective along with those of state farms.

In a bureaucratic structure, productivity must also depend on reliability of information available to decision makers. Hence, in gauging conformity to the first efficiency rule, we must recognize that while Soviet statistics generally are dubious, those compiled for agriculture have been notoriously so.[9] Under Stalin, however, distortions were largely the result of reporting practices initiated at the center; in any event, it should not have been too difficult for superior agencies to obtain reliable data by discounting for such distortions as occurred. Under Khrushchev, as he himself has made clear, "simulation" (*ochkovtiratel'stvo*), including

8. K. Kondratev, cited in Nimitz, *Soviet Agriculture since the September 1953 Reforms*, p. 94.

9. See Abram Bergson, "Reliability and Usability of Soviet Statistics," *American Statistician* (June-July 1953); *Real SNIP*, pp. 58–59; Willett, in *Dimensions*, pp. 96 ff.

even patent falsification (for example, forgery of procurement receipts) has become pervasive. Consequently, even superior agencies must often be in doubt as to the actual state of affairs. However, reporting may have become more accurate since the publication in May 1961 of a decree calling for criminal prosecution of, and a prison sentence of up to three years for, persons guilty of making "inflated entries in state accounts or other deliberate distortions of accounts on the fulfillment of plans."

Finally, we still know little about the procedure by which different members of the collective farm are assigned to different tasks. No doubt qualifications generally are an important determinant, and conformity to the first efficiency rule is to be viewed accordingly. From the same standpoint, however, we must also realize that in the 1930s, especially when wholesale collectivization was under way, the party often found it expedient to favor political reliability at the expense of agricultural expertise in filling the strategic post of chairman. Thus it was in 1929 that the famous action was taken to dispatch to the country 25,000 politically tested industrial workers, chiefly to staff collective farm chairmanships. More recently, greater emphasis appears to have been given to agricultural knowledge; but, curiously, as late as 1955 the party again filled chairmanships in a wholesale way through recruitment of urban workers. Particularly, it then undertook to recruit for such posts some 30,000 urban "volunteers" from among experienced party, Soviet, administrative, engineering and technical officials, workers, and employees.[10] Avowedly this was done to strengthen executive capacities generally, but it was felt necessary to warn in-

10. *Current Digest* (May 18, 1955), pp. 11–13. In considering recruitment of chairmen from outside the collective farm, I am going beyond my initial supposition that collective farm inputs are given, but there should be no misunderstandings if the first efficiency rule is understood correspondingly in the sense that account is taken of the "opportunity cost" incurred in shifting industrial personnel to the collective farm.

dustrial organizations not to repeat "past mistakes," including the recommendation for agriculture of "unsuitable" persons who were unwanted by their employers. In any case, the number of chairmen with party status probably was increased (Table 10.1). In the last few years, however, col-

TABLE 10.1.

Chairmen of Collective Farms by Party Status, Education, and Tenure

	NUMBER OF CHAIRMEN (PER CENT)			
	July 1, 1953	*April 1,* 1956	*April 1,* 1959	*April 1,* 1962
Party members and candidates	79.6	90.5	93.5	n.a.
Graduates of universities	2.6	7.8	11.8 ⎫	60.1
Graduates of middle special schools	15.4	29.3	38.6 ⎭	
Having served as chairmen:				
Up to 1 year	23.8	29.7	4.6	9.7
From 1 to 3 years	35.6	33.9	38.9	37.1
3 years and more	40.6	36.4	56.5	53.2

Sources: TSU, *Sel'skoe khoziaistvo SSSR* (Moscow, 1960), p. 474; *Narkhoz, 1961*, p. 466.

lective farm chairmen have tended to be increasingly well-trained and experienced, although to what extent in agricultural specialties is uncertain. These gains have been realized without any sacrifice in respect of their party status.

Yet, in January 1959 Khrushchev still could complain:

> Why is it that collective . . . farms do not organize their work as well as factory personnel? Because some collectives have been headed by poor chairmen for long stretches of time; some have brought as many as three collectives to ruin and are heading toward a fourth. . . . And the party organizations put up but a weak fight against such an evil.[11]

We may safely conclude that the collective farm has hardly conformed to the first efficiency rule in any pro-

11. Lazar Volin, in *Comparisons,* Part I, p. 311.

nounced way. The member has had an incentive to be productive, even though not a very impelling one. Through the years presumably he has also learned somehow to accommodate himself to the vast, intricate, and ever-changing bureaucracy that has hovered over him. But for output to be much below the maximum must not be unusual.

The second rule requires in effect that the worker receive in return for further effort the entire increment in product resulting from the exertion. Because of the government's onerous exactions this has hardly been the case. The government in principle might still have observed the rule by limiting the exactions to the rent of land, but at least on the less productive farms the exactions must exceed such rent, and on all farms they tend, unlike rent, to absorb additional output due to additional effort. Moreover, as was explained, even if the exactions should happen to be limited to land rent, they might often have adversely affected material incentives, and in that case effort too would be impaired. So far as effort has been a variable, therefore, it should have been less than necessary for conformity to the second rule.[12]

12. Should exactions correspond to rent at any one level of output, it might be suggested that they need not be especially adverse to incentives if they diverge at others. Thus, while the dividend generally might suffer as a result, might not the individual farmer still find the opportunity to increase his own share a sufficient inducement to exert something like an optimal effort? Possibly so, but so far as farm members generally exert themselves to increase output none would find his share increased, and the variation in exactions would be discouraging to all alike.

Even if exactions correspond precisely to land rent, it should also be observed that incomes of collective farm members would correspond to marginal productivity on the average, but the extent of correspondence for individual members would depend on the degree to which their differential returns reflected differences in productivity. Also, some of the income remaining after government exactions properly is viewed as a return to capital rather than to labor; but if the government should expropriate only differential rent, the returns to capital and labor together should reflect their marginal productivities.

OTHER FARM PRODUCTION

While supplying labor services to the collective farm, member households also cultivate small plots that have been assigned for their individual use. On such homesteads, collective farm households also keep livestock. Although individual holdings have been minuscule in the aggregate, the homestead herds have accounted for a sizable fraction of Soviet livestock (Table 2.3). Chiefly for this reason, the homesteads in 1937 accounted for more than one-fifth of Soviet farm output. Since 1937, their share of Soviet livestock herds has fluctuated, but in the course of time it has declined sharply and their share of the total output must have varied more or less correspondingly. But the collective farm homesteads still produced one-fifth of the country's milk in 1958 and one-third of its meat in 1959.[13]

As to resource use in these plots, the reader will be able to judge tendencies to conformity to the two efficiency rules if I explain that under Stalin the homestead was called on to make obligatory deliveries at least of crops, at rates higher than those of the collective farm.[14] Furthermore, the homestead was also subject to a money tax, and while for a time this essentially was a very limited poll tax, with the amounts varying according to the region, the government from 1939 on levied instead a tax on actual and imputed income, ex-

13. J. A. Newth, "Soviet Agriculture: The Private Sector 1950–1959 —Animal Husbandry," *Soviet Studies, 13* (1961–62), 423, 427. This is a sequel to J. A. Newth, "Soviet Agriculture: The Private Sector 1950–1959," *Soviet Studies, 13* (1961–62), 160–71.

14. On the economics of the collective farm homestead, see, in addition to the writings of Newth just cited, Karcz, *Soviet Agricultural Marketings and Prices, 1928–1954*, pp. 62–68; Nove, *Soviet Studies, 5* (1953–54), 162 ff.; Holzman, *Soviet Taxation*, pp. 186 ff.; Jasny, *The Socialized Agriculture of the USSR*, pp. 688 ff.; Nove, *The Soviet Economy*, pp. 57–59; A. N. Sakoff, "The Private Sector in Soviet Agriculture," United Nations, Food and Agriculture Organization, *Monthly Bulletin of Agricultural Economics and Statistics* (September 1962).

clusive of labor day earnings from the collective farm. The rates initially varied from 7 to 15 per cent, depending on the income, but by 1951 they had risen to 12 to 48 per cent.

Nevertheless, households probably retained for their own use a larger share of net income produced on their homesteads than of net income produced on the collective farm, and it must have been partly for this reason that before the war, earnings for a day's work on the homestead much exceeded those received from the collective farm for a corresponding effort. In fact, the former is estimated to have been as much as two and one-fourth times the latter. How these relative earnings varied subsequently under Stalin is uncertain, but the differential in favor of homestead work probably had declined by the late 1940s.

Soon after Stalin's death the government reduced obligatory delivery quotas for collective farm homesteads, and in 1958 it eliminated them altogether, although apparently it is still able to procure produce from the homesteads on some scale. The government also initiated a reform in procedures for levying money taxes on the homesteads, and in the process materially reduced the total levy. Under these measures, the household must now be able to retain the bulk of the net income produced by the homestead. How earnings from this source have varied in relation to those from the collective farm is not clear, but some margin of the former over the latter ordinarily must still prevail.

As determined in the foregoing manner, the income earned by the household must have been a major factor affecting its interest in utilizing productively the resources at its disposal, but in trying to appraise the latter aspect one must also consider that the household plot has been subject to its own hazards. Thus these resources varied in the course of time for many reasons, not least because of government actions bearing immediately on them. Most importantly, after the adoption of the Model Charter in 1935 the homesteads were permitted to acquire livestock within specified limits. But beginning in 1939 collective farms were directed to increase their holdings at the expense of the homesteads, and this they did in diverse ways, including sizable "purchases" of homestead herds. After the war, the homesteads underwent a similar experience, when after having expanded their holdings they were again put under pressure to "sell" herds to the collective farm. With the permission of the government, the latter during Stalin's last years "purchased" livestock from the homestead on a wholesale scale in order to meet its quotas. After Stalin's death these practices were denounced, and the homestead apparently was allowed to increase its holdings within legal limits. But a revision of the charter in 1956 gave the collective farm authority itself to establish limits for homestead livestock holdings. How this authority has been used is not clear, but apparently with encouragement of the government, at least of local authorities, collective farm holdings have again been increasing, in part at the expense of private holdings.

The state farm is the chief remaining entity engaged in agricultural activities in the U.S.S.R. Responsible for but 9.3 per cent of total output in 1937, it has recently assumed a much increased role and is now second only to the collective farm as a producer of Soviet farm stuffs. Working arrangements affecting productivity and effort in these enterprises are similar to those in government enterprise in industry.[15] How such arrangements work in agriculture is perhaps another matter. Nevertheless, at least recently conformity to the two efficiency rules may often have been closer than in the case of the collective farm. This seems

15. See Jasny, *The Socialized Agriculture of the USSR*, pp. 235 ff.; Schwartz, *Russia's Soviet Economy*, pp. 327 ff.; Nimitz, in *Comparisons*, pp. 256 ff.

especially likely in grain production. But this is a matter on which many facts are still not clear, and it must be left for special inquiry.

THE CROP SCHEME

Apart from supplies to replace initial stocks of seed and fodder, the output of a farm enterprise normally is employed in two ways. Some of the produce is used currently in the production of further produce, e.g. as fodder. Other supplies are used for consumption by the producers, additions to seed and fodder stocks, or are disposed of for use elsewhere in the economy. From the standpoint of the individual farm, though not necessarily from that of agriculture as a whole, the former supplies represent materials for own use, and the latter, end products.

Thus far I have taken as given the structure of the Soviet farm enterprise's output, however it is used. At least, a maximum output conforming to the first efficiency rule has been understood to be one where the production of no good could be increased without that of another being sacrificed. I propose to turn now to a facet of resource use that has thus been passed by: determination of the nature of the supplies constituting materials for own use.

This facet of resource use, however, is not easily disentangled from other related ones. Thus almost inevitably choices among materials for own use have been a part of larger decisions involving choices among end products as well. Almost inevitably, too, the volume and kinds of resources employed have also changed, though one might wish to continue, as I have done thus far, to take these as given. Reference is of course to resources other than materials for own use.

But we need not be deterred by these complexities from focusing here on choices among materials for own use.

214

Where resources are given and there are no substitutions among end products, the efficiency rule that obtains is simply an extension of the one previously considered: Within limits of available economic knowledge, choices among materials for own use must be such that the output of end products is a maximum. That is, the output of no products can be increased without that of others being reduced. If resources and kinds of end products vary, this rule has to be qualified in the light of some appropriate valuation of the changes occurring. But, while by any likely accounting for such changes there must have been some tendency toward conformity to the rule in the U.S.S.R., there must also have been divergencies, and often of a very consequential sort.

Such at any rate are the conclusions to be drawn from fairly well known facts as to the Soviet practice in the sphere in question. Thus a Soviet authority has given a detailed account of how pertinent decisions were made under Stalin. Because of the rare glimpse provided into the process of Soviet decision-making at the highest level, the account deserves to be quoted at length:

> Comrades! . . . You know that right up to 1953 the grass crop rotation system devised by Academician V. R. Vilyams was intensively applied on our country's collective and state farms. Vilyams, an important scientist who enjoyed the Party's confidence, sought with extraordinary persistence in the years before the war to have grass crop rotations introduced extensively everywhere. . . .
>
> Vilyams' proposal found support at one time in the Ministry of Agriculture, and particularly in the State Planning Commission, and they were made the basis for crop rotations. The country adopted a policy of universal introduction of grass rotations, with 25% to 30% and even more of grasses in many provinces. Vilyams

saw in grasses the only way to restore the structure and fertility of the soil, with all the conclusions that followed from this. . . .

Most regrettably, many wise proposals of prominent scientists were disregarded in that period. Vilyams pushed through his farming system, elbowing the way for it; he took to sharp condemnation of his opponents outside any framework of comradely discussion. . . .

The universal and stereotyped introduction of grass crop rotations caused serious damage to our country's agriculture. . . .

Academician V. R. Vilyams was one of the talented scientists of our country. He introduced much that was new in soil science, in the theory of the soil formation process. For this we pay him due tribute.

As for Vilyams' grass crop system of farming, it has proved fundamentally wrong. . . .

Basing himself on his theory and the schedules it required for turning up the grass-bearing layer, Vilyams in effect arrived at a rejection of winter crops. . . .

Many of you know what this led to. Take the Ukraine, for example. Winter wheat is the most valuable and highest-yielding crop in the republic. It yields 30 and more centners per hectare. Yet by the rules of the grass crop system of farming, winter wheat should be driven from the fields, should give way to spring wheat, which produces only a third to a half the crop in the conditions of the Ukraine and the Northern Caucasus.

In this connection I wish to remind you of one event that was directly related to the effort to spread spring wheat in the Ukraine. A Party Central Committee plenary session was held in February 1947. The session met in a difficult situation. The severe consequences of the war and the fierce drought of 1946 had struck a strong blow at agriculture, particularly in the Ukraine. The republic had gathered a smaller harvest than in the famine year of 1921. True, it must be said that after 1946 there were years when there was even less rainfall in the Ukraine, but a harvest such as that of 1946 never happened again. The trouble was that 1946 was the first year after the war, the soil was tilled with cows and even by hand, people often dug the soil with shovels and even harnessed themselves to the plow. We are not afraid of such an admission. The people had devoted all their efforts to routing the enemy and had won a historic victory. (*Applause.*) There were neither machines nor fuel in the villages, but people realized that the wounds would be quickly healed.

T. S. Maltsev, a field worker of the Lenin's Behests Collective Farm, Shadrinsk District, Kurgan Province, spoke at the February Central Committee plenary session. He spoke of the bumper crop of spring wheat in the Trans-Urals. Please understand me correctly, Terenty Semyonovich, you spoke wonderfully, you showed by your example the tremendous possibilities of obtaining high crops in the Urals and Siberia. If I speak of you, it is not by way of reproach, but to illustrate my thoughts.

When Maltsev began to speak of the bumper crops of spring wheat, I thought immediately that Stalin would try to force this crop in the Ukraine, too. The fact is that he and I had had a talk about this even before the war. I said then that spring wheat should not be sown in the Ukraine. Spring wheat would not yield a high crop there. The more we sowed it, the less grain would we get. He agreed with me at that time. But here it was 1946, crop failure, no grain in the country, and now Maltsev was delivering a speech and advocating spring wheat. The misgivings arose that Stalin, without understanding that the Ukraine and the

Trans-Urals are different zones with entirely different conditions, would draw the conclusion that I was wrong and Maltsev right and would say, "Let's sow spring wheat in the Ukraine."

That is what happened. The session came to an end. In the intermission we entered the room where the Politburo members gathered. Stalin immediately asked me:

"You're for winter wheat?"

"Yes," I replied.

"Yet you heard what Maltsev said?"

"Yes, I heard, but that is the Urals, that is Siberia, not the Ukraine or the Northern Caucasus."

He did not agree with me and said: "But after all, you have chernozem soil."

"Yes, we have chernozem," I replied, "but spring wheat does not yield in Ukraine conditions."

Nevertheless Stalin said: "Put down in the plenary session decision that the Ukraine is lagging seriously in raising spring wheat and that farms are instructed to see to enlarging the sowings of this crop."

This was included in the decision of the February 1947 Central Committee plenary session.

The introduction of spring wheat sowings might have ruined Ukraine agriculture. The republic began to sow spring wheat. The newspapers and magazines were dotted with reports that the collective and state farms were overfulfilling the plan for sowing spring wheat. Although later M. A. Posmitny, the collective farm chairman who is famous in the Ukraine, told me: "I reported that I was sowing spring wheat, but I sowed winter wheat." (*Laughter, applause.*)

Time passed. In 1948 the Ukraine harvest recovered. Not thanks to spring wheat, of course. The collective

218

and state farms continued lovingly to cultivate winter wheat.

I told Stalin that if the sowing of spring wheat continued in the Ukraine there would be no grain. He was obliged to admit this and agreed to a reconsideration of the decision of the February Central Committee plenary session, only not by a Central Committee decree but, as they say, by a roundabout way. Stalin permitted a gathering of the scientists and practicing farmers to assemble and to discuss the question of what to do about spring wheat in the Ukraine.

In 1948 the Party Central Committee of the Ukraine assembled scientists and farmers and submitted for their consideration the question: Which wheat is better to sow—winter or spring wheat? Of course we knew that the winter wheat was the answer, but the scientists had to state this publicly.[16]

In thus describing for the benefit of Novosibirsk agricultural workers the experience under Stalin, Khrushchev must have been aware that he himself emerged in a favorable light. But, by Western as well as Soviet accounts, policies on crop schemes under Stalin, including those where materials for own use were in question, were formulated and implemented in a notably centralized way. No doubt decision makers at all levels sought to conform to the stated efficiency rule or some variant thereof which might apply where inputs and quality and variety of end products change. But given the centralization of decision making, use of available agronomic knowledge often left much to be desired, to say the least.[17]

16. *Current Digest* (December 27, 1961), pp. 3–4.

17. On pertinent working arrangements under Stalin, and on more recent corresponding ones to which I come below, see Lazar Volin, *A Survey of Soviet Russian Agriculture* (Washington, 1951), pp. 88 ff.;

Reference has been to the practice under Stalin. By the decree of March 9, 1955, the party and government called for a marked change in planning procedures for determining crop schemes, including those affecting materials for own use. Decisions which for collective farms previously had been taken in good measure by government and party organs, and often at the highest levels, were now to be left largely to the collective farms. In formulating its plan for land use and outputs of different products, however, the collective farm was required to take into account its obligations to deliver produce to the government.

Under this decree, Soviet authorities claim that crop schemes are now determined with due regard to local conditions. No doubt in some measure this is the case. But only a few months before the new arrangements were adopted, Khrushchev called for a sharp expansion in the corn-sown area, and by now that expansion has occurred. Indeed, five years after Khrushchev spoke, the corn-sown area had increased 23.9 million hectares. Moreover, the campaign to extend the corn-sown area has now become part of a still larger program to change crop patterns generally. Thus in 1961 Khrushchev called for a sharp reduction in the area under grasses, forage legumes, oats, and summer fallow, and a corresponding expansion in intensive feed crops such as corn, sugar-beets for feed, and beans. Under this program, some 40 million hectares are to be replanted within a few years.

Nimitz, *Soviet Agriculture since the September 1953 Reforms*, pp. 134 ff.; A. Tolupnikov, "Planning and the Balanced Development of Various Branches of Agriculture," in *Problems of Agriculture* (Moscow, 1956), as translated and published by U.S. Department of Agriculture et al.; *Direktivy, 4*, 365 ff.; Volin, in *Comparisons*, Part I, pp. 309 ff.; Nove, *Foreign Affairs, 40* (1961–62); U.S. Department of Agriculture, *The Agricultural Situation in 1961–62 in the Soviet Union and Other Eastern European Countries* (Washington, D.C., September 1962); *Current Digest* (March 21, 28, 1962).

Without questioning the possible value in the U.S.S.R. of an increased emphasis on corn, Western authorities believe that because of the extraordinary scale and the sweeping manner of its implementation the corn program has often led to unsuitable use of land. This is evident from the fact that the area sown to corn already had reached its present magnitude by 1956, but had to be reduced by nearly one-fourth before it could be expanded again. As for the more general reform in crop patterns now being implemented, what will be achieved will depend on many circumstances difficult to foresee, including the availability of fertilizer. But again, if only because of the wholesale and abrupt nature of the changes being made, it has been held that dubious results will often be unavoidable.

The corn program and the general program for the substitution of intensive feed crops for grasses and the like were both initiated before the latest reorganization of agricultural administration in 1962. In proposing the latter reform to the party Central Committee, Khrushchev explained that:

> We have abandoned the old system of planning, have condemned the unsuitable practice of handing down the plan for sown areas from above, and we were right in doing so. But some comrades, as is now evident, have an oversimplified concept of the new system of planning and consider rejection of the planning of sown areas from the top as rejection of any intervention in the planning of collective and state farm production.
>
> This is not right. We abandoned the faulty practice of planning in order not to determine the specific plan for sowing of individual crops for the collective and state farms from the top, since it is impossible from the center to take into account the specific features of each zone. But the planning of production and procurements on the collective and state farms should be a

221

firm rule and law. Naturally, therefore, once the plan is drawn up and the assignment given, the production administration, in order to know how the collective farms are ensuring fulfillment of their pledges, should conduct check-ups, exercise control, and disclose and quickly eliminate shortcomings.[18]

Despite his ambiguities, Khrushchev presumably made it clear enough that the discretion granted the collective farm in 1955 to determine its own crop scheme was to be further curtailed with the organization of a territorial-production administration (TPU) "to advise" it.

THE VOLUME OF FARM EMPLOYMENT AND ITS DISPOSITION AMONG FARM ENTERPRISES

We have by no means exhausted the interesting facets of agricultural resource use in the U.S.S.R., but for the present it may suffice to refer to only one other. Substitutions between end products, at least for agriculture generally as distinct from those for one enterprise, are still passed by. Also, for each enterprise, inputs of resources other than labor are still taken as essentially given. Of concern, therefore, is the determination of the volume of employment of labor in agriculture and of its allocation among individual farm enterprises. To refer first to the latter aspect, the efficiency rule that applies is simple: For labor of any one kind, marginal productivity must be the same in all farm enterprises employing it, or at least all in one locality. Not surprisingly, this rule is one that has hardly been approached in the U.S.S.R.

Thus, collective farm households have systematically devoted to their homestead plots a disproportionately large share of their labor. In 1960, for example, their plots accounted for but 3.5 per cent of the sown area of homesteads and collective farms together. But they devoted over one-fourth of their labor to the former and less than three-fourths to the latter.[19] Because of their relatively large livestock holdings, the households probably also have held a disproportionately large amount of capital. But the presumption must be that the marginal productivity of labor on the plots has tended to be less than that on the collective farm.

If this has been so, the explanation may be found in two opposing forces. On the one hand, the households at least during protracted periods have been able to retain a larger share of the net income produced on their homestead than of that produced on the collective farm. They have had an incentive, therefore, to devote their labor especially to the homestead, so far as they have been free to do so. On the other, they have not been entirely free to do so, for the government has sought in various ways to ensure that they would labor on the collective farm.[20] Specifically, adult members were expected from the outset generally to participate in collective farm work, but in early years many persons, especially women, worked little or not at all on the collective farm, often concentrating their efforts on their homestead. Hence, the government found it expedient in 1939 to establish a minimum number of labor days which each collective farm member had to earn yearly by work on the collective farm. Depending on the region, the minimum varied from 60 to 100. Subsequently the minimum requirement was increased, and by 1954 varied from 100 to 150 labor days. More recently each collective farm has been allowed to fix the minimum number of labor days to be

19. *Narkhoz, 1961,* p. 316; below, Appendix B.
20. Jasny, *The Socialized Agriculture of the USSR,* pp. 391 ff.; Nimitz, *Soviet Agriculture since the September 1953 Reforms,* pp. 128–30; *Direktivy, 4,* 605 ff.

required of its members. It seems doubtful that this discretion has often been used to reduce the minimum.[21]

We know little about transfers of labor from one collective farm to another, but they probably have been limited.
Where a member has wished to leave the collective farm,
he has not been entirely free to do so, and while the restrictions have borne partly on departures, the member desiring
to leave one collective farm in order to enter another has
as a rule required the approval of the general assembly of
members in both farms.[22] Since the member apparently

21. The requirement that for any kind of labor marginal productivity be the same in different farm enterprises applies strictly only if
effort per unit of time is also the same. If effort varies, marginal
productivity should vary more or less similarly, depending on the
worker's own valuation of additional exertion. If the government has
found it difficult to recruit labor for the collective farm, however, it
should have found it still more difficult to assure that the labor recruited would exert a commensurate effort. By limiting their exertion
on the collective farm, the members can husband their energies for
the more remunerative work on the homestead. By the same token, the
marginal productivity of labor on the homestead plot should have been
greater than it otherwise would have been; but when allowance is
made for the extra effort exerted, the efficiency rule must still have
been violated.

I argued above that effort on the collective farm has been too limited.
This should have been so even if the member had no alternative opportunity for employment, but effort must have been even more
limited, because the member could devote his energies instead to the
household plot.

I am indebted to Miss Nancy Nimitz for stressing the possible importance of this aspect.

22. On restrictions of the members' freedom to leave the collective
farm, to go either to another or to industry, see N. D. Kazantsev
et al., eds., *Kolkhoznoe pravo* (Moscow, 1955), pp. 97 ff.; Schwarz, *Labor
in the Soviet Union*, pp. 53 ff.; Volin, *A Survey of Soviet Russian
Agriculture*, p. 36; Vladimir Gsovski, *Soviet Civil Law, 1* (Ann Arbor,
1948), p. 714; Abramov, *A Day in the "New Life,"* pp. 84–85, 108–09,
128–30.

could take with him little or none of the capital, the farm he was leaving may have had some incentive to approve. But by the same token, the farm which he might wish to enter should have been less enthusiastic, especially if it happened to be the more prosperous one.

Nevertheless, there may have been transfers from farms where labor was relatively scarce, but where earnings of members of different collective farmers have diverged, they can have done little to stimulate transfers that might equalize them. However, the drift from collective farms to industry (see below) no doubt occurred more often from the less prosperous farms. For this reason, the variation in earnings among different collective farms should have been somewhat restricted. But it has been marked, and probably persistent. Where earnings have varied, conceivably marginal productivities might still have converged, but since the government exactions have borne heavily even on the less prosperous farms, this is unlikely to have happened often.

The procedures for the allocation of labor among state farms appear to have been similar to those regarding the allocation of labor among industrial enterprises. The pertinent procedures for the allocation of labor between state and collective farms have yet to be studied, but they must have been more or less similar to those followed in respect of the determination of the volume of employment in agriculture generally. In any case, it may be as well to turn at once to the latter procedures.

On the eve of the five-year plans, the U.S.S.R. was still predominantly an agricultural country, with some three-fourths of the population supported by farm pursuits. The expansion of nonfarm employment, therefore, has occurred on a sizable scale through transfer of population from the farm (Table 10.2). It follows that the volume of employment in agriculture has turned essentially on the volume

The Economics of Soviet Planning

TABLE 10.2.

Net Rural-Urban Migration, U.S.S.R.

	Millions
1929	1.4
1930	2.6
1931	4.1
1932	2.7
1933	.8
1934	2.5
1935	2.5
1929–35	16.6
1926–39 (census dates)	23
1950–55	>9

Sources: See Warren Eason, *Soviet Manpower* (processed), (Princeton, 1959), pp. 87 ff.; Eason, "The Labor Force," in Bergson and Kuznets, eds., *Economic Trends in the Soviet Union.* Figures for migration probably include the population of areas classified as rural at some previous census date and reclassified as urban during the intervals to which the figures relate.

of labor transferred to industry, and it is with these transfers that we must be concerned here. How have they been determined?

As we have seen, in deciding on the volume of end products to be sought from nonfarm sectors, the government endeavors to ensure that at any time requirements for labor correspond to available supplies.[23] By implication, where the supply of nonfarm labor can be supplemented through transfers from agriculture, the volume of end products to be sought from nonfarm sectors may still vary. But in contemplating this aspect the government must consider that transfers of labor from agriculture also affect the output of agricultural end products. Hence, if for the present we sup-

23. In Ch. 6, above, pp. 104 ff., reference was to the determination of the total output of nonfarm sectors, but in view of the discussion in Ch. 7, we may now refer instead to the determination of the output of nonfarm end products.

226

pose that the relative volume of end products to be sought from the two spheres has been decided, the volume of labor required to be transferred from agriculture is in principle determined. With labor quotas in nonfarm and labor utilization in farm enterprises determined in ways that have been described, the required transfers are also determined in practice, at least after allowance is made for nonfarm labor forthcoming from sources other than transfers from agriculture.

At the same time, to guarantee a corresponding supply, the government has been able to exercise substantial, although by no means complete, control over the material incentives that might induce the needed transfers, particularly the relative real earnings in industry and on the farm. In any event, the farmer on the eve of the plans probably could have increased his real earnings by shifting to industry. While industrial real wages sharply declined thereafter, wholesale collectivization and the resultant wholesale disorganization in agriculture may have enhanced incentives to enter industry. Nevertheless, where the farmer sought to respond, he could be and sometimes was obstructed by the collective farm itself. Also, the government, after having relied primarily on autonomous transfers, in 1931 instituted the so-called "organized recruitment" of peasants for industry by contracting with collective farms. Under this system, the individual peasant supposedly was a party to the agreement; but as Soviet sources make clear, he was not always an influential one. Hence he might often find himself willy-nilly bound for a time as to both occupation and place of work.[24]

In these ways the government sought to obtain from

24. On trends under the five-year plans in relative real earnings of farmers and industrial workers, see the sources cited above p. 191, n. 12, and *Real SNIP,* p. 8. On methods of recruiting farm workers into industry, see those cited above, p. 94, n. 1, and p. 224, n. 22.

agriculture the recruits it needed for industry under the First Five Year Plan. After this plan was completed, the industrial worker's margin of superiority over the farmer regarding real wages fluctuated, but it probably has tended downward from the preplan level. For a time, however, the government found it expedient to continue to rely extensively on organized recruitment as supplemented by autonomous transfers. But for both the farm population and persons already attached to industry the year 1940 brought additional controls. In fact, the chief of these pertinent here is the labor reserve school law already mentioned. Under this decree, farm as well as urban youths were subject to draft for vocational training and to subsequent administrative assignment to jobs. To what extent other controls were established after the Nazi attack is unknown, but the law of October 1940 remained on the books until the mid-fifties, although use of the draft probably had tended before then to decline. Since abolition of this decree, the farmers appear to be more or less free to stay on the farm. While organized recruitment continues currently on some scale, it now appears to be employed without the violation of the workers' freedom of choice so common in the 30s. In order to leave the collective farm for industry, however, the member for long has required approval of the farm management.

By these procedures the government has been able under the five-year plans to add substantially to its nonfarm labor force. Moreover, the latter has corresponded more or less to requirements, as manifest in wage funds placed at the disposal of nonfarm enterprises. Whether the government has been able to realize the relative volume of farm and nonfarm end products it has sought is another matter. It is also an elusive one, but interestingly the nonfarm labor force has tended systematically to exceed targets set for it. This has been so in respect to the targets of the long-range plans (Table 5.2), and frequently also in respect to those in the annual plans. By implication, recruitments from agriculture must often have exceeded and the labor force remaining in agriculture have fallen short of targets set for them. The record of fulfillment of nonfarm output targets has been uneven, but as a rule far superior to that for output targets in agriculture. Output targets, as is often suggested, do not always represent what is really sought in the U.S.S.R., and the violation of the plan for labor recruitment from agriculture has to be viewed accordingly.

In relation to industry, however, agriculture has not always fared as well as the system's directors themselves have sought regarding outputs generally. So Khrushchev himself has suggested:

> Since the party agencies are set up on the territorial principle, it is their duty to deal with industry and agriculture alike. But in practice, matters frequently shape up in such a way that the province and territory party committees and the Central Committees of the union-republic communist parties are obliged to scatter their energies, to take up first one and then another matter. All this gives rise to a campaign method in party guidance: Now the party agencies focus on agriculture and to some extent slacken attention to industry and other problems of communist construction, now they switch completely to industry and slacken the guidance of agriculture.[25]

The desire to assure a more sensitive response to priorities apparently was a major reason for the reform of the party and governmental apparatus in the latter part of 1962. I refer particularly to the extraordinary decision to establish separate hierarchies for rural and urban affairs.

The efficiency rule that applies in the sphere of resource

25. *Current Digest* (December 12, 1962), p. 5. Capitalization modified to accord with our style.

229

use in question requires ideally a volume of recruitment of labor from agriculture for nonfarm pursuits that will permit realization of the relative volume of farm and nonfarm end products sought. With supplies corresponding to requirements in this sense, the margin between real earnings in industry and in agriculture is supposed to correspond to the related transfer price—that is, the differential required to induce the needed volume of migration voluntarily. The extent of conformity with this rule must be judged from the facts already set forth. Presumably there has been some such tendency in the case of the volume of recruitment of farm labor for industry, although perhaps not as pronounced as might be supposed. Any correspondence of the differential in real earnings between nonfarm and farm pursuits to transfer prices must at best have been very proximate.

CONCLUSIONS

Since our efficiency rules are desiderata when consumers' welfare is the end, the degree of conformity with such rules for agriculture is also indicative of economic rationality from this standpoint. So far as consumers' welfare has been the end, therefore, economic rationality has been limited indeed in agriculture. In this sector, however, the system's directors have been concerned first of all with farm marketings, particularly their volume and the terms on which they might be obtained. Does not the use of resources in agriculture, as often is suggested, become more rational economically when seen in this light?

Four of the five rules that have been set forth bear on resource use within agriculture and one bears on the allocation of labor between it and industry. Of the four, one requires that total output obtained from inputs to any farm producing unit must be a maximum. Another requires that the choice of farm materials for own use be such that the output of farm end products be a maximum. A third requires that the marginal productivity of labor be the same in all farm-producing units. Evidently, all these primitive precepts must be observed in order for the volume of farm end products of any desired structure obtained from given inputs to be a maximum. For the system's directors, therefore, the precepts should still be impelling even if the concern is primarily with farm marketings. If the output of end products is less than the maximum, the possibility is open that marketings can be increased, and without the material lot of the farmer being made any the worse.

That is to say, in respect to these rules resource use in agriculture is really no more rational economically with farm marketings as the first concern than it is if consumers' welfare is the sole end. Furthermore, the last of the four rules requires only that the effort of each worker be such that additional output from more intensive work be just sufficient to compensate him for the exertion. Where this rule has been violated, the effort must have been less rather than greater than called for, and the system's directors could not consider this to the good. After all, by exerting additional effort the farmer at the very least might improve his lot without reducing marketings or making them more expensive. Possibly marketings could be increased or cheapened to boot.

For the system's directors, however, the rules could be observed only so far as a desired volume of marketings could be extracted on appropriate terms. In principle this is possible, for by employing here again a lump-sum tax, the government might conceivably exact marketings without impairing household incentives. If incentives are not impaired, there is no bar to conformity with the rules. In practice, however, to levy on any scale any tax, lump-sum or other, which does not damage incentives, is not apt to

231

be feasible. In order to ensure marketings of a volume and on terms such as have obtained in the U.S.S.R. the tax would have had to be large. Even if it does not become more rational economically, therefore, resource use in Soviet agriculture becomes more understandable when we consider the marketings have been the primary concern.

But granting that a "first best" has been precluded, the government has hardly achieved a "second best" in any meaningful sense. In any case, many of the working arrangements must be understood otherwise than in terms of the need to generate marketings. Consider, for example, an outstanding feature under Khrushchev: the sweeping and abrupt transformations of crop patterns. So far as these measures have been wasteful, the reason is administrative deficiencies. Yet such wasteful programs, it has been argued, are unavoidable in Soviet conditions because of the need at the center to counter inertia below. For inertia below, however, the government is partly to blame, and while its exactions must be an important factor, its other actions must have played a role. Probably not the least of these have been the reforms in crop patterns, with, for many farmers, their demoralizing results. Moreover, in the economy generally the system's directors have had diverse reasons to favor centralized decision making. It would be surprising if they did not have such reasons here.

In general, the system's directors have acknowledged that their policies and practices in agriculture have frequently been dubious, and this is surely not an overstatement. Although resource use has to be understood in terms of the directors' own material ends, administrative deficiencies have had their place here as elsewhere. No doubt, as was just suggested, there have also been nonmaterial ends.

I refer to policies and practices that have been pursued within the framework of prevailing ownership forms, including the predominant collective farm. If the government had never taken its fateful decision in favor of wholesale collectivization and had chosen instead to continue to rely on independent peasant farms, how Soviet agriculture might have performed is conjectural. Students of the Soviet economy (including this one) have assumed that the record achieved regarding marketings could not have been approached. Even without collectivization, however, the government would have been able to fix the terms for marketings. It could also have induced marketings by levying taxes, which it had some power to enforce. Thus it still could have achieved much. Productivity, it is true, might have suffered. But it has suffered much in the collective farm, and this says nothing of the wholesale losses that attended institution of this form of organization to begin with.

Still and all, in order to match the record regarding marketings, some sort of war economy probably was unavoidable in early years. But one wonders whether the commitment to the collective farm would have been in order if the system's directors had not also had nonmaterial ends. Most importantly, in the U.S.S.R. it has long been axiomatic that even a cooperative organization represents an ideological advance over the independent peasant farm. In the West, the system's directors have been held to be less concerned with such ideological aspects than with power. They have no doubt found appealing from this standpoint the supplanting of twenty-five million peasant households (which with small-scale production generally Lenin had held to be breeding "capitalism and bourgeoisie continually, every day, every hour, spontaneously and on a mass scale," [26]) by several hundred thousand collective farms that were relatively amenable to political control.

26. V. I. Lenin, *Sochineniia, 31* (Moscow, 1950), 7–8.

In place of the independent peasant farm, the government has made use of both the collective and the state farm, relying chiefly on the former. Although the comparative performance of the collective and state farms from the standpoint of my efficiency rules is not considered here, the essential reasons for the government's primary reliance on the former are not difficult to surmise.

Thus in the U.S.S.R. the state farm is ideologically superior to the collective one, but especially in early years the former might have aroused even more opposition among the peasants than the latter. Anyhow, the initial experience with the state farm came to "nothing short of a catastrophe." [27] While this reflected many transitory circumstances, the government understandably found it discouraging. More recently, the system's directors until the latest years must have been in doubt about the comparative "costs" of production in the two sorts of farms. This is in respect to costs in the Soviet sense referred to earlier.[28] Even in the U.S.S.R. such costs are understood to be insufficient for appraisal of comparative productivity of the state and collective farm.

The state farm probably has come to be considered as often superior from this standpoint, but for the government the collective farm still has the virtue of placing chiefly on the farm household the burden of harvest fluctuations, since the dividend is a residual share. In the state farm the farm worker is a government employee paid a money wage, and the government assumes much of the burden of harvest fluctuations. Moreover, information on the relative earnings of collective farmers and state farm workers is incomplete. But if the government should have felt obligated to pay the former in accord with wage scales

27. Jasny, *The Socialized Agriculture of the USSR,* p. 246.
28. Above, p. 166. On Soviet calculations of comparative state and collective farm costs, see Nimitz, in *Comparisons,* Part I, pp. 256 ff.

prevailing for the latter, it would often have had to raise materially the earnings of the collective farmers, particularly those employed in the less productive farms.[29]

The government's reasons for relying primarily on the collective farm apparently are no longer as impelling as they were formerly, for, as was stated, lately it has been using the state farm to an increasing extent. The latter has been employed in the implementation of the New Lands Program, and many collectives have been converted to state farms.

In its 1961 program the party declared itself in favor of a gradual rapprochement of the two forms of organization, and one must read partly in this light some further recent developments that have tended to limit differences between the two. As a result, the choice between them is no longer as consequential as it was formerly. I refer for one thing to the recent extension, with government encouragement and support, of the practice of paying collective farmers part of their money dividend at intervals in the course of the year rather than at the end of the year. As was explained, some farms have also begun to guarantee their members regular payments of specified amounts per labor day, and in some instances the guarantee has been expressed simply in relation to output. Working arrangements in the state farm are also being altered, apparently in a manner to make them less different from the collective farm. Thus, under a new wage system introduced in 1961, state farm earnings to a greater degree than was true before are to vary with the quantity and quality of output.

Since the latest reorganization of agriculture state and collective farms have both been "administered" (guided) by the same bureaucratic apparatus. The institution of this

29. *Real SNIP*, pp. 118 ff.; Nimitz, in *Comparisons*, Part I, pp. 256 ff.; Nove, "Incentives for Peasants and Administrators."

arrangement, too, is to be seen in relation to the 1961 party program.[30]

Under the working arrangements for agriculture, the government has determined, among other things, the distribution of income among farm households. In this connection the system's directors presumably have considered equity. But in agriculture, as in industry, income at present is viewed as appropriately distributed "according to work done," although in the case of agriculture accrual to the household of some differential rent apparently is not thereby precluded. This should have been a source more of conformity with than of divergence from the efficiency rules. Distribution according to work done has been held to be appropriate even though the resultant inequality has been marked. Such inequality is already suggested by the working arrangements described, but is seen more clearly from data such as these: in 1960, collective farm members in 6.5 per cent of the collective farms earned per labor day only 20 to 33 per cent as much as was earned by collective farm members generally. Collective farm members in 5 per cent of the farms earned 200 to 300 per cent more than was earned by collective farm members generally. Reportedly the inequality in 1960 was less than it had been in 1954–55.[31]

I have been considering economic rationality without regard to the time period, but working arrangements in Soviet agriculture have evolved in the course of time. Has there been any corresponding trend in economic rationality? The changes have occurred chiefly since Stalin's death. The

30. As this study goes to press, the Soviet government reportedly is considering a proposal that at long last the collective and state farm be supplanted by a single form of organization administered by a regional producing and marketing association. In the new organization, farmers would be paid wages relatively to gross income. See *New York Times* (February 13, 1964).

31. T. Zaslavskaia, "O ravnoi oplate za ravnyi trud v kolkhoze," *Voprosy ekonomiki*, No. 10 (1962), p. 28.

more consequential of these must sometimes have been adverse to economic rationality, but no doubt they have more often been favorable. Among adverse changes are the seemingly enhanced tendency toward wholesale reforms in crop patterns and the increase in frequency of organizational change. Among favorable changes are those in farm prices and in other aspects affecting collective farm incentives, the abolition of the machine tractor station, and the increased use of the state farm.

Reference is to economic rationality from the standpoint of our efficiency rules. Perhaps there has also been a gain in economic rationality in terms of the aims pursued by the system's directors, but this is not as evident, and appraisal becomes the more difficult because the aims themselves may have varied. Specifically, the priority accorded marketings in relation to output may not be quite so pronounced under Khrushchev as it was under Stalin.

Why have the system's directors been so concerned with marketings? The excess of marketings exacted over manufactures offered in return evidently represents a form of savings. As such it has constituted a major source of finance for investment under the five-year plans. The concern for marketings, therefore, is but a manifestation of the larger one referred to at the outset, that for the future relatively to present. But further discussion of the latter concern is postponed.[32]

Resource use in agriculture has also diverged from the fifth of our efficiency rules, that regarding the allocation of labor between farm and nonfarm pursuits. According to this rule, this allocation must permit realization of the relative volume of farm and nonfarm end products sought. Also, the margin between real earnings in industry and in agriculture is supposed to correspond to the related transfer price. There must have been some tendency toward con-

32. See below, Ch. 13.

formity with the former aspect. Perhaps here again, however, resource use becomes more understandable when we consider that the system's directors have been less interested in end products generally than in marketings, but this is difficult to judge. As for the relation of earnings to transfer prices, even as an expedient the government cannot have been especially concerned to pay farm recruits for industry their transfer price. But, if we exclude the war and immediate postwar years, the government relied on compulsory measures chiefly in the 1930s. For this it must have had diverse reasons, but presumably one was a desire to ensure a politic relation between urban and rural earnings. In this sense, resource use, at least at this point, may have borne the special stamp of equity.

As was explained, on the eve of the five-year plans the vast bulk of the Soviet population was agricultural. Despite the continuing transfers to industry that have occurred since, even today almost two-fifths of the total population are supported by farm pursuits. Under such circumstances, many economists assume that a substantial part of labor in agriculture is apt to be surplus: the marginal productivity of labor in this sector not only is zero but would remain so after significant withdrawals. Hence even without any consequential investment of capital, labor could be withdrawn without any loss of output.

The validity of this supposition generally is not a matter to be explored here, but in this chapter I have assumed that in the U.S.S.R. there has been no consequential surplus of labor in agriculture, at least for some time. I should explain, therefore, that on the eve of the plans the existence of surplus farm labor was widely assumed among Soviet economists. Whether and to what extent there was a surplus in the sense pertinent here is another matter, for the prevalent view rested chiefly on calculations concerning the number of farm workers who might be dispensed with if agriculture generally were to function as efficiently as the "better" farms and without use of any more labor time, male or female, than was actually employed there.[33] Alternatively, reference was to the excess of available over actual labor time generally, but with the inclusion in available time of seasonal surpluses and the like. A surplus in these senses, of course, is not at all tantamount to one in the sense now pertinent.

But if there ever was a surplus of the latter sort in the U.S.S.R., it could not have been long-lived. To begin with, transfers to industry were especially large in early years (Table 10.2), and occurred while turbulent events—including, chiefly, wholesale collectivization—were exacting in agriculture a toll of human lives. In consequence, the labor force available to agriculture, which initially numbered 71 millions, within less than a decade fell some 17 million persons.[34] The number in surplus at the outset, even according to some Soviet calculations, was far less. Then, too, collectivization meant the wholesale destruction of Soviet draft animals. Instead of the 25.2 million work horses available in 1929, Soviet farmers in 1935 had to cultivate their fields with 12.0 million.[35] Although the supply of mechanical power had increased meanwhile, it was not until 1938 that the total power of all sorts at the disposal of agriculture matched that of 1929. Concomitant with the loss of work horses was a loss of livestock generally, which reduced the volume of work that had to be done. But the early years also witnessed an increase in the sown area, and this had a contrary effect. In any case, it is not surprising that collective farms, even at an early stage, sought not to encourage but to discourage departures of labor for industry.[36] Or,

33. I am indebted to Mr. Barney Schwalberg for advice at this point.
34. Eason, *Soviet Manpower*, p. 133.
35. Jasny, *The Socialized Agriculture of the USSR*, p. 458.
36. See above, p. 227.

rather, it is not surprising if the surplus of labor had already been dissipated, if indeed it ever existed. If there still was a surplus, however, such conduct by collective farms would be difficult to understand.

11 CHOICE OF TECHNOLOGY

Thus far I have taken as given the stocks of fixed capital in different productive enterprises and branches. I turn now to the working arrangements for determination of these stocks. They may vary in diverse ways, but by far the most important are those which, whether to replace or to complement old capital goods, entail use of new ones. Hence, there is an appropriation, for a particular activity, of part of the investment in fixed capital that the community is currently undertaking in the economy generally. How much will be appropriated must depend on the total volume of investment; but if we put aside for the present the determination of the latter, what remains for consideration is the allocation of investment. It is to procedures for determining this matter that attention is now directed.

The allocation of investment in fixed capital must also depend on the output mix to be produced with it, but as has been done hitherto, I take as a datum the structure sought for end products. Strictly speaking, reference previously was to the structure of end products sought in any one economic sector and to the relative volume of such goods sought for different sectors. At this point, we begin instead with the structure of end products desired for the economy as a whole, i.e. the structure desired for final products.[1]

Investment in fixed capital contributes to output only *after* it is made. Moreover, it contributes for a more or less protracted period depending on the service lives of the capital goods involved. For the allocation of fixed capital investment in any period, therefore, what counts is not the mix of end products sought for that period but the series of mixes sought for subsequent periods during which investment is to be exploited. This means only that all these mixes must be taken as a point of departure, although it must be understood that mixes sought for distant periods are apt to be less well defined than those sought for proximate ones.

In a modern community, the mix of final products is one thing, that of total outputs is quite another. But for the U.S.S.R. we have already considered how in relation to any structure sought for end products the structure of total outputs is determined. While this has been done for restricted sectors, for present purposes the problem is taken to have been sufficiently explored for the economy generally. Also, we considered previously the determination of total outputs first in the plan and then in actuality, but it poses no new problem if (as must be so here) concern is primarily with the former aspect.

On the other hand, reference previously was to the total outputs projected for a single year, while here we are concerned with total outputs as these might be projected over

1. See above, pp. 127–28.

242

a protracted future period. Moreover, total outputs were supposed before to have been produced with given stocks of fixed capital in different enterprises and branches. Where these stocks are variable, for any mix of end products sought there may be different mixes of total outputs. In any enterprise or branch, input coefficients, including those for materials, will often depend on the stocks of fixed capital employed, and almost inevitably, therefore, the mix of materials corresponding to any mix of end products is also dependent on such stocks.

Thus the task of determining total outputs, which already was extraordinarily intricate, now becomes even more so. Granting this, there is little occasion to reopen this question here. In any event, I propose to take as a point of departure the structure sought not only for end products but for total outputs. It is understood, however, that the structure of the latter could be determined only in a provisional way until the allocation of investment itself is settled. Also, as for end products, reference is to total outputs desired not only currently but in the future.

Among the final products of any period, of course, are new capital goods themselves. Furthermore, these goods often are specialized in their uses. Hence, if the mix sought for these goods should be taken as given, little of the problem of investment allocation might remain to be settled. One might wish, therefore, to consider the mix sought for capital goods for any period as open to determination, at least in some degree, in the light of that sought for final goods generally, including capital goods, in subsequent periods. How we should proceed at this point, however, is rather academic in view of a limitation in the scope of the inquiry generally. Thus allocation of investment involves allocation of money investment. Within the limits of these sums, it also entails allocations of different capital goods. Whether the mix sought for the latter is considered given or variable, the problem of resource use has its parallel in the sphere of industrial materials supply, which we have already examined. The pertinent working arrangements also appear to be broadly similar. Hence, I shall focus on the allocation of money investment, although that of capital goods cannot be wholly ignored.

Depending on the allocation of investment, together with that of cooperating factors, the volume of total outputs may vary even if their structure is prescribed. But the problem of allocation still has two facets: (i) determination of the capital to be employed, together with cooperating factors, to produce any given volume of output in one or another branch; (ii) determination of actual output to be realized in any branch in the light of the desired mix of total outputs. The two facets are related, for the amount of capital employed per unit of output will depend on the volume of output. But they do differ, and attention will be directed chiefly to the determination of the capital employed together with cooperating factors to produce a given volume of output—at this point, decidedly the more novel matter.

In any period, of course, some fixed capital ordinarily will already be employed as a result of previous investments, and our concern here is only with new investments. But new investments may be used not only to establish new stocks of fixed capital but to replace old ones. If we inquire here into working arrangements for determination of the former, however, we may also gain some insight into those for determination of capital replacement, and for the rest it may suffice to recall two familiar features, although the consequences for capital replacement must be conflicting. On the one hand, maintenance outlays in the U.S.S.R. probably are often below those required for realization of intended service life.[2] On the other, Soviet economists for long apparently considered obsolescence a phenomenon

2. Berliner, *Factory and Manager*, pp. 138–39, 234–35.

Choice of Technology

peculiar to capitalism, and hence as having no meaning in the U.S.S.R. In the last several years, however, opinion on this matter has changed.[3]

Replacement aside, the new investment still may not add to existing capacity in any branch, for depending on the volume of output sought the concern might be only to free for other uses cooperating inputs previously employed in the branch. More usual, however, is the case where capacity is expanded, although the volume of cooperating inputs might still vary in diverse ways. Whatever the circumstances in these respects, we are led here to consider Soviet working arrangements for dealing with the famous problem of "capital intensity" of production methods. In economics, this problem is often referred to as one concerning the choice of technology. A familiar efficiency rule applies to it.

Consider for the moment the case where capacity is to be expanded in any branch. Supposedly to realize the expansion a choice may be made between alternative projects involving different outlays on capital goods in the current and possibly future periods, and different amounts of operating expense as the new investment is exploited. Reference is to the operating expense associated with the introduction of the additional capacity; in other words, the operating expense over and above that previously incurred. The rule is simply that the project selected be such that

(11.1) $$\sum_{n=0}^{N} (K_n + V_n)(1 + i)^{-n} = \text{minimum}.$$

Here K_n represents the capital outlays and V_n the operating expense in year n, while i represents the rate of interest. The requirement, therefore, is that the total costs of realizing the given increase in capacity be a minimum.

3. Robert W. Campbell, *Accounting in Soviet Planning and Management* (Cambridge, Mass., 1963), pp. 152 ff.; Nove, *The Soviet Economy*, p. 151.

245

Total costs include both capital outlays and operating expense, but in each case reference is to the present value at the given rate of interest.

The latter must itself be determined by reference to the costs incurred in some one of the many diverse projects undertaken in the economy generally. Specifically, for the project in question the interest rate must be such that total costs are *necessarily* a minimum. In other words, the rule requires that, at an interest rate for which costs are a minimum for any one project undertaken, costs for all other projects undertaken must also be a minimum.

It is useful to put the rule somewhat differently. Consider for any project undertaken, j, the corresponding "internal rate of return," m_j, on a marginal investment. This is given by the formula

$$(11.2) \qquad \sum_{n=0}^{N} (\Delta K_n + \Delta V_n)(1 + m_j)^{-n} = 0 \ ,$$

where ΔK_n represents the difference in capital outlays and ΔV_n the difference in operating costs between project j and any alternative very similar to it. The rule, then, requires simply that the internal rate of return on a marginal investment be the same for all projects undertaken. In other words, for each m_j,

$$(11.3) \qquad\qquad m_j = i \ ,$$

where i is a rate of interest so fixed that the relationship necessarily holds for some one project. The rate of interest so determined is precisely the one defined previously, while for any project the stated rule comes to the same thing as that requiring costs to be a minimum.

That this is so probably is evident, but we may better grasp the nature of the requirement if we consider that, among alternative projects being appraised, where investment is greater operating expense ordinarily should be less,

246

although the situation where both investment and operating expense are greater is also entirely possible. According to formula 11.2, investment in any activity must be carried up to, but not beyond, the point where additional sums allocated to this purpose are compensated for by resultant economies in operating expenses. Both the additional investments and economies in operating expense are understood to be expressed in terms of their discounted present value. Also, the rate of interest is such that 11.2 necessarily holds for some one project. This comes to the same thing as the requirement that total costs, at their discounted present value, be a minimum, where the rate of interest is such that 11.1 necessarily holds for some one project.[4]

Reference has been to the case where capacity in every branch is to be increased. If this is not so and capacity in some branches is to be unchanged, it must be understood that in one of the projects being appraised in such branches there are no new capital outlays whatsoever, and operating expense accordingly continues at the previous level. But given this, formula 11.1 still applies, and formula 11.2 may also, but it is now possible that the project with no new capital outlays may be the least cost one. Moreover, on the margin economies in operating cost may fall short of rather than equal the investment needed to realize them.[5]

---

4. This presupposes that there is only one project for which the internal rate of return on a marginal investment equals the rate of interest. There may, of course, be several such projects. Thus, when different projects are arrayed in terms of their total cost, there may be a succession of "local" minima, each of which satisfies 11.2 and 11.3. In this case, therefore, this requirement is insufficient to determine the choice to be made, and it is only by appealing to 11.1 that this can be settled. The latter provides a basis for choice, since it in effect calls for selection of the "minimum minimorum."

5. I have been considering investment in fixed capital. Given the capacity to be established, there ordinarily should be little variation among projects in the volume of investment in inventories, but if

247

I have also referred to *the* rate of interest, this being determined by reference to some one project undertaken. This is entirely proper only so far as the "marginal productivity" of capital is expected to be constant over the service lives of projects appraised. Where the marginal productivity of capital is expected to vary, different projects may have to be appraised in terms of somewhat different interest rates. The rates must vary to the extent that the projects differ in respect of the time distribution of capital outlays and operating expenditures. For example, if the marginal productivity of capital is expected to decline, projects with lengthy service lives are subject to a lower rate of interest than those with short service lives.[6]

---

such variation is consequential, the efficiency rule must be reformulated somewhat. In inquiring into Soviet working arrangements for determination of capital intensity, I shall pass by this complexity. Hence there is no reason to pursue it on a theoretic plane.

6. To consider a simple case, suppose that among the projects to be appraised now and in the future there are for any "year" a number of more or less lucrative ones for which capital outlays made in any one year would be fully liquidated in the next. In other words, each such project has a service life of one period. Among such projects all that are selected for introduction in any year must still have a common internal rate of return on marginal investments. That is to say, among these projects formulas 11.1 and 11.2 still apply provided only that the rate of interest considered for any year corresponds to the internal rate of return on marginal investments in some one of the one-year projects introduced in that period. For any year, let us designate as the "primary" rate of interest, the rate of interest that is so determined.

Suppose now that the primary rate of interest is constant over time. In terms of a rate of interest corresponding to the common value of all primary rates, then, formulas 11.1 and 11.2 also continue to apply to projects generally. Suppose, however, that the primary rates vary in the course of time. In this case, for all projects other than those of the one-year sort, selection as before must be based on the "present" value of future capital outlays and operational expense at the time the project is to be initiated. But capital outlays and operating expense

Choice of Technology

We saw earlier that ruble prices for materials and labor often diverge from pertinent efficiency rules. This is also true of ruble prices for capital goods, for these are fixed according to essentially the same principles as the prices of materials.[7] The efficiency rule regarding project selection, however, presupposes ideally that the prices in terms of which capital outlays and operating expense are expressed also correspond to relevant efficiency principles. For the U.S.S.R., therefore, the rule must be less impelling than it would be otherwise. But it may still serve as a point of departure in the inquiry into Soviet working arrangements for project selection.

For an economy generally, project appraisal embraces selection of projects in both nonfarm and farm sectors. While I shall focus here on the former, properly conceived choice among projects in the nonfarm sector involves allo-

---

during any future year are now discounted to the present by reference to the series of primary interest rates applying to intervals between the present and the future period in question. Similarly, for each project selected the internal rate of return on a marginal investment is now to be equated to a corresponding "weighted average" of primary rates, the weights depending on the distribution over time of the increments in investments and operating expense.

Here as before (above, n. 4) there may be a number of local minima. That is, there may be different local minima for different classes of projects with different time distribution of capital outlays and operating expense. This, I believe, poses no new question of principle if the different projects have the same service lives, but if service lives differ, in choosing among the different sorts of projects one must consider comparative total costs, in terms of discounted present value, for a period of operation corresponding to that of the shorter-lived projects, but with due allowance for the discounted present value of residual capital stocks in the case of the longer-lived projects. The residual capital stocks represent the discounted value of future operating cost economies still to be extracted by their use.

I am indebted to Professor Paul A. Samuelson for advice on the foregoing and on the nature of the resultant optimum (below, n. 19).

7. See the sources cited above, p. 162, n. 6.

cation of investment not only within this sector but between it and agriculture. This still leaves unsettled choices among farm projects which involve allocation of investment only within the farm sector. But from the discussion of appraisal of nonfarm projects and from familiar facts regarding agricultural institutions, particularly the collective farm with its self-financing of investment projects through accumulation at established norms and its lack, at least until recently, of meaningful cost data, the reader can surmise the essentials of the appraisal of farm projects as this involves investment allocation within agriculture.

CRITERIA FOR PROJECT SELECTION

Choice among investment projects in the U.S.S.R. has become the subject of a sizable Western literature. Attention usually is focused chiefly on the treatment of this question in Soviet economic thought, but from these writings and related Soviet ones we can learn something about its treatment in Soviet practice, particularly in the sphere now of concern.[8]

8. See especially Holland Hunter, "Planning of Investments in the Soviet Union," *Review of Economic Statistics, 31* (1949), 54–62; Norman Kaplan, *Capital Investments in the Soviet Union, 1924–1951*, RAND RM-735 (November 28, 1951); Norman Kaplan, "Investment Alternatives in Soviet Economic Theory," *Journal of Political Economy, 60* (1952), 133–44; Gregory Grossman, "Capital Intensity: A Problem in Soviet Planning" (dissertation, Harvard, 1952); Gregory Grossman, "Scarce Capital and Soviet Doctrine," *Quarterly Journal of Economics, 67* (1953), 311–43; David Granick, "Economic Development and Productivity Analysis: The Case of Soviet Metalworking," *Quarterly Journal of Economics, 71* (1957), 205–33; T. S. Khachaturov, "Capital Investment Decisions in the USSR," *American Economic Review, 48S* (1958), 368–84; "Vsesoiuznaia nauchno-tekhnicheskaia konferentsiia . . . ," *Voprosy ekonomiki,* No. 9 (1958); T. S. Khachaturov, ed., *Ekonomicheskaia effektivnost' kapital'nykh vlozhenii i novoi tekhniki,* (Moscow, 1959); David Granick, "On Patterns of Technological Choice in

Choice of Technology

Determination of nonfarm projects to produce given outputs has been the responsibility of diverse agencies, but for long it has been a relatively centralized task. Even where additions to the plant and equipment of a single enterprise have been involved, investments of any magnitude have been subject to substantial control by higher agencies, and such agencies have also been responsible for decisions concerning a new factory or similar works. Thus in industry, under the ministerial system that prevailed until 1957, projects to be undertaken were determined by many authorities but most important were so-called project-making organizations, which functioned immediately under the ministries. After 1957 decision making on projects was somewhat decentralized in the sense that the enterprise gained slightly in influence. Predominantly responsibility was still borne by superior agencies, although project making organizations that formerly were subordinate to the industrial ministries now functioned under diverse authorities, including the regional and republican economic councils, committees and councils under the U.S.S.R. Council of Ministers, and so on. As a result of the reorganizations initiated in the latter part of 1962, responsibilities for project determination apparently are now concentrated in the all-union committees for different industries, together with a central authority administering construction.

As to the basis for decisions, this has not always been systematic but so far as it has been, for consequential investments the responsible agencies apparently have vacillated between two main approaches. In both, alternative projects are evaluated in terms of their comparative costs, but in one approach reference is made to operating expense exclusive

Soviet Industry," *American Economic Review*, *52S* (1962), 149–57; Nove, *The Soviet Economy*, pp. 209 ff.; Alfred Zauberman, "The Soviet and Polish Quest for a Criterion of Investment Efficiency," *Economica*, *29* (1962), 234–54.

of any allowance for interest on capital outlays. In the other, in one way or another, account is also taken of interest on capital outlays, although it has generally been found expedient not to refer to it as such.

According to incomplete information, the latter approach was widely applied at the outset of the plans, but in 1931 it was largely supplanted by the alternative where interest is omitted. Costs continued to be considered in the more inclusive sense, however, in some sectors, including railway transportation, highway construction, and electric power. Moreover, while interest continued to be omitted in most sectors for long after 1931, recently the consideration of costs including interest has again become a widely used approach. Thus allowance for interest in effect was sanctioned in 1958 by an all-union conference on the "problems of determining the economic effectiveness of capital investment and new technology." This conference was held under the sponsorship of the Institute of Economics of the Academy of Sciences of the U.S.S.R. and the Committee on the Economics and Organization of Production of the All-Union Central Council of Trade Unions (VTSSPS). This approach is also reflected in *Tipovaia metodika opredeleniia ekonomicheskoi effektivnosti kapital'nykh vlozhenii i novoi tekhniki* (*Typical Method of Determining the Economic Effectiveness of Capital Investment and New Technology*), a volume published by the Academy of Sciences in 1960. The instructions set forth were avowedly cleared with Gosplan U.S.S.R. and other interested government agencies. Curiously, they still are not declared to be binding on those responsible for project appraisal, but with the appearance of *Tipovaia metodika,* allowance for interest costs, at least implicitly, must be viewed as official policy. We still do not know how generally this approach is employed in practice, but presumably it is now, or is in the process of becoming, preeminent.

Choice of Technology

This procedure must therefore be of chief interest here, but before considering it further it may be well to state explicitly that where interest has been neglected, the choice between projects has been made simply by reference to the criterion

$$(11.4) \qquad \bar{V} = \text{minimum},$$

where $\bar{V}$ represents annual operating costs. In contrast to the operating expenses considered before (V), these costs are understood to include depreciation. As with V, however, $\bar{V}$ includes no charge for interest. The procedure followed for cases where annual operating expenses might be expected to vary is not clear. Probably reference has been made to an average of expenses in different years, or, where such costs would be expected to decline as experience accumulated, to the level of expense that might prevail after the project had struck its gait.

Where interest has been considered, this has been done in different ways, but by far the most important is that where reference is made to a "coefficient of relative effectiveness" of capital investment. Indeed, it is this method that was sanctioned by the 1958 conference referred to above, and that is elaborated in *Tipovaia metodika*. We may properly focus on this procedure.

Here in any particular case the CRE itself is given by the formula

$$(11.5) \qquad e = \frac{\bar{V}^b - \bar{V}^a}{K^a - K^b},$$

where $\bar{V}^a$ and $\bar{V}^b$ represent the annual operating costs of two alternative projects for producing the same output, A and B, that are being compared, and K^a and K^b the corresponding capital outlays. As before, $\bar{V}$ includes depreciation. If A is the project for which capital outlays are greater, ordinarily it will also be the one for which operating expense is less.

253

Hence e represents the economy in operating expense realized per ruble of additional capital outlay.

Under the CRE method, alternative projects are subjected to either of two formally equivalent tests. In the first, the choice between two projects depends simply on whether

$$(11.6) \qquad e \gtrless E,$$

where E is some CRE taken as a standard. Thus A is selected if $e > E$; B if $e < E$; and the two projects are equally desirable if $e = E$. In the second test, the choice is viewed as depending on the relation:

$$(11.7) \qquad \bar{V}^a + EK^a \gtrless \bar{V}^b + EK^b.$$

In this case, in effect the total cost including interest on capital outlays is calculated for each project, and preference is accorded the project for which such costs are less.

What if there are more than two projects in question? Preference supposedly is accorded to the project for which, when a comparison is made with any other that is more capital intensive, $e < E$. When a comparison is made with any other that is less capital intensive, $e > E$. Alternatively, one simply chooses the project for which

$$(11.8) \qquad \bar{V} + EK = \text{minimum}$$

where $(\bar{V} + EK)$ as before represents total costs. Use of 11.8 is expressly recommended in *Tipovaia metodika*.

Capital outlays have been assumed tacitly to be made in some initial period, and operating costs to be constant over time. In fact, capital outlays often have to be made over a period of years, and operating costs also often vary. How such complexities are treated in Soviet practice is not clear. But it would be surprising if capital outlays have not often been treated still as if they occurred in one initial period. As for operating expenses, alternatives probably have been simplified here also; for example, as where interest is not al-

Choice of Technology

lowed for, by reference to the level to be reached after the project strikes its gait.

In other words, in one way or another, alternatives have been reduced to a form amenable to appraisal by the tests applied where capital outlays are made in an initial period and operating expenses are constant. But another procedure has probably also been employed, especially in recent years. This involves reformulation of the CRE criterion as

$$(11.9) \qquad \sum_{n=0}^{N} (\bar{V}_n + K_n)(1 + E)^{-n} = \text{minimum}.$$

Thus the project selected must be one for which total costs are a minimum, where total costs are the sum of the present values of operating expenses and capital outlays, with E serving as the rate of discount. Use of 11.9 was recommended before the appearance of *Tipovaia metodika*, but by implication it now has the stamp of approval of this document.

Those concerned with the task of appraising projects in the U.S.S.R. have found it convenient often to refer not to the CRE but to a "period of recoupment." This is understood as the reciprocal of the CRE. Since the period of recoupment for any two projects considered is compared with a standard period which is the reciprocal of the standard CRE, use of one procedure rather than the other is a matter of form and not of substance. This is now made clear in *Tipovaia metodika*. The period of recoupment procedure, therefore, is nothing more than the CRE method in another guise, and was so considered when it was said above that the latter method is the chief one in which interest charges are allowed for in project appraisal in the U.S.S.R.

PROJECT SELECTION VERSUS THE EFFICIENCY RULE

Given the manner in which it has been conducted, how has nonfarm project appraisal in the U.S.S.R. compared with that called for by our efficiency rule? To repeat, nonfarm project appraisal has two facets so far as it involves investment allocation—on the one hand, within the nonfarm sector and, on the other, between that sector and agriculture. If for the present we consider it only in the former context, our efficiency rule properly is also understood as relating only to this sphere. In other words, projects selected are required to be of minimum cost in terms of a rate of interest corresponding not necessarily to the internal rate of return on marginal investments in any project but to that in any nonfarm project. Alternatively, the internal rate of return on marginal investments must be uniform not necessarily for projects generally but for nonfarm projects. How then does Soviet practice compare with this requirement?

Under the five-year plans, I assume that with investment allocation conforming to our efficiency rule the internal rate of return on marginal investments in the nonfarm sector would have been positive and not zero. If so, where projects have been appraised without reference to interest costs our rule has been violated. Under this procedure, projects selected ideally must be such that the internal rate of return on marginal investments is zero. In fact, given the limited supply of new capital available, this requirement cannot have been met generally. It follows, then, that the method can only have provided partial guidance. To some degree, the supply of new capital has had to be rationed on some basis other than that established by the method itself. But investments actually made in any case must often have yielded less operating cost economy than alternatives excluded.

But while this approach has often been widely employed, it apparently is now being superseded by another approach where interest costs are considered. How has project appraisal in this case compared with that called for by the rule? This alternative approach, as represented by the CRE method, must also often diverge from our rule, but its rela-

Choice of Technology

tion to the latter is rather complex. I have yet to consider how the standard CRE is determined, but for sake of clarity we may assume at the start that the coefficient employed is uniform. Also, at the established coefficient all projects undertaken are supposed for the moment to conform with the method. Hence, the coefficient employed is in effect a "clearing" one in respect of the available capital supply. How might the resultant investment allocation compare with that called for by the efficiency rule?

The CRE procedure is most readily applicable to the simple case where capital outlays are made only in an initial period and operating expenses are constant. To refer first to this case, our efficiency rule, as given by 11.2, reduces to

$$(11.10) \qquad \frac{-\Delta V}{\Delta K} = i + \frac{i}{(1 + i)^N - 1} \ .$$

On the right, the first term is the rate of interest called for. The second represents the annuity which, when compounded at a rate i, will accumulate after N years to a unit value. The requirement, therefore, is that per unit value of capital the annual cost economy resulting from a marginal investment must equal the rate of interest plus an amount which ultimately will suffice to replace the unit value of capital. For assets with the same service life the latter amount is the same. Hence, the requirement more basically is that, per unit value of capital, the annual cost economy resulting from a marginal investment must be the same in all projects with assets having the same service life. Where assets vary in service life, the cost economy must vary also, to ensure that differences in service life are compensated for by the cost economy.

Consider now the tests used in the CRE procedure. For the simple case in question, three are employed, but it suffices to refer to that given by 11.8. The latter applies more generally than the other two given by 11.6 and 11.7. As will

257

be recalled, 11.8 requires that the project selected from among alternatives considered to produce any given output be one for which total cost $(\bar{V} + EK)$ is a minimum. By implication, if capital is allocated on this basis

(11.11) $$\Delta \bar{V} + E\Delta K = 0,$$

where $\Delta \bar{V}$ represents the difference in operating expense between a project undertaken and any alternative similar to it, and ΔK is the corresponding difference in capital outlays. Since $\bar{V}$ includes depreciation, we may reformulate 11.11 as

(11.12) $$\frac{-\Delta V}{\Delta K} = E + \frac{\Delta D}{\Delta K},$$

where ΔD represents the difference in depreciation charges between the project selected and the alternative with which it is compared.

In comparing the resulting allocation with that required by the efficiency rule, we must remember that in the U.S.S.R. depreciation charges generally are determined by the "straight-line" formula. Hence, as with the sum required for capital replacement in 11.11, depreciation per unit value of capital, $\frac{\Delta D}{\Delta K}$, must be the same in all branches wherever assets have the same service life. It follows that, if E is uniform as between projects, under the CRE procedure $\frac{\Delta V}{\Delta K}$ will in fact be equated for marginal investments in different projects undertaken. Moreover, where service lives vary, the required cost economy varies also. But in this case it varies somewhat differently from that called for by the rule, so that the CRE procedure may favor unduly some assets over others. Depending on the service lives and clearing coefficient, the bias may vary, but ordinarily long-lived assets should be favored over short-lived ones. The effect on resource use, however, should not be consequential. Furthermore, to favor long-lived assets might be in order anyhow if account should be taken of the complexity referred to at the outset: variation in the marginal productivity of capital. In the U.S.S.R., as elsewhere, so far as the marginal productivity of capital varies over time it presumably tends to decline.[9]

9. To say that the CRE method might tend to favor unduly long-lived assets may seem paradoxical, for under the straight-line formula the charge for depreciation is generally high relative to the sum that must be invested annually to assure capital replacement, but it is higher for long-lived than for short-lived assets. Hence, under the CRE method one might suppose that the cost economy required would tend to be relatively too large for long-lived assets and relatively too small for short-lived ones. But if depreciation charges are generally high, the clearing CRE must be lower than the internal rate of return if the latter is properly computed, and hence also lower than the interest rate called for by our efficiency rule. By the same token, the annual cost economy required by the efficiency rule, apart from that needed for capital replacement purposes, is for all assets higher than that corresponding to the clearing CRE, and in contrast to even the straight-line depreciation charge the extra annual cost economy thus required is not dependent on service life. Rather, it depends only on the initial investment and the interest rate called for by the rule. In consequence, the annual cost economy required under the efficiency rule might well be relatively higher for long-lived than for short-lived assets, in comparison with the situation where the CRE procedure is employed.

From hypothetical cases, however, I find that the bias is not apt to be serious. Under the CRE procedure, for example, if the standard coefficient were 20 per cent, the annual cost economy required for an asset with a 50-year service life would be 73.3 per cent of that required for an asset with a 10-year service life. Taking the corresponding clearing rate of interest called for by the efficiency rule as 24 per cent (or approximately the internal rate of return on an asset with a 20-year service life that was admissible under the CRE method), the annual cost economy required for the asset with a 50-year service life may be calculated as 88.4 per cent of that required for an asset with a 10-year service life.

All of this is based on the supposition that regardless of service life, appraisal is in terms of a single rate of interest. If the marginal productivity of capital varies, this assumption is inappropriate. Fur-

What if capital outlays are made over a protracted period or operating expenses vary? It is self-evident that depending on the actual time patterns of expenditures the CRE method must become quite crude so far as, through one simplification or another, tests given by 11.6, 11.7, and 11.8 are still applied.

To deal with the case in question, however, the test given by 11.9 is also used. On the face of it, this criterion is formally the same as that called for by our efficiency rule. But in 11.9 operating expenses include depreciation. In the tests given by 11.6, 11.7, and 11.8 this was to the good, but for that given by 11.9 such a conception of operating expense represents a divergence from our efficiency rule. In effect, capital outlays are improperly counted twice as part of total cost, once when made and once in the form of depreciation. Under the circumstances, one wonders whether the Soviet conception of operating expense may not be modified at this point. But if so, this fact has not been reported.

It was also assumed provisionally that a uniform CRE is taken as a standard, and that it is at a clearing level. In the U.S.S.R., however, reference has been made not to one standard, but to many.[10] This was the practice before the issuance of *Tipovaia metodika,* and it has now been endorsed in this document. Thus according to *Tipovaia metodika,*

> Normative coefficients for separate branches in the present time must be not less than 0.15 to 0.3, which correspond to periods of recoupment of not more than 3 to 7 years. For separate branches (transport, electric power) the normative periods of recoupment may be longer,

thermore, if the variation entails a decline in the latter, application of a single rate of interest would result in a bias favorable to short-lived projects.

10. See Grossman, *Capital Intensity,* pp. 119 ff., 175 ff.; *Voprosy ekonomiki,* No. 9 (1958), 121; *Tipovaia metodika,* p. 10; Nove, *The Soviet Economy,* p. 213.

but not more than 10 years (normative coefficient of effectiveness of not less than 0.1).

In earlier years, norms varied not only between but within branches, and sometimes widely.

As we have seen, under the CRE method, where a uniform CRE is applied, investments in long-lived assets probably are favored somewhat in comparison with those in short-lived assets. Relative to the results obtained under our rule where use is made of a single rate of interest, however, such a tendency might not be inappropriate if the marginal productivity of capital is expected to decline. And, on the same basis, it might not be inappropriate even to vary the standard CRE with service life, as apparently has been done in the U.S.S.R. One wonders, however, whether the variation might not have been excessive. At any rate, there is little evidence that it reflects the kind of calculation that might be in order at this point. The variation with service life is illustrated by the especially low norms fixed in *Tipovaia metodika* for electric power and transport. The CRE has also varied in other ways, for which there is no place at all under our efficiency rule. Among other things, it has varied with the importance of the branch. From the standpoint of the efficiency rule, such preferences between branches are properly considered in determining the desired output mix. To consider them also in determining the CRE violates the rule.[11]

11. According to *Tipovaia metodika*, p. 10, "normative coefficients of relative effectiveness, differentiated by branch, must take into account the structure of capital and peculiarities of the different branches, their tempos of technical progress, and the attainment of levels of advanced foreign techniques." While cryptic, this does not seem inconsistent with the view of Soviet policy in determining differential norms that I express in the text, but the reference to "tempos of technical progress" may betoken a concern to compensate for errors in depreciation allowances due to insufficient allowance for obsolescence, and where norms vary on this account they need not represent

Granting that the standard CRE has sometimes varied improperly, have the diverse norms employed tended to be at clearing levels? Reportedly, in the earliest years Gosplan required that in decision-making on projects 6 per cent be taken as a standard return, but the basis for this figure is unknown.[12] Possibly it originated in the rate of discount used by Tsarist banks in 1913. Subsequently under Stalin, determination of the standard CRE appears to have been left to the authorities concerned with different industries and regions, and here, too, the procedure employed must often have been rather conventional. In any event, there is little basis to suppose that either for the nonfarm sector generally or for individual branches the norms tended to be at clearing levels. In fact, the rates employed were criticized even in the U.S.S.R. as too low from this standpoint. The situation was probably the same for a time after Stalin, but the conference that led to *Tipovaia metodika* called for a relatively systematic inquiry into the effectiveness of capital investment. While *Tipovaia metodika* still does not seem incisive regarding the nature of and basis for determining pertinent norms, it may not be accidental that, despite the great increase in the capital stock that has occurred since, the norms recommended are as high as, and often higher than, rates employed previously. For example, while 10 per cent is the suggested minimum coefficient for transport and electric power, it is reported already to have been the usual one in rail transport before the war. The standard rate in electric power was said in 1958 to have usually been about 6 per cent. To what extent clearing levels have now been approached is uncertain.

a departure from our efficiency rule. For the nonfarm sector, how sensible it is to seek to match "advanced techniques" is a familiar issue in the economics of development. For the U.S.S.R., I consider it later.

12. See especially Grossman, *Capital Intensity,* pp. 119 ff., 175 ff.

Under the plans generally, so far as clearing levels have not been reached, it follows that even under the CRE method capital has had to be rationed. A further divergence from our efficiency rule has also been unavoidable.

I have elaborated different ways in which project appraisal must have violated our efficiency rule. Such violations would occur even if ruble prices conformed fully to pertinent principles. They have not so conformed, however. Those concerned with project determination in the U.S.S.R. have been aware that ruble prices have their limitations. Chiefly for this reason, consideration has been given not only to money outlays but to underlying physical outlays. These have been taken into account in different ways. Reportedly, for purposes of calculating money outlays "coefficients of deficitness" have sometimes been used by which prevailing ruble prices of especially deficit inputs might be corrected. This practice has been employed particularly in the case of deficit materials.[13] Probably more often, however, some priority has been accorded to one project over another depending on the relative avoidance of use deficit materials. Both these procedures were employed before the issuance of *Tipovaia metodika,* and presumably have continued to be used since. This document, however, does not go beyond asking that calculations as to effectiveness of capital investment in money terms be supplemented by compilation of pertinent "physical indicators, characterizing the productivity of labor . . . expenditure of fuel, power, materials, utilization of equipment and productive space, application of progressive construction designs, and so forth."

But, while divergencies from our efficiency rule due to price distortions may thus have been somewhat restricted, they could not have been avoided. This is hardly possible even where money outlays are adjusted for "coefficients of deficitness," and it is even less likely where priorities are

13. Grossman, *Quarterly Journal of Economics,* 67 (1953), 340.

simply varied in the light of the volume of deficit materials employed.

Project appraisal in the U.S.S.R. would have violated our efficiency rule even if current and prospective costs and returns of alternative projects were definitely known. This, of course, has not been so, and the limitations in data often have been consequential. While their quality has improved in the course of time, deficiencies in this regard continue to be a subject of complaint in the U.S.S.R. Probably estimates of costs more often than not prove to be optimistic. This is not surprising in view of the curious manner in which premiums for project makers are determined: reportedly by reference to *planned* rather than *actual* cost reduction.[14]

In project appraisal in the U.S.S.R., whatever the method employed, we have seen that account has had to be taken of limitations in prices, and that capital rationing has been used. Under the CRE method, the CRE taken as a standard also has often varied inappropriately among and even within branches. Frequently the underlying data have been deficient. Under the circumstances, the alternative approaches that have been described, even under the CRE method, may not after all be very different from still another approach that has been advocated:

> The very problem of relating capital outlays to operating expenses has often been denied. Instead, it has been proposed to decide the question on the basis of a "total combination" of the advantages and disadvantages—political, economic, military, and others—of each alternative, i.e., in fact to abandon calculations and decide the question arbitrarily.[15]

14. See Grossman, *Capital Intensity*, p. 116; A. V. Vorobieva, *Osnovnye fondy i sebestoimost' produktsii v promyshlennosti* (Moscow, 1962), p. 178; *Ekonomicheskaia gazeta* (February 2, 1963), pp. 14, 31; (August 17, 1963), p. 16.

15. T. S. Khachaturov, as quoted in Hunter, *Review of Economic Statistics*, 31 (1949), 56.

The leading proponent of the CRE method quoted here, however, apparently assumes that the alternative does differ from it. In any event, the alternative approach too has been employed.

We may conclude that nonfarm project selection has often violated our efficiency rule no matter what method has been employed, but to a less degree under the CRE approach than otherwise.[16]

NONFARM VERSUS FARM PROJECTS

In exploring the relation of Soviet nonfarm project appraisal to our efficiency rule, project choice has been viewed as involving investment allocation only within the nonfarm sector. The selection, however, also involves investment allocation between this sector and agriculture. In the latter context our efficiency rule assumes still another

16. With this we arrive at a view much the same as is found in pertinent Western writings (see above, p. 250, n. 8), but in the latter the reasons for the divergence of Soviet practice from a principle like our efficiency rule are not always made clear. The discussion here, therefore, may illuminate this topic further. Among other things the CRE method, in the form where use is made of formulas 11.6, 11.7, and 11.8, is often described as crude. With this I agree, but the reason sometimes seems to be that it is identified with the "pay-off period" test for investment projects familiar in Western business practice. This rests on a misapprehension. Particularly where, as under the CRE method, output is given, the pay-off period test involves a comparison of the time required for the recoupment of additional capital outlays through economy of operating expense among projects being weighed with some period taken as a standard. To this extent, the test is similar to that under the CRE method in its recoupment period version. But in Western practice operating expense normally excludes depreciation. For this reason, if differences in service life are considered at all, this is only done implicitly through some adjustment in the standard pay-off period. Under the CRE method, operating expense includes depreciation. In this way differences in service life are allowed for explicitly, although Soviet economists themselves do not always seem to grasp the import of this fact.

form: In terms of a rate of interest that corresponds on the average to internal rates of return of all marginal investments, it should not be possible to reduce costs generally by any reallocation of investment, together with cooperating factors, between the nonfarm and farm sectors. This means that, on the average, internal rates of return on nonfarm projects must be the same as those on farm projects and hence on projects generally. How far has investment allocation in the U.S.S.R. conformed to this requirement?

We have not inquired into project appraisal in agriculture, but until recently if investment allocation did conform to the stated requirement, it must have been a coincidence. Nonfarm projects often were appraised without reference to interest charges, and hence in a way that required extensive capital rationing. Furthermore, even where interest charges were considered, they frequently were below clearing levels; so that here, too, capital rationing was unavoidable. Consideration also had to be given to deficiencies in prices and other special aspects. Under the circumstances, even if the government had sought to equate nonfarm with farm internal rates of return, it would hardly have known how to do so; and it did not seek such a result to begin with.

Recently, the practice of appraising nonfarm projects with some regard to interest charges has become more widespread. Furthermore, since 1960, interest charges probably have been higher than they were previously, at least in relation to the available capital supply. Conceivably, therefore, they now serve to limit internal rates of return in the nonfarm sector to levels broadly similar to those in agriculture. But ruble prices still have their limitations, and to ensure a correspondence of internal rates of return in the nonfarm and farm sector would still be difficult. In any event, we should have to know more than we do about how the nonfarm interest norms are set in order to judge this matter.

Where our efficiency rule has been violated, may we not conclude that this has occurred in a particular way? Thus, given the frequent neglect of interest, have not capital intensities tended to be too high and internal rates of return too low in the nonfarm relatively to the farm sector? Moreover, where interest has been charged but at rates below clearing levels, were these not likely also to be below internal returns on capital in the economy generally? And if so, have not nonfarm capital intensities still tended to be too high and nonfarm internal returns to be too low?

Where capital is rationed, it is not easy to judge internal rates of return from interest charges or the lack of them, but nonfarm project appraisal as conducted in the U.S.S.R. might well have given rise to the tendencies suggested. Also, actual technological choices in Soviet industry almost defy summarization, but it is easy to find possible instances of these tendencies. I refer particularly to such features as the recurring manifestation of "giantism," the repeatedly avowed commitment to the most advanced technologies generally, the notably protracted construction periods, and the like. Manifestly, however, capital outlays often have been economized in consequential ways. It suffices to recall the pervasive practice of combining in one production unit "advanced" and highly capital-intensive technologies for basic processes with "backward" and labor-intensive ones for auxiliary processes—for example, internal transport.[17]

Although difficult to interpret, tentative data available on Soviet capital stock are also illuminating. Thus the Soviet stock of reproducible fixed capital per worker is still only about 35 per cent of that of the U.S.A. For industry alone, the Soviet capital stock per worker is also less than ours, but

17. As Professor Erlich has rightly pointed out to me, even where such combined technologies have economized capital they need not have been the most economical ones to employ. For example, the labor intensive components could easily become a bottleneck. On patterns of technological choice in Soviet industry, see the articles by Granick cited above, p. 250, n. 8; also Leon Smolinski, "The Scale of the Soviet Industrial Establishment," *American Economic Review*, 52S (1962), 138–48.

by no means commensurately. It may be as much as two-thirds of the U.S. stock per worker. In agriculture capital stock per worker in the U.S.S.R. is only a very small fraction of that in the U.S.A.[18]

These differences between the U.S.S.R. and U.S.A. in relative capital stock per worker in different sectors may reflect relative differences in product mix rather than relative differences in capital intensity for individual branches in the two countries. Also, even with investment allocation conforming to the efficiency rule, relative stock per worker in different branches could hardly be expected to be the same in the two countries. They would be different even if investment allocation in the U.S.A. should conform to the rule, which presumably it does not. The Soviet capital stock per worker for the economy as a whole is less than ours. If only because of this, disproportionately large per-worker allocations to industry might be appropriate. Relative capital intensities properly might also differ in the two countries because of differences in resource endowment, although here it is more difficult to gauge the nature of the variation that might be called for. But the disproportionately large per-worker allocations to industry in the U.S.S.R. still fit in with the view that, for Soviet nonfarm projects, capital intensities have tended to be too high and internal rates of return too low.

✓ CONCLUSIONS

Conformity with the efficiency rule considered in this chapter is in order where the concern is with consumers' welfare, but we have focused primarily on the nonfarm

18. Reference is to reproducible fixed capital exclusive of housing and livestock, but relatively to that in the U.S.A., the status of agriculture in the U.S.S.R. probably improves little if at all if livestock is included. On the data on capital stock, see below, Appendix B. Data on employment are also compiled from sources cited there.

268

sector. Adherence to the rule in this sphere means that the community is able to produce a maximum output of non-farm final products of any desired structure. As theory teaches, output is a maximum in relation to the total volume of investment that is available, together with cooperating factors, for nonfarm uses.[19] Even where the concern is not with consumers' welfare, therefore, it is not easy to imagine any alternative material ends according to which conformity with the rule would not be to the good.

Whatever the ends sought, then, we must conclude that investment allocation within the nonfarm sector has often been economically irrational, for such allocation has again and again violated the rule. What is the explanation? In a dynamic economy like that of the U.S.S.R., a close approach to the rule might have been difficult in any circumstances, but the difficulty has been compounded by the nature of the ruble prices in terms of which calculations have had to be made. So far as these prices have diverged from pertinent efficiency principles, rational appraisal of alternative projects necessarily has been obstructed.

But, granting the difficulties, if our efficiency rule has been violated, a major reason has been that conformity with it in any exact sense has not been sought to begin with. And for this the explanation, of course, is to be found in a feature causing economic irrationality elsewhere: the dubious value theory. Under the labor theory of value there is no place for the subjection of investment projects to the interest test which is essential to economic efficiency at this point. If investment projects in the U.S.S.R. have been appraised with-

19. Reference is to the volume of output produced in not only the current period but in future ones. Correspondingly, one takes as a datum the structure of output in each period, and also that between periods, although in a more precise formulation a distinction is to be made between investment goods and other output. For the former, reference is properly made to stocks that are to be on hand at some terminal date.

out reference to interest costs, manifestly this has been a principal reason.

How far it has been so, we may judge from the fact that interest costs, when considered, have been considered under another name. A leading proponent of this approach has also seen fit to affirm that it "has nothing in common with the use of a rate of interest as a criterion of effectiveness under capitalist conditions." [20] Such disavowals, however, have not prevented attack on advocates of the CRE method for diverse ideological transgressions such as "idealism," adherence to "anti-scientific" principle, and subjection to bourgeois theories. Use of compound interest particularly has been held to disregard Marx's teaching that this is an "absurdity, mystification and nonsense." [21]

While application of an interest test has been held to be ideologically taboo, apparently the party never formally excluded such a procedure, and neglect of interest was never universal. Moreover, this practice is now being superseded by one in which interest is charged, although still without being identified as such. At least for the present time, therefore, ideological scruples have been repressed. But project appraisal probably continues to be hampered by the labor theory of value. At least, adherence to it must have precluded a proper grasp of the problem. Thus it is difficult to understand otherwise the continued use of varying norms of capital effectiveness which only in part could be warranted by differences in service life. Where the CRE method has been employed, our efficiency rule has also been violated because of the failure to establish norms at clearing levels. The labor theory is probably still a factor here.

So far as our efficiency rule has been violated, nonfarm sector projects in favored branches must often have been in-

20. Reference is again to Khachaturov, as quoted in Hunter, *Review of Economic Statistics, 31* (1949), 56.

21. Grossman, *Quarterly Journal of Economics, 67* (1953), 333 ff.

ordinately capital intensive relatively to those in less favored branches. But the former projects might also have represented the "most advanced" technologies, and for the system's directors, if only for political reasons, this result must have had an appeal of its own. Even if they should have fully grasped the attendant economic waste, therefore, the system's directors might have sanctioned some divergence from our efficiency rule on this account.

Project appraisal in the U.S.S.R. has been a complex task. At least until recently, those charged immediately for its execution must frequently have been uncertain of the principles applying in any particular case. The procedures employed, therefore, should also have been congenial to the system's directors who in any event were reluctant to have their authority subjected to any well-defined limits. Such inhibitions, however, can no longer be quite as potent as they once were. Of this we have already become aware, but the relaxation may be seen particularly in the recent acceptance of the CRE method as the generally preferred procedure.

When superior authorities are reluctant to commit themselves to principles, arbitrariness easily comes to be considered as something of a virtue in itself. At least, this must have been so in the U.S.S.R. under Stalin, and choice of technology is one of the chief facets of resource use affected. As principles lately have gained in force, this attitude has lost ground. Hostility to principle and a flair for arbitrariness are alike seen now as manifestations of a cult of personality that must be exorcised, though apparently such attitudes still prevail:

> It is well known that in the period of the cult of personality of Stalin plans of production, capital investment, and construction not infrequently were compiled without sufficient economic basis. In style at that

271

time were the so-called volitional decisions (*volevye resheniia*). And not surprisingly at this time the significance of the law of value, profits and profitability, effectiveness of the utilization of capital investments and plant and equipment was disparaged. Arbitrariness in price formation was also allowed.

Now there are other times, other requirements, and another approach. Of course, it would be incorrect to think that the consequences of the cult of personality in the sphere of planning and economics have been fully overcome. No, here there is still much to do. People are still about who to this day do not consider the cost of construction, how much the country is damaged by the scattering of capital in many projects, the dragging out of the period of introduction of capacity and the freezing of capital in uncompleted construction. With us to this day people still sometimes decide the problem of the direction and volume of allocation of means not by a calculation with a pencil in hand, but more quickly by a subjective decision—in dependence on this, how it is necessary to manipulate affairs in order to "ram through" (*protashchit'*) the decision. . .[22]

Deficiencies in ruble prices have been due to many causes. Among these, not least here again are adherence to the labor theory and the generally centralized nature of decision making.

Reference has been to nonfarm project appraisal as it involves allocation of investment within the nonfarm sector. To the extent that such appraisal entails allocation of investment between the nonfarm and farm sectors, conformity with our efficiency rule still assures a maximization of output, now of farm and nonfarm products together. Thus, given the allocation of investment and cooperating resources

22. *Pravda* (September 24, 1963).

within agriculture, output of all final products is a maximum in relation to the total volume of available investment, together with cooperating factors, for use in the economy generally.

For this reason, the rule should be as impelling as within the nonfarm sector, and any violations seem again to betoken economic irrationality. In seeking to conform to the rule at this point, however, the system's directors might no longer be able to exercise complete discretion as to the mix of final products. Particularly, in Soviet circumstances conformity to the rule would have required an even larger transfer of farm workers to the city than has occurred. Through a concomitant reallocation of investment in favor of agriculture, nonfarm and farm products might still have been produced in the same proportions as actually prevailed, and the output of both might even have increased. But, given a larger industrial population, presumably urban housing and urban facilities would have had to be stressed more. The advantages of the reallocations, therefore, would have depended on the values attached to such products. Soviet preferences among final goods are yet to be discussed, and I do not plan in any case to deal particularly with preferences for housing and urban facilities, but obviously the system's directors have not valued housing and urban facilities simply from the standpoint of consumers' welfare. In relation to rural standards, urban consumption per employed worker for long probably has not been as high as is often assumed,[23] but to the system's directors further recruitment of farm labor into industry must also have seemed dubious, since it might compel larger allocations to consumption generally at the expense of investment.

This is not to say that, where investment allocation between nonfarm and farm sectors has been involved, nonfarm

23. See above, pp. 227–28.

project appraisal has been economically rational after all. Considering the nature of such appraisal, it would be surprising if anything like an optimum has been achieved even in terms of the system's directors' own values, but resource use has not been quite as inefficient as might be supposed.

12 CONSUMPTION STRUCTURE

In any modern community working arrangements for resource use must delimit myriads of economic magnitudes, but the process may be viewed broadly as one of determining two large matters: the volume of final goods of any given structure that is produced, and the structure and disposition of such final output.

Thus far we have referred chiefly to procedures bearing on the former. In this chapter and the next I consider procedures for determining the structure and disposition of final output, particularly those bearing on two outstanding aspects, (I) the volume of final output devoted to capital formation relative to that devoted to other major final uses, especially household consumption, and (2) the structure of household consumption. Working arrangements concerning the latter aspect are considered in this chapter, those concerning the former in Chapter 13.

We thus come to a facet of resource use where a famous

efficiency rule applies: In relation to each other supplies of different goods made available for household consumption must be such that their prices are everywhere proportional to the marginal costs of their production. The prices are understood to be such as prevail in an open market. Also, they should be at clearing levels, in the sense that, for each product, demand corresponds to available supplies. Also, costs should reflect factor prices determined in familiar ways often indicated in previous chapters.[1]

In the U.S.S.R. some consumers' goods become available to households in the form of farm and other income in kind, but I shall focus primarily on supplies which are distributed to households at money prices. For many years, these supplies have constituted the bulk of household consumption. The stated rule is applied most readily to these goods. Then, too, consumers' goods that have been disposed of at money prices have often been rationed in the U.S.S.R., but of chief interest here is the period since December 1947, when the open market required by the rule prevailed. Even during this period, however, prices have often diverged markedly from clearing levels, although there has been some tendency in the latter direction. Moreover, although our inquiries into Soviet factor charges have not been exhaustive, clearly such charges also must frequently have differed from those called for. In short, that the structure of consumption in the U.S.S.R. has diverged from that required by our efficiency rule is a foregone conclusion. How then has it been delimited?

FORMULATION OF THE PLAN

As was done in considering disposition of consumers' goods, I shall focus on foodstuffs and manufactures.

1. In the present context, only proportionality of prices to marginal costs is relevant, although elsewhere equality is necessary. See above, pp. 122 ff.

276

Consumption Structure

In the U.S.S.R. allotment of foodstuffs and manufactured goods for household consumption necessarily is determined initially in economic plans. We must try first, therefore, to grasp how pertinent aspects of the programs are formulated.

Expressly or by implication, supplies of foodstuffs and manufactures for household consumption are delimited in both the annual plan and plans for longer periods. Because of its relatively operational nature, however, the annual plan is of prior interest. Nevertheless, we now consider alternative mixes of supplies requiring alternative distributions not only of labor and materials but of capital. For this reason, here especially we must bear in mind that the annual plan is formulated in the perspective of longer period programs.

In the annual plan, supplies of foodstuffs and manufactures for households are recorded in accounts of supplies of and requirements for different products. Such accounts for industrial goods were described previously; similar accounts are compiled for nonindustrial goods, including those that in some degree find their way to households. Most products which to a significant extent are consumed by households are included in accounts considered by central authorities, including Gosplan. Probably, however, some of limited importance are covered in accounts considered only by lesser agencies.

In effect, then, for supplies of foodstuffs and manufactures for household consumption there are explicit targets in the plan. How are these targets formulated, at least in relation to each other?

In determining the planned mix of these consumers' goods, reference apparently has been made to several aspects.[2] One of these is consumers' demand, as it will manifest

2. See the writings on price formation cited above, Ch. 4, especially n. 11; and those on industrial materials allocation cited in Ch. 7. especially n. 4. See also I. M. Khrekin, *Pokupatel'naia sposobnost'*

itself in the retail market under the plan. This necessarily has been seen, however, in the light of the relation of current consumers' demand to current supply, as manifest particularly in inventory charges. Nevertheless, an attempt has been made to project consumers' demand to the period of the plan. This has been done by diverse agencies, among them not least those administering wholesale and retail trade. The latter on this basis determine the "orders" which they will present for fulfillment in the plan.

But, such investigation must have limitations. The state of demand studies in the U.S.S.R. is evident from the following statement by two Soviet students of consumption planning in 1959:

> Unfortunately, the organization of work on the study of the demand of the population for commodities still suffers from serious deficiencies which adversely affect the satisfaction of the population needs. . . . So, for example, at the request of trading organizations of a series of republics the production of green bohea tea was reduced, and then it was discovered that the supply on the market was inadequate, as a result of which it was necessary again to switch over to production. In 1954–56 at the request of trading organizations in Moscow and Leningrad significantly more potatoes were delivered than were required for sale to the population.

naseleniia i tovarooborot (Moscow, 1958); K. M. Skovoroda and S. I. Grigor'ev, *Balansy tovarov narodnogo potrebleniia i metody ikh razrabotki* (Moscow, 1959); S. Partigul, "Spros i predlozhenie tovarov pri sotsializme," *Voprosy ekonomiki*, No. 10 (1959); K. Skovoroda, "Spros i predlozhenie tovarov v sotsialisticheskom obshchestve," *Voprosy ekonomiki*, No. 11 (1960); S. P. Figurnov, *Real'naia zarobotnaia plata . . .* (Moscow, 1960); S. S. Vasil'ev et al., *Ekonomika torgovli* (Moscow, 1962), chs. VI–VIII; P. Lokshin, "Proizvodstvo tovarov i platezhesposobnyi spros," *Planovoe khoziaistvo*, No. 1 (1963); Philip Hanson, "The Assortment Problem in Soviet Retail Trade," *Soviet Studies, 14* (1962–63), 347–64.

Consequently, the potatoes had to be shipped back from Moscow to other oblasts.[3]

More recently, demand studies have also been described by another Soviet authority:

> up to this time, the determination of the volume of demand and its commodity structure has not been placed on a scientific basis. . . . Organizations of retail and wholesale trade have some experience with diverse methods and forms of study of demand. Among them are: orders and expressed preferences of purchasers; sample studies in separate stores on the course of sales and movement of stocks for different sorts of goods; exhibit sales, surveys of new models and forms of products in specialized stores . . . conferences of buyers . . . travel of product managers in wholesale bases into the retail trade network in order to take orders. . . .
>
> However, the accumulated experience in the study of demand is not generalized; observation of the condition of demand and its satisfaction does not have a systematic character; on a country-wide scale continuing, effective work in the study of demand has not been undertaken. Trading organizations, orienting themselves by reference to current demand, tolerate many errors in evaluating it for the future, as a result of which industry does not receive a correct orientation and an irregularity is injected into trade.[4]

While attempting to estimate consumers' demand, the authorities concerned with the determination of the planned mix of foodstuffs and manufactures for household consumption do not feel bound to take such demand at face value. Rather, depending on its urgency as seen by the

3. Skovoroda and Grigor'ev, p. 33.
4. Lokshin, *Planovoe khoziaistvo* (January 1963), pp. 28–29.

authorities, consumers' demand for some products may be either discounted or stressed relative to that for others. So at any rate Soviet sources imply, and probably with good reason.

For example, to the authorities concerned, demand for children's things usually has seemed relatively urgent. Possibly this has also been true of basic foodstuffs and hygienic supplies. For alcoholic beverages, jewelry, perfumes, and the like, however, demand has not been considered urgent.[5]

Account necessarily is also taken of costs. For different products, these apparently are viewed as proportional to the "socially necessary labor time" expended in their production. Soviet economists understandably hesitate to be explicit on the manner in which such costs have been gauged, but in practice reference is made to the costs recorded in the books of enterprises. Under Soviet accounting practice, of course, the latter ultimately do resolve for the most part into labor charges, including earnings of collective farm households, but not entirely. Most importantly, the turnover tax is levied at widely varying rates, and not only on fabricated goods allotted to final uses but often on materials to be processed further. This has been especially true of materials of agricultural origin, for here the tax has been levied in good part on procurement agencies and processors of semi-fabricates.[6] Consequently the turnover tax is part of the cost of fabricates of many goods destined for household consumption. So far as materials prices allow for planned profits, such charges too must be reflected in costs of these final products.

In accord with the accepted understanding of "socially

5. See Turetskii, *Ocherki planovogo tsenoobrazovaniia v SSSR*, pp. 407, 418–19.

6. Before the establishment of uniform procurement prices in 1958, such levies were used as offsets for industry to differential payments to farmers.

necessary labor time," reference has been made to average costs. In the formulation of plan targets for supplies of food-stuffs and manufactures for household consumption, how-ever, availability, as reflected in capacity limitations, ease of expansion of labor and materials, competing uses and the like, has also had to be considered. By implication, if only in the most proximate manner, some attention has been given to variations in costs that are associated with variations in output.

In the light of the foregoing aspects, just how are plan targets for supplies of foodstuffs and manufactures for house-hold consumption determined? The procedure apparently presupposes that prices normally are more or less propor-tional to costs as estimated. Variations from this standard are introduced, however, depending on the relative urgency of consumers' demand for different products, as seen by the authorities, and in such cases it is the resultant prices that are viewed as "normal." Prices may also vary from costs in order to limit consumers' demand to currently available sup-plies, but such manipulation is not attempted often, or if at-tempted is unsuccessful.[7] In any case, in formulating targets for supplies, the authorities try somehow to alleviate deficits and surpluses that are experienced, or would be experienced at prices "normally" related to costs. In the process, account somehow is taken of availability.

But Soviet accounts are not clear, and one cannot be sure that even the foregoing broad principles are observed at all systematically. And even where they are observed, the targets must frequently be arbitrary.

Unavoidable in any case, the arbitrariness must be com-pounded by the arrangements employed, including the Method of Balanced Estimates, to assure that accounts com-piled for supplies and requirements balance.[8] If we may

7. See above, pp. 55 ff.
8. Above, Ch. 7.

judge from the experience in spheres considered previously, under these arrangements the government encounters special difficulties in expressing any mix of final products in the plan targets. Moreover, if the mix sought cannot readily be translated into targets for all final products, this must be no less true for supplies for household consumption in particular. In fact, under prevalent priorities, if to achieve a balance a change has had to be made in supplies allotted to final uses, it has tended to be made first in supplies allotted to household consumption. For this reason, the mix sought must be realized to a less extent in targets for supplies for household consumption than in those for supplies for final uses generally.

IMPLEMENTATION OF THE PLAN

I have been discussing determination of the mix of foodstuffs and manufactures allotted to household consumption in the plan. The Soviet government for long has published only scant details on its annual plan, and the record of its fulfillment in respect of the supplies in question is correspondingly incomplete. Manifestly the record has been uneven, but it has probably been more so than the limited and often dubious official releases suggest (Table 12.1).[9]

This is not surprising, but the Soviet performance here can better be understood if one recalls that working arrangements for fulfilling the plan have been such as to amplify as well as correct distortions in the mix of final products sought. Also, under prevailing priorities, the authorities have been primarily concerned to assure supplies for end uses other than household consumption. Consequently, the mix of supplies for household consumption must be distorted the more. Then, too, in the U.S.S.R. the volume of

9. See also above, pp. 83 ff., 89.

Consumption Structure

12.1.

Goals of Annual Plan for 1960 and Their Fulfillment, U.S.S.R.
(percentage of 1959)

	Goal	Actual
National income	109	108
Industrial production:		
Total	108.1	<110
Means of production	108.8	<111
Means of consumption	106.4	>107
Railway freight turnover	106.5	105.2
Fixed capital investment	111	112.4
Production of:		
Coal	101.7	101.0
Crude oil	111.1	114.1
Electric power	111.2	110.3
Steel	108.4	108.9
Chemicals	110	111.3
Cement	117.3	117.3
Cloth	101.2	103.8
Leather shoes	104.5	107.5
Grain	120.8	106.5
Meat	119.1	97.8
Milk	116.7	100.0

Sources: Pravda (October 28, 1959); *Narkhoz, 1960*, pp. 152, 223, 243, 254, 272, 276, 308, 321, 337, 375, 378, 536, 591.

foodstuffs and manufactures depends much on agricultural performance. While the government has held some stocks to offset harvest fluctuations, these still leave their imprint on current allocations to household consumption.

Not surprisingly too, supplies have been marketed at relative prices often differing widely from "socially necessary labor time" according to any likely understanding. Of this we may judge from estimates of retail and factor cost values of different foodstuffs and manufactures sold to households in government and cooperative retail shops (Table 12.2). Factor cost differs from retail value chiefly because of the turnover tax, but for some products this charge is largely

283

TABLE 12.2.

Government and Cooperative Retail Sales to Households at
Retail Prices and Factor Cost, U.S.S.R., 1937

	Sales at Retail Prices (billion rubles) (1)	Sales at Factor Cost (billion rubles) (2)	Col. 1 as Per Cent of Col. 2 (3)
Foods:			
Grain products and legumes	27.07	10.63	254.7
Meat and poultry	6.32	5.69	111.1
Fish	2.92	1.57	286.0
Sugar and confectionery	11.52	4.13	278.9
Fats (including butter)	4.23	1.31	322.9
Milk and milk products	1.39	2.02	68.8
Eggs	0.49	0.55	89.9
Vegetables and fruit	3.96	5.10	77.6
Salt	0.21	0.07	300.0
Tea and coffee	0.83	0.21	395.2
Alcoholic beverages	10.48	2.68	391.0
All foods	69.41	33.96	206.0
Manufactured goods:			
Textiles	8.40	4.50	186.7
Garments	7.23	4.64	155.8
Knitwear	2.44	1.59	153.5
Shoes	5.15	3.71	138.8
Haberdashery, notions	2.19	1.34	163.4
Soap, drugs, etc.	2.96	1.58	187.3
Housewares	2.56	1.60	160.0
Reading matter	1.54	1.51	102.0
Cultural, sport goods	3.37	2.64	127.7
Kerosene, matches	1.01	0.22	459.1
Tobacco products	3.73	0.74	504.1
All manufactures	40.59	24.07	168.6
All commodities	110.00	58.03	189.6

Source: Real SNIP, p. 432.

or entirely offset by subsidies and extra collective farm earnings in the collective farm market. To the extent that the latter compensate collective farm labor for low government procurement prices, they seem properly to be allowed for in the computation of factor cost.

Consumption Structure

Regrettably, data like those shown for 1937 are not available for a recent year. Nor do we know to what extent divergencies between relative retail prices and factor costs that prevail in any one year persist in subsequent years. However, prices probably were more nearly at clearing levels during 1937 than in many other years under the five-year plans. The divergencies between relative retail prices and factor costs, therefore, presumably reflect to some extent variations in the degree of urgency of consumers' demand for different products, as seen by the authorities. But they must also reflect divergencies of supplies from requirements at prices "normally" related to costs. Of course, for some products demand must be relatively inelastic, and the relation of prices to factor cost must have only a limited impact on household requirements. No doubt this aspect, too, has been considered by the authorities in determining relative prices.

Although data on retail prices and factor costs are not at hand for a recent year, it is pertinent that procurement prices paid the collective farmer for different crops in

TABLE 12.3.

Collective Farm Production Costs and Corresponding
Government Procurement Prices, U.S.S.R., 1960

	Production Cost (rubles per 100 kilos)	Procurement Prices (rubles per 100 kilos)	Procurement Prices as per cent of Production Cost
Cereals	4.0	6.2	155
Potatoes	3.2	4.7	147
Sugar beet	1.4	2.3	164
Raw cotton	20.7	34.1	165
Milk	13.3	11.4	86
Cattle	91.6	59.1	65
Pigs	122.6	82.3	67
Poultry	140.5	82.2	59
Eggs	93[a]	60[a]	65

Source: *Economic Bulletin for Europe* (November 1962), p. 14.
a. Rubles per 1,000 eggs.

1960–61 still varied notably in relation to his "costs" (Table 12.3). Here costs are calculated on the basis of state farm wage norms. The extreme disproportions observed, however, were partially rectified in June 1962, when procurement prices for animal products were raised along with the corresponding retail prices.

Interestingly, the resultant structure of supplies by major groups does not differ radically from that in a Western country with a similar standard (Table 12.4). Apparently, the Soviet government has found it both feasible and expedient to provide its people with a mix of products broadly like that generated in a market economy. Reference, however, is only to major product categories, and even among

TABLE 12.4.

Consumption per Capita, U.S.S.R. and Italy

	IN U.S. 1955 DOLLARS	
	U.S.S.R., 1955	*Italy,* 1955
All products	492	524
Food	193	216
Clothing	29	38
Durables	7	4
Housing	27	31
Other, including education and health care	236	235

	IN U.S. 1950 DOLLARS	
	U.S.S.R., 1955	*Italy,* 1950
All food	178	168
Cereal products	65	51
Meat, poultry, fish	32	30
Dairy products	26	24
Fruit and vegetables	40	46
Alcoholic beverages	21	39

Source: Rush V. Greenslade, "Measurement of Consumption in the Soviet Union," typescript (February 27, 1963).

these there are sometimes significant differences in consumption structure.

The mix of foodstuffs and manufactures provided
households in any community has three facets: the structure
of supplies by more or less distinct product categories; for
any one product category, the assortment of products with
concrete specifications, such as materials employed, styles,
colors, sizes, and the like; and for each product the standards of quality observed. Thus far, I have focused on the
first of these aspects; I now turn to the latter two. While
foodstuffs and manufactures supplied households are partly
unprocessed, of chief interest are commodities processed by
industry.

As to the determination of the assortment of these goods,[10]
the annual plan for any agency administering industry for
long has embraced not only a target for total output but
(where appropriate) further targets for specific products
constituting such output. This has been true at all administrative levels, although the assortment program has been
elaborated in most detail at the level of enterprise. Similarly,
plans for procurement and sale of organizations engaged
in trade have been elaborated in varying detail depending
on the agency involved.

How are the targets for assortment determined? What of
their fulfillment? The working arrangements that apply
are broadly the same as those for targets for broader categories, but in determining assortment the government has
encountered special difficulties.

10. Berliner, *Factory and Manager*, ch. VIII; Nove, *The Soviet
Economy*, pp. 155 ff.; Goldman, *Soviet Marketing*, ch. 3; Lokshin,
Planovoe khoziaistvo (January 1963); I. A. Orlov, "O povyshenii
kachestva tovarov narodnogo khoziaistva," *Voprosy ekonomiki*, No. 1
(1963); Hanson, *Soviet Studies, 14* (1962–63).

In order to understand these, one must recall the success criteria confronting the management of the industrial enterprise. Until 1959 by far the most important criterion was fulfillment of the target for total output. Since 1959, fulfillment of the output target apparently has no longer been the primary test of success, but it has only given way to another aggregative feature, fulfillment of the plan for cost reduction. Success throughout has also been judged on other bases, among them performance in respect of the assortment. But there are limits to the detail in which assortment can be planned, and further limits to the detail in which violations of the plan for assortment can be observed. Furthermore, such violations have not always been an impelling concern for superior authorities who themselves have been judged primarily by performance in respect of targets for output and costs, and who almost inevitably have assortment targets formulated in even less detail than the enterprise. In any case, enterprise management apparently came long ago to understand that success was to be judged primarily in terms other than performance in respect of assortment. This understanding has persisted.

Of course, failure to conform to the assortment plan has meant that producing enterprises and *glavki* could not make deliveries in accord with agreements reached beforehand with purchasing agencies. But under circumstances of recurring shortage purchasing agencies have hesitated to reject shipments or seek damages, as they have had the right to do. Moreover, the producer might obtain without great difficulty funds to pay damages, for here as elsewhere financial controls have not been stringent.

But, granted that success has been judged mainly otherwise, should the enterprise management still not have been concerned to produce an appropriate assortment? At least should it not have been as much concerned to produce this as any other assortment? It must often have been, but often too it must have been otherwise impelled. Thus the enterprise's goal for total output has been expressed as a rule in value terms, and in seeking to fulfill it, the management has had to consider the relative prices of different products. With resources at its disposal limited, it has also had to consider relative per-unit costs. This was so even before 1959, but relative per-unit costs have been of more concern since then. Yet prices have often varied markedly from costs, and while such variations sometimes might have encouraged or discouraged production of different products in conformity with the assortment plan, this has by no means always been so. Hence, as Soviet sources freely acknowledge, the manner in which the target for total output has been calculated has in itself invited violation of the plan for assortment. In addition to costs, management has had to consider availability of material and other inputs needed for different products, but the incentive to violate the assortment plan has not been less on this account.

Actually there have been several targets for total output, including at least two main ones: one for "gross" and the other for "marketed" output. Also, output has been valued differently depending on the concept. Thus gross output has usually been valued in constant and marketed output, in current prices. At least until 1959, the target for marketed output was supposed to have priority, but apparently success still is sometimes judged primarily by performance in respect to the target for gross output. Moreover, until 1949 the latter target invariably was expressed in ruble prices of 1926–27, and the consequences for incentives to produce different products were often strange indeed. At that time, however, even valuation in current prices must often have operated similarly. Since 1949, the valuation year employed in the computation of gross output has been

289

a more or less contemporary one, and partly for this reason the difference in pricing between the target for gross and that for marketed output has not been consequential.

Necessarily targets for individual products elaborated in the assortment plan have themselves often been aggregative. By the same token, depending on the relation of prices and costs, management here, too, might find it advantageous to produce an odd assortment. While still conforming to the letter of the assortment plan, it might be tempted to deviate materially from it in spirit. I refer to cases where, as for total output, aggregation has been in terms of prices. Often for different products aggregation has instead been in terms of physical quantities. Here, therefore, there has been an incentive to produce disproportionate amounts of products bulking large physically. For example, with output expressed in tons, it might have been advantageous to produce items that are heavy relative to their costs. Reportedly performance in respect not only of individual products but of output generally, or at least of major components, sometimes has been judged by reference to targets in physical units. In such cases interest in fulfilling the assortment plan would have been affected similarly.

The foregoing working arrangements have prevailed in industry generally, and hence also in branches producing consequentially for household consumption. The concern to produce an appropriate assortment must have been even less here, however, than elsewhere. Thus, under the prevailing priority scheme, assortment has been of less concern even to the government in the case of products destined primarily for households than in the case of industrial goods generally. Then, too, the purchaser of the former supplies from industry has been a trading organization, and any concern of the latter regarding departures of the producer from the planned assortment has been tempered by the realization that the products received might be readily disposed of in a retail market where demand has tended to exceed supply.

In any event, managerial interest in producing an appropriate assortment of foodstuffs and manufactures has been limited. And the management has acted accordingly. This is the burden of accounts of former Soviet citizens, although these relate chiefly to early years, and of complaints made in the U.S.S.R. itself. The latter are voluminous even by Soviet standards.[11] Thus industrial enterprises at various times have reportedly overfulfilled the plan for woolen dresses and underfulfilled it for children's suits and similar items because the former happened to be more profitable; stressed unduly bandage over shirt cloth simply because of the relative ease of producing the former; produced small-sized men's shoes rather than large-sized boys' shoes, because of the higher cost norm allowed for the former than for the latter; produced inordinate amounts of small-sized raincoats, apparently for similar reasons; neglected inexpensive cloths, which tend to bulk small in total output, and narrowed the width of cloth generally, because output was measured in linear meters; accepted from trading organizations orders for heavy, more readily than for light, household enamelware because the former requires relatively less labor; underfulfilled orders for small and overfulfilled orders for large electric bulbs, because gross output thereby is made larger.

Violation of the assortment plan has been held to be "one of the most prevalent forms of simulation" in the U.S.S.R.[12] On reviewing the evidence, one can only agree.

Violation of the plan must have resulted again and again

11. Berliner, *Factory and Manager*, pp. 120–24; Nove, *The Soviet Economy*, pp. 158 ff.; Lokshin, *Planovoe khoziaistvo* (January 1963), p. 26; Orlov, *Voprosy ekonomiki*, No. 1 (1963); Hanson, *Soviet Studies, 14* (1962–63); *Current Digest* (July 24, 1963), pp. 5 ff.

12. Berliner, *Factory and Manager*, p. 114.

in production of an inappropriate assortment, but the plan itself has left something to be desired, and perhaps sometimes matters were no worse than before. Thus by a decree of August 1960 the product assortment was to be based on orders from trading organizations, but in 1961 production targets for different kinds of textiles ranged from 30 to 250 per cent of orders.[13]

In seeking to control the quality of its industrial goods, the Soviet government has had to grapple with a twofold task, to determine standards of quality and to assure that they are observed.[14] In the U.S.S.R. norms of quality have always been left in some degree to the discretion of the producing enterprise, but the government has sought to ensure that such standards should generally be controlled by superior agencies. And it has achieved this result to a great extent in the course of time. This has been done for industrial goods generally, hence for goods intended primarily for household consumption. For example, there are now in effect some 8,000 so-called state standards establishing technical norms for different industrial goods, while such standards embrace some 53 per cent of the distinct manufactured consumers' goods supplied. A corresponding figure for processed food products is not at hand.

The state standard (GOST) is issued chiefly by the all-union Committee on Standards, Measures, and Measuring Equipment, and applies on an all-union scale. Since 1957, however, the Council of Ministers in each republic has had considerable authority to amend all-union standards for

13. Hanson, *Soviet Studies*, *14* (1962–63), 354. Neither Hanson nor the Soviet source he cites is clear as to the territorial scope of the figures.

14. On control of the quality of industrial products see *Zakonodatel'nye akty*, *1* (Moscow, 1961), 495 ff.; Berliner, *Factory and Manager*, ch. IX; Orlov, *Voprosy ekonomiki*, No. 1 (1963); Nutter, *Growth of Industrial Production in the Soviet Union*, ch. 3.

consumers' goods produced by enterprises subordinate to it, and besides those included in the GOST, technical norms for consumers' goods are established by the republican ministerial council and by other subordinate agencies, particularly the regional economic council. The volume of industrial consumers' goods now subject to some standard must therefore be very large, although the precise share of the total produced is not known.

How are the standards fixed? The cardinal concern avowedly is to ensure output of high quality, for "the systematic improvement in quality is an obligatory requirement for the growth of the economy." But apparently the precise norms are subject to some negotiation, and one encounters here as elsewhere reflections of a concern on the part of industrial management to establish a "safety factor" for their operations. Of course, quality must ordinarily be purchased at a cost. One might wish to know at what point such an effort is felt in the U.S.S.R. no longer to be worth while, but the facts on this interesting question are obscure.

As for the observance of the established standards, there is no basis to question the familiar view that it has often been in the breech, though surely less often in recent than in early years. We have properly been warned not to take at face value Soviet self-criticism,[15] but the constantly repeated complaints are illuminating. Thus Khrushchev's comment at the November 1962 plenum of the party central committee is only one of the latest of a long series:

> Questions of the struggle for quality of output, against those who create spoilage and thereby inflict harm upon all of society as a whole and upon each working person, are deserving of special attention.
>
> Many complaints of poor-quality industrial goods

15. Alec Nove, "The Pace of Soviet Economic Development," *Lloyd's Bank Review* (April 1956), pp. 11–12.

and consumer goods reach the Central Committee and the Council of Ministers. Here are two small examples. Matters reached such a state at the Zhdanov Clothing Factory in Nikolayevo, under the Kherson Economic Council, that only 15 out of each 100 inspected articles were of satisfactory quality. It takes some contriving to produce 85% spoilage!

Or take the Neman-3 brand of television sets produced at the Minsk Radio Plant, directed by Comrade Shapoval. I wish to quote a letter addressed to Comrade Shapoval by Comrade Krasnova in Riga, who bought a Neman-3 set.

"For a long time I could not get a television set. But now, thanks to the solicitude of the state, my dream has been realized and I have been able to buy a television set on the installment plan. I paid 293 rubles for it and pinched on many things to do so.

"I bought a Neman-3 set of your production on Feb. 3, 1963. By Feb. 28 it had ceased to work and my torments began.

"The television set does not work. I want to know whether, turning out such an expensive product at your plant, you are not troubled at all for those persons to whom you bring disillusion instead of joy and satisfaction. I am not writing this letter casually; since acquiring the television set which you manufactured, I have obtained my 'entertainment' not from the set but from the television repair shop. [*Laughter in the hall.*]

"You can imagine, of course, what kind of entertainment it is to deal with a television repair shop. The factory director who received such a letter should burn with shame! An end must be put to such disgraces, comrades! People who only babble about how our goods should be the best in the world but themselves turn out shoddy goods should not be allowed, as they say, within cannon-shot of the management of enterprises!" [*Prolonged applause.*][16]

Losses due to production of defective goods by industrial enterprises under all-union jurisdiction reportedly totaled 3 billion rubles in 1951. Such losses together with other "unproductive outlays" amounted to 6 billion rubles in 1955.[17] Reference probably is to defective goods discovered, which is not necessarily the same as defective goods produced. Among products examined in the first half of 1962 by inspectors of the Ministry of Trade of the RSFSR, 32.7 per cent for clothing articles, 25 per cent for knitwear, and 32.6 per cent for leather shoes were rejected or reclassified in a lower quality category.[18] Among clothing and knitwear articles inspected by the Ministry of Trade of the Ukraine during 1963, 20 to 25 per cent had to be condemned as defective.[19]

Production of defective goods, of course, is inevitable in any economy, and it no doubt has been greater in the U.S.S.R. because of the recent emergence from a state of economic backwardness. But if, as seems likely, defective products have been inordinately consequential, this would not be surprising in view of the prevailing stress on quantity. In seeking quantity, the management of the industrial enterprise is obligated to conform to established standards of quality, and defective goods are supposed not to count or not to count at full value toward fulfillment of the output target. But imperfections are not always easy to detect, and within the enterprise those charged with observing

16. *Current Digest* (December 26, 1962), p. 10. On earlier Soviet statements, see the sources cited above, n. 14.

17. Berliner, *Factory and Manager*, p. 137.

18. Orlov, *Voprosy ekonomiki*, No. 1 (1963), p. 61. See also *Current Digest* (July 24, 1963), pp. 5 ff.

19. *Pravda* (September 30, 1963).

them, like their fellows, have reasons to honor the claims of mutual support. If one eye is out for losses, therefore, apparently the other is often out for the bosses.

Then, too, the purchaser can demur, and either refuse merchandise or seek financial compensation. But, as in the case of departures from the agreed assortment, chronic difficulties in procurement have fostered tolerance. For the trading organization, purchasing for ultimate resale to households under conditions of excess demand, tolerance has been only the greater.

Those responsible for production of defective goods also become liable to punishment personally. Thus, by a decree of December 8, 1933, production of substandard goods became a penal offense for responsible industrial executives, the guilty persons being subject to a minimum sentence of five years' deprivation of freedom. By a decree of July 10, 1940, the principle of criminal prosecution for such offenses was reaffirmed, and the penalty was fixed at five to eight years' loss of freedom. Still more recently the penalty apparently has been limited to three years' loss of freedom, at least in the RSFSR, but for long the law seems not to have been frequently invoked. Perhaps the draconian penalties have only impaired its effectiveness as an instrument of control.

On working arrangements for determination of both assortment and quality of consumers' goods, this recent summary by a Soviet authority surely is not unduly critical:

> Under circumstances of shortage of goods and insufficiently exacting trade organizations, many industrial enterprises have permitted a reduction in quality of goods, and have not tried to refresh assortment. The assured demand has given rise among industrial and trade workers to less attentiveness to appearance, finish and quality of goods, neglect of the requirements of

the market. . . . We not infrequently encounter such phenomena as where much goods are on sale, but to select in accord with one's taste a coat, dress, cut of cloth or pair of shoes is not always possible. In 1961, retail stocks of cloth, clothing and leather shoes increased by 1260 million rubles, or by 21 per cent, but sales of these goods, taken together, did not increase at all. In 1961 almost 10 per cent of currently supplied woolen cloth and clothing was left in stocks. Almost all of the increase in the marketable supply of shoes in 1961 was left in stock. One of the chief reasons for this situation is the lack of correspondence of assortment and quality to demand.[20]

To improve performance regarding quality and assortment understandably is among the major aims of recent proposals for further reform in planning, particularly success criteria for enterprise management.[21]

CONCLUSIONS

At the outset of this chapter I stated the efficiency rule regarding determination of the mix of consumers' goods. A divergence of resource use in the U.S.S.R. from it, however, seemed unavoidable, and such a divergence surely has occurred in fact. The reasons for this are fairly evident. In order to conform to the rule, supplies provided households must be determined in the light of consumers' demand. In the U.S.S.R. the authorities concerned sometimes have sought to determine supplies in this way, but they have departed from the standard to take account of their own sense of urgency. More basically, the efficiency rule is an imperative for economic rationality only if the end sought

20. Lokshin, *Planovoe khoziaistvo* (January 1963), p. 26.
21. Goldman, *Foreign Affairs, 41* (1962–63).

is consumers' welfare. By construing consumers' demand in accord with their own sense of urgency, however, the authorities often have in effect been concerned with planners' preferences.

In so construing consumers' demand, the authorities sometimes have probably not intended to replace household by planners' preferences. Rather the concern has been only to achieve a desired redistribution of real income. In other words, resort has been made to a second best in the interest of equity. Where the departure from consumers' demand has been more than transitory, however, one wonders whether the desired income redistribution might not have been achieved more directly without a violation of the efficiency rule. In any event, here as well as where planners' preferences supplant household preferences, the rule is violated.

However consumers' demand is construed, economic rationality still has its imperatives, and, equity apart, there must be conformity either with our efficiency rule or with an analogous one reflecting planners' preferences. By the same token, in seeking to understand resource use in the sphere in question, we must also consider that conformity with any such rule has been impeded by the attempt to apply the labor-value theory. Here as elsewhere this theory has been construed elastically, but efficiency probably has been none the greater on this account. Because of the limitations of ruble prices, even application of the labor theory has been difficult. While the limitations are in part due to use of the labor theory itself, they must have impaired efficiency still more. Last but not least, pursuit of any principles has been impeded by administrative deficiencies.

The last of these sources of inefficiency has been particularly important in the determination of assortment and quality. Here the government has been unable to devise suitable and effective controls over managerial behavior.

In view of their persistence, one wonders whether the government is as much concerned with these deficiencies as it avows. But manifestly it has not been able to devise controls that would not be unduly costly in terms of other desiderata, particularly total output.

It remains to observe that the government is beginning to use input-output analysis in coordinating planned targets. If such techniques should facilitate achievement of a desired mix of final products generally, they should do so as well for consumers' goods. For purposes of improving demand estimates, some use lately has also been made of econometrics. It is not yet clear, however, that this "bourgeois" tool may be employed in this sphere with impunity.[22]

Even if consumers' demand comes to be more accurately appraised on this basis, however, the mix of consumers' goods may not be much affected. At any rate, while household preferences have often been supplanted by those of planners, apparently this is now to be done, if it is not already being done, more systematically than previously. Such at least would appear to be the import of the "rational norms" of consumption which diverse Soviet agencies have lately been compiling.[23] Representing the volume of consumption "necessary for assurance of the harmonic physical and spiritual growth of the individual," such norms have already been established for food products and for many manufactured consumers' goods.

Thus it has been calculated that the typical Soviet consumer requires annually 120.0 kilograms of grain products,

22. See Goldman, *Soviet Marketing,* p. 76.
23. In addition to the studies cited above, p. 277, n. 2, see I. Iu. Pisarev, ed., *Metodologicheskie voprosy izucheniia urovnia zhizni trudiashchikhsia* (Moscow, 1959); 2 (Moscow, 1962); P. Krylov, "Nekotorye voprosy metodologii perspektivnogo planirovaniia povysheniia urovnia zhizni naroda," *Planovoe khoziaistvo,* No. 8 (1960); B. Smirnov, "Ratsional'nye normy potrebleniia," *Sovetskaia torgovlia* (November 1961).

in flour equivalent; 95.0 kilograms of potatoes; 164.0 kilograms of vegetables and melons; 110.0 kilograms of fresh fruits and berries; 40.0–44.0 kilograms of sugar; 90.0–100.0 kilograms of meat and meat products, and 184.0 kilograms of milk. For many product categories, these standards only represent aggregates of more detailed norms compiled for different subcategories. Similarly, it has been calculated that a member of an ordinary worker's family requires each year, on the average, 5.4 meters of woolen cloth, 37.2 meters of cotton cloth, and so on.

How are such norms established? For foodstuffs the norms are the result of a substantial research effort conducted under the leadership of the Nutrition Institute of the Academy of Medical Sciences of the U.S.S.R. For persons of different age, sex, and occupation an initial step was to formulate "physiological norms" for consumption of different food elements, i.e. calories, fats, minerals, etc., and then to construct an appropriate diet. This diet supposedly also takes into account "the tastes of the population living in different parts of the country and its habits of life. Besides, attention is given to the economic expediency of production of substitute products and certain other factors." [24]

Because specific physiological requirements do not obtain, the calculation of rational norms for nonfood goods admittedly has been difficult, but "rational limits for the utilization of clothing, shoes, cloth and many other goods can still be established with sufficient exactness. Of course, reference is understood to be to the reasonable needs of healthy, culturally developed people." [25]

How the norms have been compiled may be judged from calculations of those for cloth. Among other things, these

24. N. P. Kuznetsova and N. Ia. Kirichenko, "Ob opredelenii nauchno-obosnovannykh potrebnostei naseleniia v produktakh pitaniia," in Pisarev, ed., *Metodologicheskie voprosy, 2,* 242.

25. Smirnov, *Sovetskaia torgovlia* (November 1961), p. 14.

entailed the determination for persons of different age, sex, and region of an appropriate inventory of clothing. This inventory was arrived at in this manner: "So it was arbitrarily (*uslovno*) assumed that 100 per cent of all (sic) women of each zone must have one everyday and one dress suit, one between seasons coat, a dress and a skirt of woolen cloth; in a zone of cold climate only 30 per cent of the males must have rain coats; in a temperate zone—40, and a hot zone—50 per cent." [26]

The rational norms often differ widely from present-day consumption standards in the U.S.S.R. For example, at current prices bread and grain products are projected to absorb 8.4 per cent of the average household's food budget, in place of the 18.5 per cent now allotted to these products. Outlays for meat and meat products are to rise from 19.3 to 24 per cent of total food expenditures.

The norms, therefore, are most readily applicable in the formulation of plans for the long run. Indeed, their chief application thus far has probably been in the work on the twenty-year plan that was recently published.[27] However, the norms are probably also being considered in the formulation of annual plans, although this is not certain.

So far as rational norms reflect household tastes, they are but a concrete representation of consumers' demand, and their consideration in principle introduces no new factor into the determination of targets for supplies of foodstuffs and manufactures for household consumption. However, they apparently also reflect tastes as the authorities feel they should be, hence planners' preferences. By implication, such preferences are now to be applied generally and in detail.

26. I. I. Nemchinov, "O ratsional'nom urovne potrebleniia sovetskim narodnom tkanei, odezhdy i obuvi," in Pisarev, ed., *Metodologicheskie voprosy, 2,* 266.
27. Actually, the norms cited above, pp. 299–300, refer to the population structure of the future, although at what dates is not clear.

In view of the limited study of consumers' demand in the
past, however, the rational norms may sometimes provide
a basis for determination of the mix of consumers' goods
more in accord with this standard than has been the case
thus far.

13 CAPITAL FORMATION

Concerning the determination of the share of the community's income devoted to investment in a Soviet-type economy, three theories might suggest themselves. All of them refer to the relation of the volume of investment to that of noncommunal consumption. Hence it is understood that all would have to be elaborated if allocations between investment and other final uses, including communal consumption, defense, and other collective goods, were also in question.

(1) The system's directors seek to ensure for any period a volume of investment corresponding to the savings households might wish to undertake. Reference is to the savings of households if the entire income of the community were at their disposal, although some of this would have to be taken from them in taxes to finance collective goods. The savings would also depend on the rate of interest offered.

Supposedly this corresponds to the rate of return, either "internal" or "external," on marginal investments.

(2) The concern is to realize the highest possible rate of growth of the community's income, or the highest possible level of income at some future time. The volume of investment is determined accordingly, but on the understanding that for any period, the larger is the volume of goods and services devoted to investment, the smaller must be the balance available for consumption. Depending partly on the previous level of consumption, workers might in consequence become progressively less interested to exert themselves. In fact, in the course of time, they might exert themselves less even if consumption only failed to increase. If standards were sufficiently reduced, workers would also become less capable of exertion. Hence as the volume of consumption is curtailed, the community's current income itself would tend to diminish, and beyond a point this would be true also of the additional income to be obtained subsequently from additional current investment. By implication the concern is to achieve a relatively high volume of investment, although not necessarily the maximum possible in any period.[1]

1. To be precise, investment is at a maximum during any period when on the margin a further reduction in consumption would cause an equal reduction in total output. For the simple community illustrated, investment and consumption exhaust the total output, and

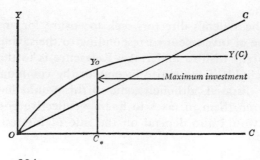

Capital Formation

(3) While seeking a large volume of investment in the interest of rapid growth, the system's directors consider that consumption standards not only affect effort but may have political consequences that have to be heeded. Perhaps more rather than less consumption is also regarded as desirable for its own sake. Hence, depending on the expansion of output that has occurred relative to a previous period, consumption standards may be allowed to rise concomitantly. At least, they tend to be higher than they might be where the concern is with their impact on effort alone. The consequences for investment and future growth, however, still are weighed.

To which, if any, of these theories does resource use in the U.S.S.R. conform? Western students of the Soviet economy seem often to assume that the rate of investment has tended to approach that called for by the second hypothesis. At least, this supposedly was so under Stalin. By implication I began this essay on the supposition that the rate of investment in any event must have surpassed that required by the first hypothesis. Neither theory, however, is definite as to the required allocation, and the third hypothesis is even less so, but the different principles may serve as a point of departure for an attempt to gain insight into the policy pursued. I first set forth some data on several pertinent aspects, and then consider the question at issue.

---

the maximum investment would be achieved when consumption, C, is at C_o, and output, Y, is at a corresponding level. The latter is understood to vary positively with the level of consumption over some range, though presumably after consumption has risen beyond a certain level further additions to it would have little effect one way or another on output. In realizing a maximum volume of investment, the system's directors might conceivably be sacrificing growth, or at least future output, if with a smaller investment and a larger consumption allocation workers might exert themselves more and use the available capital stock to produce a larger volume of output both currently and in subsequent periods.

305

The Economics of Soviet Planning

GROWTH AND ALLOCATION OF INCOME

The aspects to be considered are the rate of growth of the community's income that has been achieved, the allocations made to investment and consumption, and resultant trends in consumption standards.

Rate of Growth. Under the five-year plans the national income of the U.S.S.R. has grown rapidly, although not nearly as rapidly as official claims might suggest. During the period 1928–60 the gross national product grew at an estimated average annual rate of 4.5 per cent (Table 13.1). For "effective years," the corresponding figure is 5.2 per cent, i.e. the

TABLE 13.1.

Rate of Growth of Real Gross National Product, U.S.S.R.

| | AVERAGE ANNUAL RATE OF GROWTH, PER CENT, WITH OUTPUT | |
	In Ruble Factor Cost of 1937	As Composite Series, 1937 Base
1928–37	4.8	11.9
1937–40	3.4	3.4
1940–50	2.1	1.8
1950–60	7.0	7.0
1928–60	4.5	6.3
1928–60, "effective years"	5.2	7.3

Sources: Underlying indices have been adjusted for changes in territorial coverage. In the calculation of the rates of growth for effective years, the entire growth for 1928–60 is imputed to the twenty-eight peacetime years. For output in both ruble factor cost of 1937 and as a composite series, with 1937 base, serial data compiled in *Real SNIP*, pp. 210, 217, 261, for the period 1928–55 have been extrapolated to 1960 by reference to a computation in terms of 1955 ruble factor in Stanley H. Cohn, "The Gross National Product of the Soviet Union," in *Dimensions*, p. 75. The index numbers in *Real SNIP*, p. 210, represent the growth of output before adjustment for territorial changes. On the latter adjustment, see *Real SNIP*, p. 218. Also, of two alternative series compiled in terms of 1937 ruble factor cost, reference is to the one where the factor cost revaluation is extended within retail sales.

306

Capital Formation

average annual rate of growth, if the entire growth realized during the thirty-two-year period is imputed to the twenty-eight peacetime years. This is a crude but probably conservative way of allowing for the effects of the war. Thus the Russians did not reattain the 1940 level of output until 1948. The expansion of output to this level and beyond was facilitated, however, by reparations and by the fact that for a time there were partially damaged plants which might be renovated and restored to full use with limited investments.

I refer to the growth of the gross national product calculated in terms of "ruble factor cost" of 1937. The period of the five-year plans witnessed a radical change in the structure of the Soviet economy in respect of both output and costs. For this reason, the measures of growth are rather different if instead of the series in terms of ruble factor cost of 1937 one considers an alternative series obtained as a composite. In the latter the underlying index numbers for different years are supposed to approximate those that would result if each comparison with 1937 were made in terms of ruble factor cost of the given year. Although the resulting series is of a novel sort, it has a claim to be considered along with the more conventional one in terms of 1937 ruble factor cost.[2] According to the "composite series, 1937 base," the gross national product grew during 1928–60 at an average annual rate of 6.3 per cent. For effective years the corresponding figure is 7.3 per cent.

These are rates of growth for the period of the five-year plans generally. The change in economic structure that has occurred under these plans was concentrated especially in the years of the first two plans. For this reason our two series yield widely different measures of growth for this interval, one being at about the average level for the entire period 1928–60, the other much above this level. Within

2. *Real SNIP,* ch. 3.

307

the period of the first two plans, the tempo probably was relatively slow under the first and relatively rapid under the second. At least, this was so for the measures in 1937 ruble factor cost.[3] Corresponding measures in terms of the composite series are not available.

Under the third five-year plan, up to the war, the tempo of growth declines according to both measures, although much more markedly according to the composite series. The war, of course, brought a decline in output. For this reason, with either sort of measurement, the rate of growth for the entire decade 1940–50 remains low despite the rapid recovery in the postwar years. For the years since 1950 the two series converge and growth is again relatively rapid. However, the tempo probably was lower in the late than in the early 50s.

Allocation of Income. On the eve of the five-year plans, the Russians were already devoting to investment a notably large share, some 25 per cent, of their gross national product (Table 13.2). In the years immediately following, they devoted still more to investment, although in 1937, the final year of the Second Five Year Plan, the rate of investment was again at the 1928 level.[4] Subsequently, in the years

3. The data are to appear in a study by Richard Moorsteen and Raymond Powell now in progress on the Soviet capital stock.

4. In other words, the rate of investment rose after 1928 and then declined to the 1937 level. Reason to think that it did so is found principally in the calculation in Francis Seton, "Social Accounts of the USSR in 1934," *Review of Economics and Statistics, 36* (1954), 290–308. Seton finds that in 1934 the Russians allotted 26.5 per cent of their gross national product to investment. The corresponding figure for 1937, according to my own calculations, was about 20 per cent. Reference is to the rate of investment in terms of prevailing rubles, but I believe the difference between 1934 and 1937 would be similar for the rate of investment in terms of prevailing ruble factor cost. It is on the latter that I focus in the text. On trends in this rate, see also below, n. 6.

Capital Formation

TABLE 13.2.

Shares of Final Uses in Gross National Product, U.S.S.R.
(percentages)

		Calculations of Real SNIP, Extended						Calculations o Bornstein-Cohn	
	1928	1937	1940	1944	1950	1955	1958	1955	1960
Household consumption									
In current ruble factor cost	64.7	52.5	51.0	36.4	45.5	49.2	50.0		
In 1937 ruble factor cost	79.5	52.5	49.4	31.8	45.7	48.0			47.1
In 1955 ruble factor cost									
Communal services									
In current ruble factor cost	5.1	10.5	9.9	9.1	10.8	10.0	9.5		
In 1937 ruble factor cost	4.6	10.5	10.3	7.9	10.2	8.7			
In 1955 ruble factor cost									10.1
Household consumption, incl. communal services									
In current ruble factor cost	69.8	63.0	60.9	45.5	56.3	59.2	59.5	58.9	
In 1937 ruble factor cost	84.1	63.0	59.7	39.7	55.9	56.7			
In 1955 ruble factor cost								58.9	57.2
Government administration, including NKVD									
In current ruble factor cost	2.7	3.2	3.8	3.7	4.8	2.6	2.0	2.9	
In 1937 ruble factor cost	2.1	3.2	3.9	3.0	4.3	2.1			
In 1955 ruble factor cost								2.9	
Defense									
In current ruble factor cost	2.5	7.9	16.1	36.8	10.9	10.3	6.8	13.0	
In 1937 ruble factor cost	1.3	7.9	17.3	44.1	12.9	13.1			
In 1955 ruble factor cost								13.0	10.2
Gross investment									
In current ruble factor cost	25.0	25.9	19.2	14.3	27.9	27.9	31.6	25.2	
In 1937 ruble factor cost	12.5	25.9	19.1	13.1	26.9	28.1			
In 1955 ruble factor cost								25.2	32.6

Sources: *Real SNIP*, p. 237; Nancy Nimitz, *Soviet National Income and Product*, RAND RM-3112-PR, p. 16; Morris Bornstein, "National Income and Product," in *Comparisons*, Part II (Washington, 1959), p. 380; Stanley H. Cohn, "The Gross National Product in the Soviet Union," in *Dimensions*, p. 72. As between *Real SNIP* and Bornstein-Cohn data, the different end use categories often vary in scope. Among other things, "defense" in the latter probably includes some outlays classified elsewhere in the former. Note also that in the Bornstein-Cohn data "government administration" in 1960 was included under "government consumption," which is here shown as "communal services."

before the German attack, the rate of investment declined, and during the war it fell still further, but by 1950 it was again at a relatively high level, surpassing even that of 1928 and 1937. More recently it has tended to increase still more, amounting to 31.6 per cent in 1958.

The share of household consumption in the gross national product has also fluctuated, but here the trend has been downward. Thus in 1928 household consumption accounted for 64.7 per cent of the gross national product. Toward the end of the First Five Year Plan the corresponding share was much reduced, and, while it probably rose subsequently, in 1937 it was but 52.5 per cent. By 1940 it had fallen somewhat more, and during the war it dropped precipitously. After the war it rose again, but as late as 1958 it still had not surpassed the 1940 level.

Reference is to household consumption other than communal. In considering the foregoing trends, therefore, it should be observed that under the five-year plans communal consumption, particularly health care and education, have tended to rise relative to the gross national product. Both household consumption and investment have also had to compete throughout with defense outlays. The latter too have tended upward since 1928. Such outlays, however, rose sharply immediately before and during the war, and then fell immediately after.[5]

I have been considering shares in the gross national product calculated in current ruble factor cost; that is, the gross national product of any year is calculated in ruble factor cost values currently prevailing. While such measures are of interest, so also are the shares in the gross national product measured throughout in terms of ruble factor cost of a single year, 1937. Thus from the former one can gauge the changing allocation of available resources; from the latter, one can judge the changing disposition of the real volume of output.

Because of the changes in structure already referred to, particularly those in costs, the trends in shares in terms of constant ruble factor cost differ somewhat from those in terms of current ruble factor cost. Most importantly, under the plans, the share of investment still tends to increase

5. I refer essentially to defense outlays recorded in the government budget of the U.S.S.R. Particularly for recent years, these probably do not cover all military expenditures as generally understood. See *Real SNIP*, pp. 75–76, 362–63.

and that of household consumption still tends to decline. But especially under the first two five-year plans these movements are both distinctly more marked for shares in constant ruble factor cost. Allocations to communal consumption vary much as they did in current prices, but the upward trend in defense outlays observed before becomes more pronounced.[6]

From the data used in the computation of shares of the gross national product in constant ruble factor cost, we may also determine shares in increments of the gross national product during different intervals (Table 13.3). Thus gross investment absorbs nearly half of the increase in output realized under the first two five-year plans, and 60.7 per cent

TABLE 13.3.

Shares of Final Uses in Increment of Gross National Product, U.S.S.R.
(percentages)

	1928–37	1940–50	1950–55
Household consumption	9.1	29.4	53.2
Communal services	20.0	9.6	5.3
Government administration, including NKVD	5.0	6.1	(−) 2.8
Defense	18.5	(−) 5.8	13.5
Gross investment	47.5	60.7	30.9

Source: Real SNIP, p. 128. The underlying data are in 1937 ruble factor cost.

6. As was explained, under the first two five-year plans the share of investment in income in terms of current ruble factor cost probably rose and then declined. For output in constant ruble factor cost, I believe there was no comparable fluctuation, but probably the rate of investment rose much more sharply under the First Five Year Plan than it did under the Second. Moreover, toward the end of the former plan, the share of investment must have leveled off for a time, while at one point, 1933, even the volume dropped. There may also have been a decline in investment in constant prices in 1937. I rely here chiefly on data on investment in the forthcoming study of Moorsteen and Powell.

of that achieved from 1940 to 1950. For the interval 1950–55 the share of gross investment in the increment of output falls but is still 30.9 per cent. The share of household consumption in the increase in output under the first two five-year plans is only 9.1 per cent. For 1940–50, the corresponding figure is 29.4 per cent, but from 1950 to 1955 it is 53.2 per cent. Other final uses claim varying amounts of the increment of output during different intervals.

Attention has focused on gross investment. For net investment, trends have been much the same, but as rates of net investment go, those in the U.S.S.R. have been especially high (Table 13.4).

TABLE 13.4.

Share of Net Investment in Net National Product, U.S.S.R.
(percentages)

1928	10.3
1937	22.7
1940	15.3
1950	22.6
1955	23.3

Source: Net investment and net national product are calculated from data on gross investment, gross national product, and depreciation in 1937 ruble factor cost in *Real SNIP*, p. 128, and Abram Bergson, "National Income," in Bergson and Kuznets, eds., *Economic Trends in the Soviet Union*, p. 36. In the latter source net national product is net not only of depreciation but also of part of capital repairs. Net national product here is net only of the former.

To return to the rate of investment in current ruble factor cost, while this was already high in 1928, it probably only had become so in the course of a few preceding years. Thus according to official data the rate of net investment on the eve of the five-year plans was:[7]

7. Gosplan, *Kontrol'nye tsifry narodnogo khoziaistva SSSR na 1928–1929 godu* (Moscow, 1929), pp. 82–83.

Capital Formation

	Net investment ÷ national income (percentages)
1925–26	15.9
1926–27	22.9
1927–28	21.3
1928–29 (plan)	23.0

These data refer to national income according to the Soviet concept,[8] and valued in ruble prices of 1925–26. But a sharp upward trend is indicated in the rate of investment in terms of the national product as understood here and valued in current ruble factor cost.

Consumption Standards. By 1928, per capita consumption probably had fully recovered from the extraordinary losses suffered under the impact of World War I, revolution, and civil war. Even the low Tsarist standard was enjoyed only briefly, however, for under the First Five Year Plan per capita consumption again declined. Of this decline we have no accurate quantitative measure, but that it occurred is evident from the reduction in farm output by one-fifth under wholesale collectivization, the expanding exports of such products and familiar facts concerning the concomitant widespread shortages, and in some rural areas actual famine.

It is chiefly to this period that Western authorities attribute the "deficit" of many millions in Soviet population that is observed in the late 1930s. Although the loss was only partly due to the reduction in consumption, it speaks more eloquently than any statistical measure of consumption of the privations that were endured.[9]

8. *Real SNIP*, p. 3.
9. On farm output, see Johnson and Kahan, in *Comparisons*, p. 205. On population trends, see Frank Lorimer, *The Population of the Soviet Union* (Geneva, 1946), ch. IX, and Eason, *Soviet Manpower*, pp. 16 ff. Famine conditions have been reported primarily for early 1933, immediately after the conclusion of the First Five Year Plan.

313

Under the Second Five Year Plan, per-capita consumption rose and by 1937 was again at the 1928 level. I refer to per-capita consumption in ruble prices of 1937 (Table 13.5). As for national income, the trend is more favorable if

TABLE 13.5.

Indices of Household Consumption per Capita and per
Employed Worker, and Nonfarm Real Wages
(1937 = 100)

	1928	1937	1940	1944	1948	1950	1952	1954	1955	1958
Household consumption per capita										
In ruble prices of 1937	103	100	95.6	66.0		116			160	191
Composite, 1937 base	82.2	100	95.6	64.3		110			155	
Household consumption per employed worker										
In ruble prices of 1937	131	100	95.2			103			145	172
Composite, 1937 base	105	100	95.2			97.9			140	
Real wages of nonfarm workers, net of taxes and bond subscriptions, but gross of pensions										
In ruble prices of 1937	180	100	93.3	70.5			116	145		167
Composite, 1937 base	123	100	89.5	63.3			107	137		

Sources: For 1928–55, for household consumption per capita and per employed worker, see *Real SNIP*, p. 252. In each case, for purposes of calculating household consumption, housing, services and farm income-in-kind were valued initially at ruble prices, but then revalued to assure greater comparability with foodstuffs and manufactures included at ruble prices. Data on nonfarm real wages are those of Janet Chapman as adapted in *Real SNIP*, p. 256. While ruble values are unadjusted, I believe the results would be little affected if housing and services were revalued as is done in the calculation of household consumption. Here, of course, no farm income in kind is included. For 1958, for household consumption per capita I cite an index derived in Janet Chapman, "Consumption," in Bergson and Kuznets, eds., *Economic Trends in the Soviet Union*, p. 238. As Mrs. Chapman explains, this index may be too high. The corresponding index for household consumption per employed worker is derived from Mrs. Chapman's index for consumption per capita. For real wages, I allow for a 15 per cent increase from 1954 in the light of data compiled in Chapman, *Real Wages in Soviet Russia since 1928*, pp. 181 ff.

reference is made instead to serial data of a composite sort, but here the more conventional measure in 1937 values is probably more reliable.[10] According to either series, however, per-capita consumption declined once more in the years before the war. During the war it fell sharply, and, while it recovered afterward, in 1950 per-capita consump-

10. See *Real SNIP*, chs. 3, 10, and pp. 249 ff.

tion was still only slightly above the 1937 level. The Fifth Five Year Plan, however, finally brought a sharp increase to new high levels, and standards have continued to improve since. Estimated 1958 levels may represent an overstatement, however, and progress in any event slowed after that year.[11]

For his years of denial under Stalin, therefore, the ordinary citizen only recently has been receiving some reward, but he would have fared worse if not for the increase in effort expended. Thus, since 1928 there has been a marked increase in the "rate of participation" of the adult population in gainful employment. Chiefly through the increase in employment of women in industry and their more intensive use in agriculture, the rate of participation has tended to increase throughout, but the rise was particularly marked under the first two five-year plans.

Relative to the labor expended to earn it, therefore, consumption has evolved even less favorably than it has relative to the population. Consumption per employed worker fell at first even more than per capita consumption, and, while here, too, the Second Five Year Plan brought a recovery, consumption per employed worker in 1937 was still below the 1928 level (Table 13.5). This is true for both measures. According to that in terms of 1937 ruble prices, however, consumption per worker fell by nearly one-fourth. After 1937, consumption per worker varied more or less as did that per capita, but in the 50s the former tended to be lower than the latter. Hence, according to the more reliable series, it is only in the late 50s that consumption per worker much surpassed the 1928 level.

Such have been the trends in consumption standards for the population generally. Interestingly, for the industrial population, consumption per capita and per employed worker have tended if anything to evolve even less favorably. At least this has been so for consumption per worker

11. Golden, in *Dimensions*.

(see Table 13.5, the series on nonfarm "real" wages), and it has probably been so also for consumption per capita. How the farm population fared is not so clear, but it should not be assumed that, because the industrial standards evolved less favorably, farm standards evolved more favorably than did those for the population generally. On the eve of the five-year plans the city worker generally lived much better than the peasant, and the divergence in the experience of the city population, on the one hand, and the population generally, on the other, must be due to some extent to the improvement that farmers often experienced simply because they came to the city. However, the city worker in the course of time has tended to lose some of his initial advantage over the rural worker.

INVESTMENT POLICY

What may be concluded as to the government's policy on investment? Of particular interest is the policy pursued in peacetime years other than those immediately preceding the war, which together with the war years clearly were rather special. For such peacetime years, the rate of investment realized in the U.S.S.R. is not unmatched in the experience of noncommunist countries, but it is not easy to find a precedent for the sharp increase in this rate to a relatively high level that occurred in the U.S.S.R., at least where measures are in constant values:

> The distinctive characteristic of the over-all capital formation proportion for the USSR is not its high level, but the rapidity with which this level was attained. With few exceptions (among them the United States) the long-term trends in capital formation proportions in most countries were upward—although this rise may not have begun until several decades after the country had entered the process of industrialization and may

have ceased while the growth of the country was still proceeding vigorously. But, with the single exception of Canada for 1896–1900 and 1901–10 among the twelve countries for which we have data, in none did the proportion double within a few years [as was so] for the USSR . . .[12]

The Soviet experience becomes the more noteworthy when it is considered that the sharp increase in the rate of investment to a high level was superimposed on sharply rising defense expenditures; and this still says nothing of the increases in allocations to communal services. Moreover, the rates of investment finally achieved also seem relatively exceptional if reference is to the net rather than the gross allocation.[13]

In any event, after the recovery from the consequences of World War I, revolution, and civil war, the Soviet citizen consumed annually perhaps $215 in goods and services at U.S. dollar prices of 1955. Even in relation to this meager standard, the years that followed under Stalin were almost all years of denial. This was so despite the increase in effort exerted. The deprivations were general, though in the course of time the industrial worker lost some of the initial advantage he enjoyed over the peasant. Under Khrushchev, standards finally have been raised, but they have been at a relatively high level for only a brief period.

In sum, for the rate of investment in the U.S.S.R., we may rule out the first of the three theories—that is, the one according to which the concern is to approximate the volume of savings households might wish to undertake. Of course, the theory presupposes that the entire income of the community is at the disposal of households, and depending on

12. Simon Kuznets, "A Comparative Appraisal," in Bergson and Kuznets, eds., *Economic Trends in the Soviet Union*, pp. 353–54.
13. Cf. Table 13.4, above, with Table VIII-13 ibid., p. 354.

the manner in which income other than that earned by the households is distributed among them, they might wish to save very diverse amounts. But in order to generate the savings required, the distribution would certainly have had to be unusual.

What of the two alternative theories? It is not easy to imagine that Stalin could have generated much more investment than he did, at least in his early years. But if Stalin was a "maximizer" in this sphere, Khrushchev must be more of a "satisficer." Partly because of Stalin's very success as a maximizer, however, Khrushchev no doubt has been more constrained by the need to provide incentives for effort. And having opted, at least for the time, in favor of a more permissive political environment, as by all accounts he has done, he must have less discretion in respect of investment for this reason too. One wonders, therefore, whether under Khrushchev, too, the rate of investment could have been much higher than it has been. But these are large and complex questions which, in the light of the facts set forth, the reader will wish to judge for himself.

In trying to grasp the policy pursued on the rate of investment, I have tacitly assumed that the system's directors have been concerned with the growth of output generally. But their concern has been primarily with the output of industry. The priority accorded to industry, especially heavy industry, obviously was a cardinal economic feature under Stalin, and continues to be so under Khrushchev, though it is not quite so overriding. The government's policy on the rate of investment must be viewed in this light, but under Soviet conditions emphasis on heavy industrial output must in any case have been in order even if the more basic concern was with total output. Thus, under the five-year plans, the government has sought systematically to limit Soviet dependence on foreign trade, although here, too, it has not been as extreme lately as it was before. Given this policy of

autarky, the Russians have had to produce the great bulk of
the investment goods needed to implement their grandiose
investment programs. Of course, heavy industry produces
not only investment goods but munitions; but we take the
government's policy on defense as a datum. Hence variations
in investment and in heavy industrial output come essentially to the same thing.[14]

I have also assumed that the rate of investment realized
has been the one sought by the system's directors. To what
extent has this been so? In the U.S.S.R., the party and government necessarily have sought to reserve for themselves
determination of the volume of available output allotted to
investment. Although central control over capital formation has been incomplete, the system's directors should have
been able to guarantee a rate of investment more or less as
they have desired, if not in any one year then in the course
of time.

Thus the all-union Council of Ministers itself passes on
plan targets for aggregate investment.[15] For government and
cooperative organizations it passes on the planned volume of
such outlays not only in the aggregate but by sector and
type. For the bulk of new investments in fixed capital, individual projects must also be approved by title at a relatively

14. As was explained, however, a high level of investment at any
one time may not ensure achievement of a high level of total output
at a future date. If this is so for output generally, it is also for heavy
industrial output. Hence, the government in effect may have had to
choose between two courses, one stressing heavy industrial output
"today" and another stressing heavy industrial output "tomorrow."
One surmises that up to a certain point it must often have been more
concerned with tomorrow, although at least in the thirties tomorrow
must have tended to merge with today as time passed, and the need
for munitions capacity became ever more pressing. From available
information, however, it is not easy to be sure that this was the policy
actually pursued.

15. See Kaplan, *Capital Investments in the Soviet Union, 1924–1951*,
pp. 1–35; Nove, *The Soviet Economy*, pp. 108–09.

high level, either by the Council of Ministers or by other agencies acting on its behalf. Decision making on investment outlays still is in some degree decentralized, but to control the volume of investment generally the central authorities are able to direct administratively not only those immediately in charge of the pertinent activities but others supplying them with funds, equipment, and materials. In the case of collective farms, central control is more limited, but even here the central authorities are able to regulate allocations to indivisible funds. They may also influence investment through control over credit and supplies of equipment and building materials. Through its authority over credit and supplies of materials, the government is also able to exercise substantial control over private investment, like that in housing.

I refer to the arrangements that have prevailed recently, but the discussion applies broadly to the entire period of the plans, at least since wholesale collectivization. Central control over capital formation, however, has only been perfected in the course of time, and conformity of the rate of investment realized to that sought must have varied correspondingly. Even before wholesale collectivization, the central authorities must have been able to exercise substantial control over the volume of investment, but especially in agriculture not as much as in more recent years.

The comparative performance regarding heavy industrial and consumers' goods, however,[16] suggests that the share of investment in total output has rarely conformed closely to the planned amount. The divergence from the plan must testify to the limitations of central control, but the rate of investment has tended to surpass rather than fall short of the goal, and this outcome is not inconsistent with the policy on investment that has been described. Conformity to plan in respect to the rate of investment probably has

16. See above, pp. 84, 283.

increased in the course of time, partly because of the increase in central control, but partly because of a change in policy.

If the rate of investment has been more or less the one sought, it need not have been sought with an awareness of the implications. For example, has the government been aware of the consequences for consumption standards? The question may seem odd, but to anyone familiar with the dubious official statistics on real national income and the strange official claims on consumption standards it is in order. But for purposes of appraising consumption standards, the government has had at its disposal a vast amount of statistical data, much of it relatively reliable, and one must assume that it has kept itself as well informed on this matter as it has desired to be.

Also to say that the government has been able to realize the volume of investment that it has sought is not at all to say that it has been able to assure that the investment would promptly come to fruition in productive use. As the ever-recurring complaints in the Soviet press testify, it actually has had notable difficulties in the latter sphere. But this is not of special concern here.

When the rate of investment has varied from the one sought, it may have exceeded as well as fallen short of the latter. Especially in the early years under Stalin, the rate of investment may sometimes have even exceeded that appropriate to a maximization of growth. In any event, in this period the government found it expedient to reduce the share of output invested from a peak reached sometime after the initiation of the First Five Year Plan. The volume of investment at one point even fell absolutely.[17]

The first theory of investment in a Soviet-type economy requires that investment correspond to the volume of savings households desire to undertake. This principle is of a piece with the efficiency rules considered for other spheres of re-

17. See above, n. 6.

source use. In other words, it presupposes a concern with consumers' welfare, construed in terms of household preferences as they see them. So far as the principle has been violated, therefore, we must conclude that the system's directors have sought ends other than consumers' welfare as so understood.

Nevertheless, even proponents of consumers' welfare as an end often find fault with this standard as so understood. Furthermore, to take household preferences as indicative of consumers' welfare, it has been urged, is especially dubious where choices are made between present and future. Owing in part to a defective "telescopic faculty," consumers systematically undervalue future utilities. Hence, properly construed, a concern for consumers' welfare may require a much larger volume of investment than households themselves might wish to generate. Indeed, for a protracted period, the rate might properly be limited only by the need to maintain incentives. In the alternative theory where the concern is to maximize growth, this also serves as a constraint. At least in this sphere, therefore, might not the concern with growth in the U.S.S.R. reflect only a concern for consumers' welfare after all? In other words, might not the system's directors have simply construed this standard as many of its proponents would have them do anyhow?

To take such a view one would have to disregard innumerable Soviet pronouncements explaining why rapid growth actually has been sought, pronouncements according to which the concern is ultimately to assure higher consumption standards but hardly less to achieve other aims. I refer to statements like this one made by the Fifteenth Congress of the Communist Party in December 1927, as it deliberated on the policies to be pursued under the projected First Five Year Plan:

> In the formulation of the five year plan for the economy, as in the formulation of any economic plan con-

structed for a more or less lengthy period, it is necessary to try to attain the most favorable possible combination of these elements: expansion of consumption of the industrial and peasant masses; expanded reproduction (accumulation) in state industry on the basis of expanded reproduction in the economy generally; a faster tempo of economic growth than is realized in capitalist countries and an unfailingly systematic increase in the share of the socialist sector, which is a decisive and cardinal force in all economic policy of the proletariat . . .

In accord with the policy of industrialization of the country, the production of means of production must be strengthened first of all, in order that the growth of heavy and light industry, transport, and agriculture—that is, the productive demand of these branches—should be essentially met from the domestic industrial output of the U.S.S.R. The highest tempo of *growth* must be assigned to those branches of heavy industry, which will raise in the shortest time the economic power and defense capacity of the U.S.S.R., which will assure the possibility of growth in the case of economic blockade, which will weaken dependence on the capitalist world, and facilitate transformation of agriculture on the basis of a higher technique and collectivization.[18]

Or like this, made by Khrushchev in presenting to the Twenty-Second Congress of the party in October 1961 a draft of its new program:

In the course of two decades the material-technical basis of communism will be created in the U.S.S.R. This is the chief economic task, the basis of the general line of the party . . . This will enable us to dispose of these most important tasks:

18. *Vsesoiuznaia Kommunisticheskaia Partiia (B) v resoliutsiakh i resheniiakh* . . . , Part II (Moscow, 1936), pp. 240 ff.

First, to create productive forces of unparalleled capacity and to [enable us] to occupy the first place in the world in respect of output per capita;

Secondly, to assure a labor productivity that is the highest in the world, which in the last analysis is the most important, most basic for the victory of a new social structure, to arm the Soviet people with the most advanced technique, to convert labor into a source of joy, of inspiration and creativity;

Thirdly, to develop the production of material goods for the satisfaction of all needs of Soviet man to assure him the highest consumption standards for the entire population . . . ;

Fourthly, gradually to transform socialist into communist production relations . . . ;

Finally, only in the process of constructing the material-technical basis of communism can we win the economic competition with capitalism, always maintain the defenses of the country at a level allowing us to smash any aggressor who might be bold enough to raise his hand against the U.S.S.R., against the socialist world . . .

Naturally the creation of the material technical basis of communism will require huge means . . . Will not the mobilization of such huge means be connected with difficulties and sacrifices, as in the period of industrialization? We have all the grounds to answer this question in the negative . . .

Heavy industry has always played and will play the leading role in expanded reproduction. The party will continue unflaggingly to concern itself with its growth, considering this as the decisive condition for the creation of the material-technical basis for swift technical progress, as the basis for the strengthening of the defense capacity of the socialist state. At the same time, the party will exert every effort in order that heavy industry in an ever-increasing degree should ensure the increased output of means of consumption.[19]

From pronouncements like the foregoing, and from Soviet technical writings, one gains insight not only into the ends sought but into the manner in which the rate of investment has been determined. Reference is made repeatedly to one principle, which, while already implied, should be explained.[20] The principle—often designated as an economic law—is simply this: The rate of growth of the "means of production" must exceed that of the "means of consumption." In Soviet discussions, these two categories of goods usually are taken to be represented by the two corresponding divisions of industrial output in Soviet statistical practice, Group A and Group B. But obviously the same law is meant to apply to means of production and means of consumption generally. In this way, as is not always made clear, the immediate consequence is the rising share of investment in the national income already observed.

While the stated law obtains under socialism generally, it is understood that the government may find it appropriate to vary the margin between tempos at different times. Moreover, such variation is held to have occurred in fact in the U.S.S.R. so far as the margin between tempos was initially wide and more recently has narrowed. This development, too, is evident in the data set forth on the rate of investment, for the latter rose sharply under the early plans. More recently it has continued to rise, but less sharply.

In describing Soviet policy on capital formation I have focused on the period up to 1960. With available data, more recent developments are difficult to gauge, but the govern-

19. *Pravda* (October 19, 1961).

20. For a recent exposition, see L. Volodarskii, "Preimushchestvennyi rost proizvodstva sredstv proizvodstva i razvitie proizvodstva predmetov potrebleniia," *Vestnik statistiki,* No. 2 (1963).

ment must be pursuing much the same policy on capital formation as it did earlier. In any event, it has been devoting to investment a share of the national income which probably is as large as and may be larger than that so allotted in the late fifties. Even so, the tempo of growth of real national income has declined.

Such a decline already had set in after 1958, but it has continued since 1960, and in 1962 and 1963 became marked. The retardation is due partly to widely reported agricultural crop failures, and hence to some extent should prove transitory, but there are other causes as well. It may be significant, therefore, that the government at least thus far has not sought to increase the rate of investment radically as an offset. Even with the rate that has prevailed, however, consumption per capita can have increased relatively little in the last several years. The task of determining policy on investment must lately have become an especially difficult one for the system's directors.[21]

21. That the rate of investment in the last several years has been as high as, if not higher than, it was in the late 50s is implied by very diverse evidence, but I am guided especially on this matter by advice of Dr. Abraham Becker.

As for the rate of growth of real national income, we can see the decline in this aspect from Soviet official claims, although these appear generally to be inflated. Thus, according to these claims, the real national income of the U.S.S.R. increased at an average rate of 10.9 per cent a year during 1950–58. In 1959 it increased 8 per cent, and in 1960 by the same amount. The corresponding figures for 1961 and 1962 are 7 and 6 per cent. See *Narkhoz, 1961,* p. 597, and TSU, *SSSR v tsifrakh* (Moscow, 1962), p. 297. According to a CIA calculation, the gross national product of the U.S.S.R. increased by but 2.5 per cent in 1962 and again in 1963. See *New York Times* (January 9, 1964).

On recent economic trends in the U.S.S.R., and the nature of the problem of formulating investment policy, reference may be made to Abram Bergson, "The Great Economic Race: USSR versus USA," *Challenge* (March, 1963), pp. 4–6.

14 ECONOMIC MERIT

In this inquiry into Soviet working arrangements for resource use I have sought to describe and explain pertinent behavior patterns. In this final chapter I turn to the economic merit of the Soviet procedures. Actually, as usually understood, economic merit comes to much the same thing as economic rationality, with which I have been concerned throughout. But we may fittingly conclude by considering summarily economic merit.

Economic rationality must be understood in terms of ends pursued, and economic merit comes to entirely the same thing as economic rationality whenever economic merit is seen from the same standpoint. But, while such a construction is customary, it need not be adopted, and in the case of the U.S.S.R. there are reasons to proceed otherwise. Thus, where the system's directors pursue planners' preferences that diverge from consumers' welfare, we wish to gauge economic merit in terms not only of planners' preferences but of consumers' welfare. In preceding chapters, a basis was provided for appraisal from the latter as well as the former standpoint, for I took as a point of departure efficiency rules reflecting consumers' welfare. But, where the concern is with economic merit, the latter standard has an interest of its own.

Economic merit, however, still turns, like economic rationality, on economic efficiency and on equity of income distribution. I have focused primarily on economic efficiency, and shall continue to do so here. But it should be observed that the Soviet government has been notably secretive regarding income distribution. For years it has published practically no systematic data on the frequency of incomes of different magnitudes, although such data are commonplace in the West. Regarding the degree of inequality, such secrecy is in itself suggestive, but it also constitutes a formidable obstacle to a factual appraisal.

However, I have explored principles of determination of earning differentials among industrial workers and collective farmers. I have also presented some data bearing on the extent of such differentials. Considering these aspects, and available evidence on earnings differentials elsewhere, I believe we must suspend judgment on the central question of interest: the extent to which inequality of incomes has been reduced relative to that under private enterprise in the West. Private property income, it is true, has been largely eliminated in the U.S.S.R., but differentials in earnings that have been reported are often impressive. The inequality in incomes generally must be less than in, say, the U.S.A., but at least if account is taken of taxes and perquisites, one wonders whether the difference can really be very marked.[1]

1. On inequality of incomes, in addition to Chapters 6, 9, and 10 and the sources cited there, see Abram Bergson, "On Inequality of Incomes in the USSR," *American Slavic and East European Review,*

Economic Merit

But inequality is not the same thing as inequity. Among other things, is not the absence of property incomes in itself a source of greater equity in the U.S.S.R.? Some proponents of socialism have so argued, and the reader will wish to decide for himself how rightly; but he should consider that if private enterprise had persisted in the U.S.S.R., much of its earnings might have been saved. To this extent, therefore, expropriation of such earnings has meant not a redistribution of consumers' goods but simply that the savings now represent the result of decisions, not by many property holders but by a small group of political authorities.

Reference has been to equity from the standpoint of consumers' welfare. As for that where planners' preferences are the standard, suffice it to say that the system's directors have been able broadly to realize the principle they embrace: distribution according to "work done." They do not seem always to have been fully at ease with this principle, however, as witness their concern sometimes to meliorate its consequences for goods distribution. Also, their control over income distribution has been imperfect generally.

SOURCES OF INEFFICIENCY

If the inquiry has thus far shed light on economic efficiency, this has been done chiefly by elaboration of sources of economic inefficiency. To try now, therefore, to summarize findings in this regard, these related but distinct features appear to be the more consequential sources of Soviet economic inefficiency:

Value Theory. In the U.S.S.R. the system's directors have never considered themselves bound by the labor theory of

_10_ (1951), 95–99; DeWitt, *Education and Professional Employment in the USSR*, pp. 537 ff., 810–13; Edmund Nash, "Teachers' Salaries in the Soviet Union," in U.S. Bureau of Labor Statistics, *Labor Developments Abroad* (March 1962).

value, and even the preferred status of the labor theory as the only analysis of value that might overtly be espoused has lately begun to erode. But the labor theory has been influential and, in diminished degree, still is. As a result, economic efficiency has been impaired in diverse ways. By far the most outstanding is that where the choice of technology is in question, and here the labor theory is no longer as influential as it once was, for, as we have seen, an interest-like criterion once considered as dubious in this light has recently received quasi-official sanction. Yet Soviet project appraisal continues to have its limitations, and for these the labor theory probably is partly responsible. Under Soviet conditions, any resultant misuse of capital has been particularly costly because of the relative scarcity of this factor.

Working arrangements for nonlabor primary factors other than capital, particularly mineral resources and farm land, have as yet been little explored. But the labor theory should have had an important adverse effect here as well. More generally, at least until recently, the labor theory has been construed not as it might be in the light of contemporary Western analysis but much as it was long ago by Marx. Most importantly, it has been construed without the benefit of the fundamental notion of marginal value.[2] Almost inevitably, then, the very concept of an economic optimum that is integral to economic rationality has been understood only imperfectly. One wonders, therefore, whether in consequence decision making has not been adversely affected in some measure almost everywhere.

I refer to dubious principles of resource use the application of which has been a corollary of adherence to the labor theory. Another closely related source of inefficiency is dubi-

2. For further discussion, though from different standpoints, see Oscar Lange and Fred M. Taylor, *On the Economic Theory of Socialism* (Minneapolis, 1938), appendix; and P. J. D. Wiles, *The Political Economy of Communism* (Oxford, 1962), ch. 3.

ous principles of price formation of similar origin, and resultant miscalculations where alternatives are appraised in monetary terms. I shall refer below to limitations of ruble prices as a source of inefficiency, and shall consider there those due to the labor theory.

Where there has been a departure from the labor theory, the alternative, at least implicitly, has sometimes been contemporary Western theory, but not always, for the alternative to the labor theory has often been no theory. And this too must have been a source of waste, for given the aversion to principle, arbitrariness was unavoidable. Such arbitrariness, however, is not easily disentangled from that originating in the feature to which I now come.

Administrative Burden on Superior Agencies. Contrary to a prevalent impression, responsibilities for resource use have been delegated to a significant extent in the U.S.S.R., even to the lowest level of the vast administrative apparatus which determines resource use—that is, to the management of individual enterprises. The fact remains, however, that economic decision making has been notably centralized.

Another source of inefficiency is found in this feature, for in seeking to carry out the onerous responsibilities which they bear, superior agencies at all levels have often found themselves without the information needed for adequate and timely appraisal of alternatives, or if such information is at their disposal, without the capacity to process and digest it sufficiently for such appraisal. Consequently, decisions again and again have had to be arbitrary, and resources again and again to be misused. This has been so not only when decisions called for positive action, but also when either purposefully or by default there has only been inaction.

Since prices are largely fixed by superior agencies, the arbitrariness necessarily has been a further cause, in addition to the labor theory, of limitations of ruble prices, and hence of miscalculations in monetary terms. But the arbitrariness also affects resource use more or less directly. Recall, for example, the difficulty, because of the sheer complexity of the task, in coordinating plan targets to assure that the projected mix of products is a desired one; the need of superior agencies to negotiate with inferior ones about targets for activities about which the former can only be partially informed; the inadequate and frequently erroneous data on the basis of which alternative technologies are appraised; and the deficient information on consumers' demand, although there probably is no impelling concern to allocate resources closely in accord with such demand anyhow.

In this study I have dealt only in part with decision making at superior levels, but among spheres where they play a cardinal role two chief ones passed by are determination of the volume and allocation of materials supply when capacity is variable, and determination of the volume and allocation of supplies of investment goods. Difficulties encountered in respect of materials supply can only have been compounded by the need to fix capacity concomitantly, and obviously also have their parallel in the case of investment goods. Gosplan no doubt has worn "steel blinkers," as Khrushchev has charged,[3] but it has not been alone in this practice, and among superior agencies generally one need not inquire far to become aware that blinkers of other materials have also been worn. This habit must originate variously, but it can only be reinforced by the fact that, even if only arbitrarily, it simplifies a most formidable task.

Given centralized decision making, the task of superior agencies would have been inordinate in any case, but in the

3. *Current Digest* (December 19, 1962), p. 9.

U.S.S.R. it must have been even more so because of the transient nature of organizational arrangements generally.

Price Formation. The extent to which ruble prices diverge from "scarcity values" perhaps is sometimes overstated, but prices must differ markedly from scarcity values where, as in the U.S.S.R., the tendency is to fix them in accord with average rather than marginal cost and with only limited concern for the current state of demand. Moreover, average cost has been calculated without any allowance for interest on fixed capital or any systematic charge for rents on extractive branches, although very recently the latter lacuna may have been filled after a fashion. And these fixed prices have been changed only infrequently.

I refer primarily to prices of basic industrial goods, but for processed foods and manufactures the only important novelty is the turnover tax with its widely varying rates. This tax brought prices of processed foods and manufactures closer to clearing levels than they otherwise would have been, but they hardly have corresponded to them, while any systematic relation to cost, either marginal or average, is difficult to perceive. We have explored the prices of other goods only unevenly, but circumstances generally could not have been very different from those described.

While such divergencies from scarcity values originate in the labor theory and the inordinate task of superior agencies, these are not the sole causes. Most importantly, while ruble prices have suffered from the labor theory, they have not benefited where the alternative has been no theory.

Whatever their cause, the divergencies have also contributed to the inefficiency. Thus, while the price system has suffered because of the inordinate task of superior agencies, this task has only been the greater because of the deficiencies in the price system itself. For being aware of these deficiencies, administrators have felt impelled to compile and

The Economics of Soviet Planning

digest even more information than might otherwise be needed, information not only of a summary monetary sort but of a detailed physical sort. And it is but another facet of the same phenomenon that deficiencies in ruble prices have been a cause as well as an effect of flexibility in regard to value theory, for principles of economic calculation usually have to be expressed in monetary terms. Given the deficiencies in ruble prices, the system's directors have only been the more hesitant to commit themselves to such principles. Thus, to refer again to the treatment of choices of technology, while application of an interest-like criterion here has been opposed on ideological grounds, that it entails monetary calculations has been an additional stumbling block. And now that an interest-like criterion has been sanctioned, the authoritative source of this endorsement still asks that project makers consider not only monetary data but also pertinent "physical indicators."

But, however much they consider physical aspects, superior agencies must still rely on monetary calculations in some degree, and the deficiencies in ruble prices become at this point a source of inefficiency more clearly in their own right, for manifestly the authorities must often have been led into miscalculations on this basis.

Not only at higher levels have monetary calculations been a basis for decisions. Under the *khozraschet* system, decisions have been affected generally. And where they have, they must again and again have been distorted.

In sum, the ruble price system fails to perform the function which, the primers teach, a good price system should —to convey reliable information on prevailing scarcities. This must be by no means the least of the causes of economic waste in the U.S.S.R.

Success Criteria. This feature is in a sense a corollary of the one just considered, for the chronic difficulties the government has experienced in formulating success criteria have

334

had various causes, but a principal one has been the limitations of ruble prices. Given these, it could not be easy to summarize in any meaningful way the results of managerial activity. At any rate, the government has not found it so, and here, too, there has been inefficiency. Managerial malpractices in concealing reserves, in violating quality standards, or in departing from the assortment plan sometimes may have permitted the system to function more effectively than it otherwise could, but they must still have been economically wasteful.

Success criteria have had to be formulated for managerial personnel both in the enterprise and at higher levels. I have focused on the former, but in engaging in dubious practices enterprise managers have often had the acquiescence if not active support of their superiors, and these too have had their foibles. Furthermore, at high levels as well as low, the dubious success criteria have been more deleterious in an environment where typically there has been a sellers' market for materials, and where materials procurement has been hazardous. Of course, such a market in a sense is but the obverse of the divergencies of prices from scarcity values.

Thus the phenomenon, curious in a planned economy, of managerial striving for self-sufficiency. This has been manifest in the enterprise in efforts to acquire excess stocks of scarce materials. It has been manifest in both the enterprise and at higher levels in the endeavor to acquire auxiliary services, to limit specialization and the like. A principal aim of the reorganization of industry in 1957 was to inhibit such practices, but departmentalism has sometimes been eliminated only to be succeeded by localism. In the *glavki*, which are subordinate to regional councils, departmentalism itself probably has not been liquidated.[4]

4. On managerial interest in "self-sufficiency" in the U.S.S.R., see David Granick, "Organization and Technology in Soviet Metalworking," *American Economic Review*, 47S (1957), 631–42; Nove, *The Soviet Economy*, pp. 196 ff.

In order to buttress more formal success criteria, the government has also relied on priorities. As revealed by the system's directors, these are supposed to guide decision makers generally, and decision makers often observe them. But as an instrument of control priorities are inherently blunt, and even choices made in their light must frequently be dubious. This must be so generally, but the distortion is only magnified where the priorities are implemented through the famous "campaign" form of administration. As the Russians themselves acknowledge, the campaign, whatever its merits, has its limitations as a method of allocating resources.

The system's directors nevertheless have still had reasons to rely on priorities as an instrument of control. But one must have been that alternative controls of a relatively sensitive kind often have to be in monetary terms. Hence here again divergencies of ruble prices from scarcity values have been a factor, for because of such divergencies monetary controls also have their limitations.

We also find here still another reason for the onerous burden of responsibility on superior agencies: the limitations of success criteria have made all the more difficult delegation of responsibility.

Collective Farm Agriculture. While I have referred primarily to nonfarm sectors, the sources of inefficiency described are found also in agriculture. The economic ills of this sector, however, no doubt have been to some extent special. This has been true particularly of the collective farm component. Even in industry incentive arrangements have had their limitations: Because of the onerous sales taxes wage rates on the margin must have tended to inhibit exertion, acquisition of skills, and assumption of responsibility. But in collective farm agriculture incentive arrangements have been especially unfavorable. The collective farmer like the industrial worker has been able to gain by using his talents productively, but as a residual claimant his reward has not been very impelling.

As a cooperative organization the collective farm supposedly has enjoyed a special relation to the government and party bureaucracy, but these authorities have not hesitated to intervene in the management of the farm, and arbitrary decision making by superior agencies cannot have been any less costly here than elsewhere. The extraordinary reforms in crop schemes, imposed with little regard to local circumstances, are only the most dramatic instances of a pervasive phenomenon. Then, too, overlapping of responsibility has been a source of difficulty generally, but especially so where the actuality of control has had to be cloaked with the symbols of autonomy.

In complex ways not easy to summarize, deficiencies in working arrangements must sometimes have been the more deleterious simply because agriculture has been the sector affected. Thus, despite all controls, the collective farmer must retain a greater measure of discretion over his productive activity than the factory worker. Hence weak incentives are the more important in the former case. Detailed circumstances of time and place must be considered in administration anywhere, but they become the more consequential in a sector where weather can be a decisive factor, and where a major input, land, is almost infinitely varied in character. If overburdened superior agencies disregard such circumstances, therefore, the costs must be especially great in agriculture.

Autarky. I have had little to say about foreign trade, but I should be remiss if I did not refer to the Soviet policy of self-sufficiency. Under this policy, since 1928 Russia's exports have averaged but 1 to 2 per cent of her national income. Exports of the United States, during the period 1869–

1913, averaged 6 to 7 per cent of total output; and while trade lately has been less important, exports in 1960 still amounted to 3.8 per cent of output.[5]

The relatively limited Soviet participation in trade may in part reflect factors other than the Soviet policy of self-sufficiency, and may have been a source of economic gains as well as losses. But the policy has been carried notably far, and the losses probably have been preponderant. Autarky, therefore, has been another source of economic inefficiency, and perhaps an important one.

We cannot always know the ends that the system's directors have pursued, but the foregoing aspects I believe have all been sources of economic inefficiency even from their own standpoint, for waste occurs equally in the light of diverse preferences. The inefficiency, it is true, has often been greater than it might otherwise have been because of the intense concern for growth. But it hardly is proper to conclude from this that the system's directors have been unconcerned about the inefficiency. But for the inefficiency, growth might have been even more rapid.[6]

Where the working arrangements have been inefficient, the system's directors have frequently had reasons to value

5. Holzman, "Foreign Trade," in Bergson and Kuznets, eds., *Economic Trends in the Soviet Union*, pp. 290, 313.

6. I am not sure I fully grasp Peter Wiles' very provocative arguments concerning "choice versus growth" (*Political Economy of Communism*, ch. XI), but it must be agreed that growth in the U.S.S.R. has had to be purchased in some degree at the expense of efficiency. Some sacrifice of efficiency has been unavoidable, since lump sum taxes that do not impair incentives are not feasible. There has thus been no way in which required investments could have been financed without some adverse effect on resource use. Then, too, when an economy expands, schedules of "costs" and "demand" (however conceived) shift, and with this an optimum must be more difficult to approach than when there is no expansion and schedules of costs and demand are unchanged. That the difficulty is also materially greater the more rapid the expansion is not so clear but may be true.

them apart from their material consequences. They have had ideological reasons, political reasons, and presumably personal reasons. Nevertheless, even from their standpoint the reasons may not always have been very good ones, and where they have been, the implication in part is only that, as with politicians anywhere, the system's directors have sometimes been constrained in their choices. But no doubt the working arrangements have often been immediately satisfying to them. Hence they should have felt compensated in some measure for the inefficiency.

Households must value the working arrangements differently, however, and from their standpoint the inefficiency is the more pronounced. Thus where consumers' welfare is the standard all the sources of inefficiency that have been listed remain so, and we must add another: the divergence of planners' from household preferences. This perhaps is not quite so great as is sometimes supposed, for the failure to conform to household preferences must often be unintentional, and therefore would represent a misallocation from the standpoint of both the system's directors and the households. But obviously household preferences have been supplanted in consequential ways. Most outstanding is that where choices are made between present and future. But household preferences have frequently been overridden also in respect to consumption structure, and with the elaboration of the new "rational norms" this practice threatens to become pervasive. Sometimes the system's directors must not have overridden but merely have been indifferent to household preferences. To the households the difference cannot have been material.

Even in terms of their own economic ends, the system's directors should perhaps have been more attentive to household preferences than they have been,[7] but the fact remains that such preferences have been violated. Where consumers'

7. See above, p. 8.

welfare is the standard, this has not been the least important source of inefficiency in the U.S.S.R.

When planners' preferences are the standard, it sometimes is assumed that there can be no economic inefficiency to speak of in the U.S.S.R. The system's directors necessarily act to assure that resource use conforms to their desires. Hence only when consumers' welfare is the standard is there economic waste. This is far from true, for even from the standpoint of the system's directors, resource use has its limitations, but no doubt the limitations are compounded from the standpoint of households.[8]

COMPARATIVE ECONOMIC EFFICIENCY

Economic efficiency represents performance relative to an economic optimum. The sources of inefficiency in the U.S.S.R. that have been described are such, therefore, to the extent that they cause resource use to fall short of this ideal. But the economic system which is the chief rival of that in the U.S.S.R., that based on private enterprise, also has its limitations from this standpoint. How does socialism as found in the U.S.S.R. compare in economic efficiency with the private enterprise system as found in the West?

Among the more important limitations of Western private

8. I said in the text that all the sources of economic inefficiency are such even where planners' preferences are taken as the standard. Strictly speaking, this would be so for autarky only if the system's directors should value a product in the same way regardless of origin, particularly whether domestic or foreign. This manifestly is not so, and while such differences in valuation as have prevailed have ultimately been political and military in origin, in accord with the usage adopted in this essay resource allocation reflecting such a difference would conform to planners' preferences, hence not represent a source of economic inefficiency from this standpoint. From the standpoint of household preferences, however, economic inefficiency still results.

enterprise are monopolistic business practices; trade union restrictions; distorting government measures, including farm controls, sales and income taxes, and tariffs; and cyclical and other extrafrictional unemployment. This is to say that sources of inefficiency in the two systems are sometimes similar; but they also differ.[9] In any case, one must weigh the respective causes of inefficiency under the two systems, and this is a difficult task. But waste due to causes of inefficiency such as prevail under Soviet socialism surely must be sizable, and related quantitative evidence, while still not very incisive, seems only to underline its magnitude. At least in comparison with private enterprise in the U.S.A., the presumption must be that Soviet socialism is the less efficient system.

The quantitative evidence consists chiefly of the results of an attempt to compare, for major factor inputs, aggregate productivity in the U.S.S.R. and U.S.A. Thus, in 1960, per unit of labor and reproducible capital the net national product of the U.S.S.R. was but 54.9 per cent of that in the U.S.A. (Table 14.1). In the calculation, output in both countries is valued in dollar prices of 1955, and labor and reproducible capital are aggregated with weights corresponding to their respective dollar factor shares. The Soviet economic system does not generate any meaningful ruble factor shares by means of which we could make a similar calculation in terms of ruble prices. But with output in ruble prices for 1955 and with labor and reproducible capital weighted by "synthetic" ruble factor shares, output per unit of major inputs is practically the same as in the

9. While similarities are evident here, they would be more marked if, following some analysts, we assumed that the business cycle is a more or less inherent feature of an industrial society, whether it be socialist or private enterprise. But even on theoretic grounds this notion is not very tenable, and one can hardly find any support for it in the Soviet experience. As we have seen, Soviet socialism has its economic deficiencies, and these are often reflected in fluctuations, but it is difficult to perceive a business cycle.

The Economics of Soviet Planning

TABLE 14.1.

Output, Factor Inputs, and Factor Productivity, U.S.S.R. versus U.S.A., 1960

| | | U.S.S.R. as Percentage of U.S.A.[b] | |
| | | With Selected Final Services Included | With Selected Final Services Omitted |
	Nature of Measurement		
Net national product	In 1955 ruble factor cost	34.1	32.3
	In 1955 dollars	67.7	63.0
Employment	Workers engaged	144.5	151.2
Employment, hypothetical	Workers engaged, adjusted hypothetically to equivalent male, eighth grade graduate	116.7	121.5
Reproducible capital, including nonfarm inventories	In 1955 rubles	34.7	48.0
	In 1955 dollars	45.6	72.8
Major inputs (employment plus reproducible capital)	With "ruble" weights[a]	62.6 (85.3)	86.2 (109.4)
	With dollar weights	123.4	140.9
Major inputs (employment, hypothetical, plus reproducible capital)	With "ruble" weights[a]	59.1 (76.9)	79.1 (95.4)
	With dollar weights	101.5	115.1
Net national product per worker engaged	With output in 1955 ruble factor cost	23.6	21.4
	With output in 1955 dollars	46.4	41.7
Net national product per worker engaged, hypothetical	With output in 1955 ruble factor cost	29.2	26.6
	With output in 1955 dollars	58.0	51.9
Net national product per unit of reproducible capital	With 1955 ruble valuations	98.3	67.3
	With 1955 dollar valuations	148.5	86.5
Net national product per unit of major inputs	With output in 1955 ruble factor cost and "ruble" weights for inputs[a]	54.5 (40.0)	37.5 (29.5)
	With output in 1955 dollars and dollar weights for inputs	54.9	44.7
Net national product per unit of major inputs, with employment hypothetical	With output in 1955 ruble factor cost and "ruble" weights for inputs[a]	57.8 (44.4)	40.8 (33.9)
	With output in 1955 dollars and dollar weights for inputs	66.7	54.7

Sources and methods are given in Appendix B.

a. Figures outside parentheses refer to calculations employing as factor input weights synthetic ruble shares, including for capital one reflecting an imputed 20 per cent interest rate. Figures inside parentheses were derived correspondingly, except that an interest rate of 8 per cent was imputed to capital.

b. The selected final services are education, health care, government administration, defense, and housing. Omission of these services means, in the case of output, exclusion of the recorded "value added" by labor and capital employed in their provision and, in the case of inputs, of the corresponding volume of the pertinent factor or factors employed.

computation in terms of dollar prices: 54.5 per cent. The synthetic ruble factor shares are obtained by imputing to labor the actual ruble wage bill, together with collective farm household earnings, and to reproducible capital a 20 per cent interest rate.

In accord with the usual Western conception, net national product includes final services, and correspondingly labor and capital include inputs of these factors to such services. We may usefully consider together with the above measurements, however, alternative ones resulting from an attempt to exclude from the net national product the recorded outputs added by labor and capital employed in certain final services, and from labor and capital employed, the corresponding inputs. I refer to these final services: education, health care, government administration, defense, and housing.

In the case of all but the last service, in the calculation of net national product output added to material inputs almosts always is measured simply by the volume of primary factors employed. Indeed, such output ordinarily is taken to correspond to employment of but a single factor, labor. This has also been the procedure here, but the inclusion of final services in this way is surely a dubious expedient, especially since the services in question have different places in the Soviet and U.S. economies. The notably high capital intensitivity of inputs to housing might alone be reason for the omission of this service, but where measurements are in ruble values, the procedure is also indicated by the inordinately low level of such values for housing services.

With the omission of the final services indicated (I shall refer to them henceforth as "selected final services"), output per unit of major inputs in the U.S.S.R. falls to 44.7 per cent of that of the U.S.A., when output in both countries is valued in terms of dollar prices of 1955 and when labor and reproducible capital are aggregated with weights corresponding to their dollar factor shares. When output in both countries is valued in terms of ruble prices of 1955 and inputs aggregated with weights corresponding to synthetic ruble factor shares, output per unit of major inputs in the U.S.S.R. falls to 37.5 per cent of that in the U.S.A.

The treatment of recorded final services apart, measurements of aggregate factor productivity have their limitations even in favorable circumstances, and the circumstances here are hardly favorable. Among other things, the comparative data on output and the two inputs are tentative and inexact, while, as was just indicated, meaningful ruble factor shares are not available. But in view of the relative scarcity of capital in the U.S.S.R. (in 1960 per worker engaged it was but 24 to 31.6 per cent of that in the U.S.A.; with the omission of selected final services, the relative volume of capital rises in the U.S.S.R., but per worker engaged it still amounts to but 31.7 to 48.1 per cent of that in the U.S.A.), a high rate of return relative to that prevailing in the U.S.A., 6.6 per cent, may be appropriate. Use of a lower rate than is assumed in any case only reduces Soviet factor productivity. To the extent that the comparative data on output and inputs are in error, however, the result probably is an understatement of Soviet factor productivity, although primarily in the measure in ruble values.[10]

10. To return to the question of the rate of return to be imputed to Soviet capital, I have argued elsewhere that for purposes such as that in mind here one might wish ideally to impute the rate that might be earned if, in relation to labor, capital were used no more and no less efficiently in the U.S.S.R. than in the U.S.A. (see Bergson and Kuznets, eds., *Economic Trends in the Soviet Union*, pp. 19–20), but probably there is more to say for referring instead to the rate actually earned on capital in the U.S.S.R. In any case, use of a relatively high rate of interest seems in order in view of the relative scarcity of capital in the U.S.S.R. However, the consequence is that the total income of capital relative to that of labor is far higher in the U.S.S.R. than in the U.S.A. Arguably, therefore, the 20 per cent rate is too high. On the other hand, this rate does not appear exces-

Economic Merit

Our concern here, however, is with economic efficiency, and from this standpoint we must consider that output per unit of major inputs as calculated does not depend on this feature alone. Furthermore, the import for the observed

---

sive in the light of the standard coefficients of capital effectiveness currently employed in the U.S.S.R. Anyhow, use of a lower interest rate reduces Soviet output per unit of inputs. Thus, with an 8 per cent interest rate, Soviet output per unit of inputs falls to 40 per cent of that of the U.S.A. (Table 14.1). With the omission of indicated services, the corresponding figure is 29.5 per cent.

In calculating ruble factor shares on the basis of the assumed rate of return on Soviet capital, it should be observed that these rates are taken to be earned on this capital as valued at prevailing ruble prices. Yet such prices for investment goods fail to reflect any interest charge on the capital used in their production, and while the prices do include "profits" and certain other nonlabor charges, the investment goods must be considered as undervalued where the interest rate is as high as 20 per cent. By implication, a factor share for capital calculated at 20 per cent of the ruble value of the capital stock actually represents what might be earned on such capital at a lower rate, perhaps about 15 per cent, when the capital is valued inclusive of interest. If an interest rate of but 8 per cent is assumed, however, the corresponding return implied on capital valued at prices inclusive of interest probably is not significantly different from 8 per cent. Of course, the standard coefficients of effectiveness employed in the U.S.S.R. also bear immediately on returns to capital when this is valued at prevailing ruble prices.

I refer below to a calculation of factor productivity in which farm land is included as an input. Where the calculation is in rubles, for this input too a synthetic factor share must be used. On this, and on the compilation of synthetic ruble factor shares generally, see Bergson, "National Income," in Bergson and Kuznets, eds., *Economic Trends in the Soviet Union,* pp. 19 ff.

Our comparative data are especially inexact regarding capital, and the Soviet capital stock probably is overstated relative to that of the U.S.A. For this reason further computations where the Soviet capital stock is arbitrarily decreased by as much as 20 per cent may be of interest: Output per unit of major inputs in the U.S.S.R. rises to 55.8 per cent of that of the U.S.A. where pertinent valuations are in dollars and to 59.4 per cent of that in the U.S.A. where pertinent valuations

difference in factor productivity of possible divergencies between the two countries in respect to other features is difficult to judge. But there is at least a presumption that a divergence in respect to economic efficiency is a factor.

Among the other features, of particular interest is the possible difference in quality between the typical Soviet and the typical American worker, and this especially is intractable.

---

are in rubles. With selected final services omitted, the corresponding figures are 45.3 and 40.3 per cent. In calculations in terms of ruble values, a 20 per cent rate of interest is imputed to capital. When valuations are in rubles, output per unit of major inputs in the U.S.S.R. may also be understated by several percentage points because of an understatement in Soviet output relative to that of the U.S.A.

In comparing output per unit of inputs in the two countries, however, one arguably should omit not only the selected final services but trade in consumers' goods, for the comparative data on output do not reflect at all the superior quality of services in such trade in the U.S.A. Additional labor and capital expended in realizing the superior quality, however, are fully represented in the comparative data on inputs. Should trade be omitted, it is safe to say that in both ruble and dollar prices the comparison would be altered materially in favor of the U.S.A.

In appraising the reliability of the comparative data on capital stocks, the reader should consider, together with the data underlying my calculations which are described below, Appendix B, related data appearing in K. Vinogradov, "Statistiki stroitel'stva—na uroven' novykh zadach," *Vestnik statistiki*, No. 2 (1962), 6; "Nauchnaia konferentsiia po voprosam metodologii . . . ", *Vestnik statistiki*, No. 6 (1963), 51; Michael Boretsky, "The Soviet Challenge to U.S. Machine Building," in *Dimensions*, pp. 69 ff.

In calculating the comparative levels of factor productivity in the U.S.S.R. and U.S.A., I have benefited from advice of Professor Simon Kuznets. Acknowledgment is to be made also to Dr. Rush V. Greenslade, who in a talk at Harvard in 1961 presented some early results of an attempt to compare relative outputs and inputs in the U.S.S.R. and the West. On the nature of the rate of return that is to be charged on capital in calculating ruble factor shares, and on the need to consider at this point the omission of interest charges from ruble prices, I have also benefited from discussions with Dr. Richard Moorsteen.

Economic Merit

Indeed, considering how different the two countries are
economically, culturally, and socially, one might wonder
whether the differences in output per unit of major inputs
could not be due entirely to this factor. Of course, if the
forces making for a difference in quality revolve about the
difference in economic systems, the observed divergence in
factor productivity still reflects in a deeper sense a difference
in economic efficiency. But other forces might also be opera-
tive. What, for example, of the fact that the two countries,
while both relatively advanced, still differ in length of their
experience with industrialization? This factor may well be
consequential here.

Of employed workers in the U.S.S.R. in 1960, however,
some 49 per cent were women. In the United States the corresponding figure was 33 per cent. Typically the Soviet
worker has had less schooling than the American worker.
Any inferiority in labor quality in the U.S.S.R. must be due
largely to these circumstances, and it seems illuminating that
a hypothetical allowance for the differences in sex and
schooling, which applies conversion factors that have been
used previously in the study of U.S. factor productivity, still
leaves output per unit of major inputs in the U.S.S.R. far
below that in the U.S.A. (Table 14.1).[11]

11. The inquiry into U.S. factor productivity referred to is E. F.
Denison, *The Sources of Growth in the United States* (New York,
1962). For the illustrative computation, a female worker in both
countries is taken to be qualitatively equivalent of 75 per cent of a
male worker. This corresponds to the rating used by Denison in the
light of differentials in earning between male and female workers
in the United States. Corresponding earnings data are not at hand for
the U.S.S.R., but the implied discount used for female labor probably
is too large for that country. In the United States, the lower earnings
capacity of females must reflect institutional barriers which the Russians claim with some basis have been removed in the U.S.S.R.

In both countries differences in schooling have been allowed for by
reference to a scale of earnings differentials imputed by Denison to
variations in schooling in the U.S.A. The scale of differentials is rather

The Economics of Soviet Planning

Output depends not only on inputs of labor and capital but on inputs of other productive factors and on other aspects. In gauging the import of this fact, we must consider that the Russians employ far more farm land than we; yet their land typically is of inferior quality. But extension of the calculation of factor productivity to include land, with Soviet inputs adjusted according to U.S. climatic analogues, appears scarcely to affect the results one way or the other.[12] As countries of continental dimensions, both the U.S.S.R. and U.S.A. are very well endowed with industrial natural resources. Both countries have also had ample opportunity to exploit economies of scale. On the average, however, the Soviet capital stock is younger than that in the U.S.A. For this reason, the former should tend to embody later technological knowledge. At least the Russians have had the opportunity to see that such is the case. But this should have resulted in a Soviet output per unit of major inputs that is higher, not lower, than in the U.S.A.[13]

arbitrary for the U.S.A., and can only be more so for the U.S.S.R. Curiously, however, the Denison scale is consistent with the reported results of a Soviet investigation into the relation of earnings and schooling in the U.S.S.R. for ordinary workers. See Aganbegian and Maier, *Zarabotnaia plata,* pp. 13–14. In any case, use of other scales for the Soviet Union seems to affect the outcome slightly.

In the calculation where selected services are included, in adjusting for differences in quality of labor it did not seem worthwhile to make any corresponding adjustment in output, though evidently this might have been in order since output is simply measured by labor inputs. In the absence of such an adjustment in output, however, there is further ground to feel that selected final services should be omitted.

Labor inputs for both countries are represented by workers engaged, the number being understood essentially as full time equivalents. In 1960 full time hours in the U.S.S.R may have somewhat exceeded those in the U.S.A.

12. See Appendix B.

13. Differences in technological knowledge embodied in different capital goods to some extent must be reflected, however, in the relative prices of such goods. This is probably more true of dollar than

Economic Merit

We have been considering features other than economic efficiency which might have produced the observed difference in output per unit of major inputs. Granted that such features cannot fully explain the difference, and that economic efficiency is also a factor, we must now consider that economic efficiency, too, has diverse facets, not all of which are reflected in factor productivity as measured. One of the two chief omissions is clearly favorable to the U.S.S.R., but important as it is, it could hardly shift the balance in favor of that country.

I have in mind, of course, unemployment. In our computation of factor productivity, reproducible capital is represented by the available stock, whether it is employed or not. Labor, however, is represented by the number of workers employed, and hence fails to reflect workers who are idle and seeking employment. In both countries some labor is unemployed. While the volume of such unemployment in the U.S.S.R. is unknown, no doubt it has been less than the 4 to 5 per cent of the labor force that tended to be unemployed in the U.S.A. during 1950–60. Therefore, relative Soviet productivity in utilizing all available factors has been somewhat greater than that in utilizing such supplies, including, in the case of labor, only employed workers. The relative improvement in the Soviet performance perhaps would be greater if account were taken also of economically

_____

of ruble prices, but so far as it is true at all the differences in technological knowledge should also be reflected in our comparative data on capital inputs. To a corresponding degree, therefore, the observed levels of productivity should be unaffected. Moreover, so far as the observed levels of productivity are affected in a manner favorable to the U.S.S.R., use of data on reproducible capital net of depreciation probably has a contrary effect, since the Soviet stock is younger than that of the U.S.A. and is subject to a smaller volume of depreciation. Yet current capital services are unlikely to be reduced correspondingly as depreciation is deducted. Hence, such services in the U.S.S.R. tend to be overstated relative to those in the U.S.A.

induced part-time work. Of course, unemployment also entails a loss of producers' surpluses—at least, if consumers' welfare is the standard—and this, too, must be considered.

The other facet of economic efficiency that output per unit of major inputs fails to reflect or reflects only imperfectly is the desirability of the output mix. Our measures of factor productivity may be viewed as indicative of the comparative capacity of the two countries to produce their respective output mixes. The implication is that per unit of major inputs the U.S.A. in 1960 was able to outproduce the U.S.S.R. in respect to either its own or the Soviet mix.

Probably this divergence is due in part to a difference in economic efficiency, but in appraising the latter we must also consider that even from the standpoint of the system's directors the output mix produced in the U.S.S.R. often leaves much to be desired. Where consumers' welfare is the end, the divergence from the optimal output mix is only compounded. Despite the limitations of the private enterprise system in this regard, the divergence from the optimum mix must be less in the U.S.A. than in the U.S.S.R., at least where consumers' welfare is the end. The replacement of household by planners' preferences in choices between present and future in the U.S.S.R. must itself lead to this result.[14]

14. On the question of the comparative capacity of the two countries to produce their respective output mixes, the calculation where output is in ruble prices bears primarily on the relative capacity in the two countries to produce the U.S. mix, while that where output is in dollar prices bears primarily on their relative capacity to produce the Soviet mix. Hence, the U.S. may enjoy a larger margin of superiority over the U.S.S.R. in respect of the U.S. than in respect of the Soviet mix.

Nevertheless, where output is in dollar prices, use is made here of market prices. As is well known, if output is so valued, the results indicate production capacity only if market prices correspond to factor cost. In the U.S.A., the degree of correspondences depends on the extent to which the output mix is optimal. But, even if the latter ideal is not realized, the comparison of output in dollar values prob-

Economic Merit

In order to appraise comparative economic efficiency, reference has been made to relative factor productivity in the two economies generally. But in view of the relatively low productivity and large number of workers in agriculture, was it not foreordained that output per unit of inputs for the economy generally would be low in the U.S.S.R.? Would it not be more interesting anyhow to compare factor productivity in industry alone? Since we are concerned with economic efficiency in the economy generally, I believe economy-wide measures of factor productivity are properly considered. The propriety of my procedure seems more evident when we consider that the calculations bear on relative capacity to produce either the Soviet or the U.S. output mix.

Relative factor productivity for industry alone, however, is an interesting question, but if we may judge from the tentative and sometimes conflicting data available, the Soviet performance must still be much inferior to that of the U.S.A. when measured in this way. The comparison for industry may be no more favorable to the U.S.S.R. than is that for the economy generally. This appears so even where for the economy generally selected final services are omitted. Even in terms of output per worker, Soviet industry probably is not as productive as is sometimes assumed. Because of the disproportionately large share of the total stock of capital employed, the Soviet performance in industry is still less impressive when measured by output per unit of major inputs.

ably would be little affected if valuation were at factor cost rather than in market prices.

In the alternative calculation, national income in both countries is valued at ruble factor cost. In fact, the valuation by this standard is only partial, and the standard itself has its limitation, but the comparative data compiled in ruble factor cost on output per worker should be broadly indicative of relative production capacity.

On the foregoing, see Richard Moorsteen, "On Measuring Production Potential and Relative Efficiency" *Quarterly Journal of Economics,* 75 (1961), 451–67; *Real SNIP,* ch. 3.

With further research, it may be possible to be more definite on this important question.[15]

What of Soviet economic growth? Has it not been more rapid than that of the U.S.A.? If so, does this not in itself testify to a higher degree of economic efficiency? As data set forth above[16] indicate, under the five-year plans the Soviet economy has grown relatively rapidly. The tempo generally has been faster than it was in the U.S.A. during the same period, and probably also than that in the U.S.A. in earlier periods. The Soviet tempo, however, has dropped markedly in the last few years. In any case, there is hardly any basis to infer from the higher Soviet tempo generally

15. The difficulty here arises chiefly from the divergence in Western estimates of the relative levels of industrial output in the two countries, but according to one which is intermediate among several that have been advanced, in 1958 Soviet industry produced 40 per cent as much as did U.S. industry. The corresponding figure for output per worker was 33 per cent. For output, I refer to a geometric mean of alternative measures in rubles and dollars. See Gertrude Schroeder, "Soviet Industrial Labor Productivity," in *Dimensions*, pp. 153–54. From 1958 to 1960, output per worker in the U.S.S.R. probably rose only slightly relative to that in the U.S.A. Hence if the 1958 relation of industrial output per worker is accepted, much the same relation must have prevailed in 1960. It also follows that relative to that of the U.S.A., output per unit of major inputs in Soviet industry must at best have been similar to that in the economy generally. Thus for the entire economy output per worker in the U.S.S.R. is also one-third of that in the U.S.A. (geometric mean of the alternative measures in Table 14.1). With selected services omitted, the corresponding relation is 30 per cent. Also, in the U.S.S.R. the government has allocated to industry a disproportionately large share of the total capital stock. Relative to the U.S.A., output per unit of major inputs in the U.S.S.R. in industry is to be judged in this light.

Of course, in both countries industry comprises only part of the nonfarm sector in any case, and this must be considered in any comparison between the performance of industry and that of the economy generally.

16. See p. 306.

any Soviet margin of superiority regarding economic efficiency. Although such an inference is often drawn, the higher Soviet tempo is explicable in terms of other factors—principally the relatively high rate of investment, which was made more potent because of the relatively limited capital stock initially available; the extraordinary opportunities to borrow Western technology, which compounded still more the effect of the high rate of investment; and probably the opportunity to raise labor quality rapidly from an initially low level.

Of course, the rate of investment in the U.S.S.R. must have corresponded more nearly to that desired at full employment levels than it has in the U.S.A. In this one respect, therefore, the rapid Soviet growth does testify to Soviet economic efficiency, but planners' rather than household preferences must be taken as the standard. Possibly, too, growth in the U.S.S.R. has benefited from a relatively efficient resource allocation in some other particulars; but for the rest, growth in each country has depended not on the level but on the rate of change in economic efficiency. Economic efficiency may have risen more rapidly in the U.S.S.R. than it has in the U.S.A. If so, however, this would testify also to the initially low level of Soviet economic efficiency.[17]

17. I have not been able to examine allocations to education and research in the U.S.S.R. Hence I must pass by now the interesting question how the two countries compare in respect of economic efficiency at this point and what the consequences may have been for growth. Because of the absence of patent restrictions in the U.S.S.R., growth in that country may have been favored by a more efficient dissemination of new technological knowledge, but the introduction of innovations there nevertheless appears often to have been impeded by inertia, if not actual resistance, on the part of lower level managerial personnel.

Of course, in the U.S.S.R. technological progress generally must have been more rapid than that in the U.S.A., but this has to be read in the light of the feature already referred to, the wholesale Soviet borrowing of Western technology. If only for this reason, the Soviet margin over

I have been referring to the growth of total output, but what has been said applies as well to the growth of industrial production.[18]

CONCLUSIONS

I referred at the outset of this study to the theoretical debate on the economic merit of socialism. Arguments advanced on both sides have been diverse, but proponents and critics alike agree that economic merit turns largely on economic efficiency. From our empirical inquiry, what may be concluded as to economic merit so viewed?

---

the U.S.A. in rate of growth need not signify any corresponding Soviet superiority regarding the rate of increase in economic efficiency, though to repeat such a margin is possible.

It was said that a relatively high rate of investment has been made more potent as a force making for growth in the U.S.S.R. because of the relatively limited capital stock initially available. The capital stock initially was limited, I believe, relative to both the labor force and the total output, and this has been advantageous in several related ways. Relative to output, the burden of depreciation has been less than it would otherwise have been. For any given rate of gross investment, therefore, the corresponding rate of net investment has been relatively great. Considered as a share of total output, a given rate of net investment has also resulted in a relatively large percentage increment in the limited capital stock. The returns to a given increment in capital stock should also have been greater so far as labor has been relatively abundant.

We must view in relation to all but the last of these circumstances a curious yet outstanding feature of the growth process in the U.S.S.R.: while the rate of gross investment there has not been altogether exceptional, the stock of capital nevertheless has grown at an extraordinary rate: in the case of reproducible fixed capital, by 9.8–11.0 per cent from 1928 to 1940, and by 10.9–11.2 per cent from 1950 to 1958. On the growth of the Soviet capital stock and on the sources of Soviet growth generally under the five-year plans see Bergson, "National Income," in Bergson and Kuznets, eds., *Economic Trends in the Soviet Union.*

18. See Raymond Powell, "Industrial Production," in Bergson and Kuznets, eds., *Economic Trends in the Soviet Union.*

On purely theoretic grounds positions taken on both sides of the debate may have seemed untenably extreme. No basis has been found in this essay to question this opinion, but the critics are seen to have been closer to the mark than the proponents. As exemplified by the Soviet experience, socialism must be less efficient economically than Western private enterprise.

Reference, however, has been to private enterprise in the U.S.A. Would not the comparison be more favorable to the U.S.S.R. if we considered private enterprise in, say, Western Europe? If Soviet socialism falls short of the U.S. private enterprise in economic efficiency, this is a matter of interest in itself, for proponents of socialism have not confined their claims to any particular country. But no doubt it would be of value to extend the comparison to other private enterprise countries.

In any event, is not the interesting question: How does socialism in Russia compare with the private enterprise system that might have prevailed there? Or how does private enterprise in the West compare with the socialism that might supplant it there? Or how might each system function relative to the other in still other countries that have not yet experienced either in any meaningful sense? And if so, are not comparisons between socialism in the U.S.S.R. and private enterprise in the West beside the point? How socialism and private enterprise might function relative to each other in one and the same country is the ultimate issue. It is also a complex one; and in judging it, the comparative performance of the two systems in countries where they now operate is among the cardinal aspects we must consider.

But then, too, socialism is still a relatively novel economic system, for which the U.S.S.R. is the pioneer. If only on this account is it not understandable that thus far it has not performed especially well? Indeed, in view of reforms even now in progress, is it not evident that important sources of inefficiency must prove transitory? Thus, have not the Russians already freed themselves in some measure from the grip of the labor theory of value, and are they not likely to continue to do so? Doesn't the increasing tendency to use mathematical techniques and advanced computers mean that centralized decision making will become more rational? What of the possibility that decision making will in any case be substantially decentralized?

In a few years, socialism will have held sway in Russia for half a century. During this period the system's directors have enjoyed a degree of discretion to fashion and refashion society that probably is without precedent in any great state in modern history. If socialism were an especially productive system, one might think that by now this fact would have been manifest.

Yet the government is more eager than it used to be to foster economic efficiency, and Soviet economists have been responsive. There have also been favorable developments in technology, particularly for information processing. But in designing working arrangements for resource use, the system's directors still are concerned otherwise than with economic efficiency: ideologically, politically, and personally. Moreover, the problem of resource use is already extraordinarily complex, and it becomes steadily more so, while more specific causes of inefficiency are often deep seated. Also, alternative procedures currently discussed inside and outside the U.S.S.R. have yet to be tried on a national scale.

In sum, economic efficiency must already have increased in the U.S.S.R. and this trend is likely to continue. But economic efficiency has risen and should continue to rise under private enterprise in the West.[19] One may wonder

19. That economic efficiency has tended to increase under private enterprise is evident from only one outstanding development—the

whether Soviet socialism will ever match the latter in this respect.

What of socialism outside the U.S.S.R.? Wherever it has prevailed on a national scale, socialism has generally been of the Soviet type, and obviously these countries have also had their difficulties. In fact, such difficulties must often have been similar to those of the U.S.S.R. If the inquiry into comparative economic efficiency is to be extended to embrace private enterprise countries other than the U.S.A., however, it should also include socialist countries other than the U.S.S.R.

But whether in the U.S.S.R. or elsewhere, has not the inefficiency been due in part to the intense pursuit of growth? And, if so, would not inefficiency have been less without this goal? The intense concern for growth apparently has been an integral feature of socialism of the Soviet type everywhere, and any other sort of socialism on a national scale still remains to be realized. But so far as it might be, the possibly favorable effect of a less intense concern for growth would have to be weighed in speculating about its economic efficiency.

In the theoretical debate on economic merit, attention has been focused on economic efficiency, but reference has also been made to equity. For reasons given, we cannot judge what gain, if any, has been realized in this respect.

In forecasting the downfall of capitalism Marx considered that ultimately this would occur because of the inability of the system to make effective use of available resources.

avoidance of great depressions lately; but there have also been other developments favorable to efficiency, to some extent of a related sort, such as the increase in information available to business firms on the state of the market and their increased ability to interpret such information correctly, and the extension and improvement of accounting and other internal controls. No doubt still other developments have sometimes been adverse, but it is difficult to believe these could have fully offset those of a favorable sort.

Inevitably, capitalism would be supplanted by an alternative, socialism, which would prove more effective economically. As it has turned out, the outstanding example of socialism that has yet come into existence has distinguished itself so far not so much for effective use of resources as for the novel and strange ends imposed on a great state. Even from the standpoint of these ends, resource use has not been especially effective, although the system's directors no doubt have sometimes experienced compensating satisfactions for the resulting economic waste; and resource use has been still less effective by any more conventional standard. This is only to say that the forces making for the rise and fall of alternative social systems have been rather different from those Marx envisaged. Perhaps, in a longer span of history, economic rationality will still come to play an important role. But the outcome could still be other than that Marx envisaged.

The two systems have also come to bear little relation to the alternatives Marx depicted, and surely they are not quite so dissimilar. Should economic rationality prove to be the potent force for social reconstruction that he anticipated, the divergence between the two systems may narrow even more. If so, however, socialism in the U.S.S.R. should have to evolve no less than its competitor in the West.

APPENDIXES

A. THE GOVERNMENT BUDGET

In the text I referred at various points to the budget of the Soviet government. Revenues and expenditures in this budget for several benchmark years are shown in Tables A.1 and A.2. I refer to what has been called since 1939 the "State Budget of the U.S.S.R.," a consolidated budget of the all-union, republican, and local governments. All figures are in terms of the ruble monetary unit adopted on January 1, 1961. At that time, ten of the rubles previously circulating were declared equivalent to one new ruble.

For present purposes, the nature of the different items probably is sufficiently indicated by the captions, but for further information on their scope and on the budget generally, the reader may refer to F. D. Holzman, "The Soviet Budget, 1928–1952," *National Tax Journal, 6* (1953), 226–49; Holzman, *Soviet Taxation*; and R. W. Davies, *The Development of the Soviet Budgetary System* (Cambridge, 1958). Among the standard Soviet Sources are K. N. Plotnikov, *Biudzhet sotsialisticheskogo gosudarstva* (Gosfinizdat, 1948); N. N. Rovinskii, *Gosudarstvennyi biudzhet SSSR* (Moscow, 1951); A. Suchkov, *Dokhody gosudarstvennogo biudzheta SSSR* (Moscow, 1955); K. N. Plotnikov, *Gosudarstvennyi biudzhet SSSR* (Moscow, 1959).

TABLE A.1.

Government Budget Revenues, U.S.S.R.
(billions of rubles)

	1937	1950	1960
Direct taxes	.40	3.58	5.60
Bond sales	.59	3.10	.91
Social insurance levies	.66	1.93	3.74
Taxes on incomes of cooperatives and collective farms	.13	.48	1.84
Transfers from profits of government enterprises	.93	4.04	18.63
Turnover taxes	7.59	23.61	31.34
Other	.63	5.54	15.02
Total	10.93	42.28	77.08

Sources: For 1937 see Plotnikov, *Biudzhet sotsialisticheskogo gosudarstva*, p. 102; Abram Bergson, *Soviet National Income and Product in 1937* (New York, 1953), pp. 20, 40, 113. For 1950 and 1960, see Ministerstvo Finansov SSSR, *Gosudarstvennyi biudzhet SSSR . . .* (Moscow, 1962), pp. 7–9.

TABLE A.2.

Government Budget Expenditures
(billions of rubles)

	1937	1950	1960
Education	1.65	5.69	10.32
Health care, including physical culture	.70	2.14	4.82
Social insurance and assistance; pensions to mothers	.75	3.84	9.79
Government administration	.44	1.39	1.09
Defense	1.75	8.28	9.30
Financing the national economy	4.34	15.79	34.12
Other	.99	4.19	3.69
Total	10.62	41.32	73.13

Sources: For 1937 see Plotnikov, *Biudzhet sotsialisticheskogo gosudarstva*, pp. 125 ff.; Bergson, *Soviet National Income and Product in 1937*, p. 40; Davies, p. 296. For 1950 and 1960, Ministerstvo Finansov SSSR, pp. 18–19.

B. OUTPUT AND FACTOR
INPUTS

In the text, pp. 340 ff., I discussed calculations of factor productivity in the U.S.S.R. and U.S.A. This appendix explains the derivation of various elements in these calculations, particularly comparative data on the net national products, different factor inputs, and aggregate factor inputs. The main calculation concerns the net national product per unit of major factor inputs—that is, per unit of labor and reproducible capital taken together. But I also computed net national product per unit of factor inputs, where farm land is considered as an input, and I refer here to elements in both computations.

The comparative data for the net national product and individual factor inputs are shown in Table B.1. These data are inexact and data used in their compilation often are especially so. While there is a basis for tentative computation of factor productivity, the calculations must be used cautiously for other purposes. In the space available, I can only present the bare bones of the sources and methods used in deriving the data, and for the most part cannot even dwell on limitations. In referring to the data on workers engaged I shall consider the related question concerning working time.

Net National Product. I take as a point of departure these figures on gross national product for 1955:

	U.S.S.R.	*U.S.A.*
In ruble factor cost of 1955, billion rubles	961.0	3,407.0
In U.S. 1955 dollars, billion	212.4	397.5

These figures, except that for the U.S.A. in ruble factor cost, are from Bornstein, "National Income," in *Comparisons,* pp. 380, 385. For the U.S.A., gross national product in 1955 ruble factor cost is derived from data on the U.S. gross national product by final use in prevailing rubles of 1955 given ibid, p. 385. I adjust this figure to ruble factor cost by reference to Bornstein data on different final outlays in the U.S.S.R. in prevailing rubles and in ruble factor cost.

TABLE B.1.

Output and Factor Inputs, U.S.S.R. and U.S.A., 1960

Item	Nature of Measurement	With Selected Final Services Included		With Selected Final Services Omitted	
		U.S.S.R.	U.S.A.	U.S.S.R.	U.S.A.
Net national product	in 1955 ruble factor cost, billion	1,183.9	3,466.4	1,202.4	3,720.5
	in 1955 dollars, billion	265.9	392.5	236.9	376.1
Employment	workers engaged, million	97.4	67.4	82.1	54.3
Employment, hypothetical	workers engaged, adjusted hypothetically to equivalent male, eighth grade graduate, million	83.7	71.7	70.6	58.1
Reproducible fixed capital, net	in 1955 rubles, billion	2,221.9	6,765.7	1,255.5	2,632.6
	in 1955 dollars, billion	395.3	976.7	260.0	386.4
Nonfarm inventories	in 1955 ruble factor cost, billion	442	902	442	902
	in 1955 dollars, billion	97.8	105	97.8	105
Cultivated arable land	million acres	549	359	549	359
Cultivated arable land, hypothetical	with hypothetical adjustment to U.S. equivalent, million acres	275	359	275	359

Data designated by Bornstein as being in "adjusted" ruble prices, are designated here as being in ruble factor cost. Essentially the latter standard is applied, although the recalculation of the U.S. gross national product in these terms involves use of ruble factor cost only in the aggregation of major final use categories.

Following Cohn, "The Gross National Product of the Soviet Union," in *Dimensions,* p. 75, I take the gross national product of the U.S.S.R. to have increased at 6.5 per cent annually from 1955 to 1960. Although Cohn refers to the GNP in 1955 ruble factor cost, I assume this rate obtains also for the GNP in 1955 dollars. For the U.S.A., the GNP in both 1955 ruble factor cost and 1955 dollars is extrapolated to 1960 by reference to U.S. Department of Com-

Output and Factor Inputs

merce, *U.S. Income and Output* (Washington, D.C., 1958), p. 119, and *Survey of Current Business* (July 1961), p. 11.

In this way, we arrive at these figures on the U.S.S.R. and U.S.A. GNP in 1960:

	U.S.S.R.	U.S.A.
In ruble factor cost of 1955, billion rubles	1,316.6	3,822.7
In U.S. 1955 dollars, billion	291.0	446.0

For the U.S.S.R. the net national product is the gross national product minus depreciation and one-half of Soviet "capital repairs." The magnitude of the latter in ruble factor cost of 1955 is estimated primarily from Bergson, "National Income," in Bergson and Kuznets, eds., *Economic Trends in the Soviet Union,* p. 36. In the light of data in Central Intelligence Agency, *A Comparison of Capital Investment in the US and the USSR, 1950–59* (processed) (February 1961), a corresponding figure in U.S. dollars is obtained by translating ruble factor cost into dollars at the rate of $.189 to one ruble.

For the U.S.A., net national product is obtained by deduction of depreciation from the gross national product. In dollars of 1955, the latter is taken as 12 per cent of the GNP in the light of calculations described in Bergson, "National Income," p. 13, n. 9. From data in the CIA study, I take one dollar of U.S. depreciation to be equivalent to 6.66 factor cost rubles of 1955.

For fixed capital goods, I take ruble factor cost to be approximately the same as prevailing rubles.

Net National Product, with Selected Services Omitted. For the U.S.S.R., I deduct from the net national product these outlays:

	In 1955 Rubles, bil.	In 1955 Dollars, bil.
Health care, education, labor earnings	67.0	32.7
Government administration, including internal security, labor earnings	19.9	8.0
Armed forces, pay and subsistence	30.7	10.6
Housing services, gross outlays, net of depreciation	(−) 3.4	2.8
All	114.2	54.1

365

For health care and education, labor earnings are calculated from employment data referred to below, pp. 369–70, and these 1955 earnings rates: for health care, 6,610 rubles and $4,625; for education, 9,180 rubles and $3,473. These rates were used by Bornstein in compiling the comparative data on U.S.S.R. and U.S. national income from which I started. Bornstein kindly informed me of them in a letter of August 7, 1963. For government administration other than internal security, Bornstein took total labor earnings in 1955 to be 10.8 billion rubles. Reference is to government administration, including "general agricultural programs." See Morris Bornstein et al., *Soviet National Accounts for 1955* (processed) (University of Michigan, 1961), pp. 48–49. He also took the 1955 ruble-dollar ratio for such activities to be 2.1 to 1 (letter of August 7, 1963), so that government labor earnings also totaled $5.1 billions in 1955. In order to obtain corresponding figures for 1960, I extrapolate by reference to employment in "apparatus of organs of government administration . . ." as given in *Real SNIP*, p. 69, and *Narkhoz, 1961*, p. 568. For internal security, labor earnings in 1960 are taken to be the same as in 1955, while for 1955 such earnings are taken to be 10 billion rubles, or two-thirds of the estimated outlays of the agencies concerned. See *Real SNIP*, p. 361. A corresponding dollar figure is obtained by application of a ruble-dollar ratio of 3 to 1, which is approximately the one implicit in Soviet and U.S. earnings rates for the armed forces considered by Bornstein. I come to these now.

For the armed forces, pay and subsistence are calculated from their average size, as given below, and these 1955 pay and subsistence rates that Bornstein employed in his calculations (letter of August 7, 1963): 9,300 rubles and $3,222.

In his calculations, Bornstein took gross outlays on housing services, including imputed rent, to be 12.8 billion rubles in 1955. See *Soviet National Accounts for 1955*, pp. 8–9. Considering the rental rates and data on housing space used in deriving this total, and corresponding data on housing space in Oleg Hoeffding and Nancy Nimitz, *Soviet National Income and Product, 1949–1955*, RAND RM-2101 (April 6, 1959), pp. 98 ff., and in *Narkhoz, 1961*, p. 614, I calculate that in terms of 1955 rental rates gross rental outlays totaled 15.4 billion rubles in 1960. The corresponding

Output and Factor Inputs

figure in terms of 1955 dollar prices is calculated at $6.4 billions. I apply here a ruble-dollar ratio of 2.4 to 1, this being adapted from one for 1950 given in Norman M. Kaplan and Eleanor S. Wainstein, "A Comparison of Soviet and American Retail Prices in 1950," *Journal of Political Economy, 64* (1956), p. 475. From the gross outlays I deduct depreciation, which is taken to be 2 per cent of the gross housing stock as calculated below (pp. 373 ff.).

For the U.S.A., I deduct from the net national product these outlays:

	In 1955 Rubles, bil.	In 1955 Dollars, bil.
Health care, education, labor earnings	42.4	20.2
Government administration, labor earnings	34.2	16.3
Armed forces, pay and subsistence	23.4	8.1
Housing services, gross outlays, net of depreciation	3.2	25.3
All	103.2	69.9

For health care and education, labor earnings are calculated from employment data referred to below, p. 370, and Bornstein's average wage data for workers in these fields. For government administration, I refer to employment as given below, and these 1955 earnings rates: 7,791 rubles and $3,710. The dollar figure represents the average earnings in 1955 for all employees in "government and government enterprises," as given in U.S. Department of Commerce, *U.S. Income and Output,* p. 213. The ruble average wage is obtained by application of Bornstein's ruble-dollar ratio for government employees: 2.1 to 1. For the armed forces, I refer to employment as given below, and Bornstein's data on average rates of pay and subsistence for military personnel.

According to the *Survey of Current Business* (July 1961), p. 15, U.S. outlays on "housing" in 1960 totaled $38.3 billions in terms of prices of 1954. Allowing for price changes to 1955, the corresponding figure in terms of prices of that year was $38.8 billions. Using the ruble-dollar ratio previously derived for housing, 2.4 to 1, I find that U.S. outlays on housing in 1960 also totaled 93.1 billion rubles in terms of 1955 prices. I allow for depreciation at the rate of 2 per cent on the gross housing stock, as calculated below, pp. 374 ff.

For fairly obvious reasons, Soviet and U.S. outlay categories with similar names need not be comparable in scope, but I believe the different categories considered, when taken together, represent fairly similar spheres. While I deduct depreciation from gross outlays on housing, one might wish to deduct also materials inputs.

Employment. For the U.S.S.R., the cited figure is obtained as the sum of:

	Millions
Wage earners and salaried workers, artisans, nonfarm	54.7
Wage earners and salaried workers, farm, except in RTS	7.1
Wage earners and salaried workers, private plots, in 280 day man-years	3.9
Collective farmers, including RTS employees and other hired labor, in 280 day man-years	19.7
Collective farmers, on subsidiary plots in 280 day man-years	7.2
Military and other	4.8

For all figures except those on "Collective farmers, including RTS employees . . ." and "Military and other," see Murray S. Weitzman, Murray Feshbach, and Lydia Kulchycka, "Employment in the USSR," in *Dimensions,* pp. 620–21. As for the figure on "Collective farmers, including RTS employees . . ." the counterpart of this in 1955 was 24.2 millions; see *Real SNIP,* p. 446. I extrapolate this to 1960 by reference to data in Weitzman et al., pp. 620–21, on employment in the collective farms, MTS and RTS.

Military employment in 1960 is taken to be 3.3 millions. See J. G. Goodair, "The Claim of the Soviet Military Establishment," in *Dimensions,* p. 43. I allow for an additional 1.5 million workers who may not be covered elsewhere—that is, penal workers, party employees, et al.

For the U.S.A. reference is to the number of "persons engaged in production", given in the *Survey of Current Business* (July 1961), p. 27.

Because of the nature of the data used, the cited figures

on employment in both countries are more or less full-time equivalents. Information on hours of work is not very satisfactory for either country, but probably there is no marked incomparability at this point. Thus, according to *Narkhoz, 1960,* p. 645, wage earners and salaried workers in the U.S.S.R. at the end of 1960 worked on the average 39.4 hours per week. This figure apparently represents working time when allowance is made for shortened hours before free days and holidays and for holidays other than usual free days. Probably it does not take into account vacation time, which according to ibid., p. 647, averaged 18.5 working days in 1958, or time lost as a result of illness, stoppages, etc. Hours were being rapidly reduced during 1960, however, and, while the work week averaged 39.4 hours at the end of 1960, for the year 1960 as a whole it may have averaged about 42 hours per week. See Central Intelligence Agency, *An Evaluation of the Program for Reducing the Work Week in the USSR* (processed) (March 1961).

By implication, the average employee worked 2,184 hours (i.e. 52 × 42) during 1960, or, say, 2,058 hours (i.e. 49 × 42) if we allow for vacations, though not illness, stoppages, etc. On advice of Barney Schwalberg, I assume that the 280-day man-year for collective farm and other farm employment is in terms of 8-hour days. Hence, each such man-year represents 2,240 hours (i.e. 280 × 8). The indicated average for all persons engaged, nonfarm and farms, is 2,202 hours a year, or 2,116, if allowance is made for vacations, though not illnesses, stoppages, etc.

In the U.S.A. in 1958 hours of work per person engaged averaged 2,057. This represents for many workers hours paid for, hence exceeds hours worked, since it fails to allow sufficiently for paid leave and the like. See Denison, *The Sources of Economic Growth in the United States,* pp. 36 ff.; John W. Kendrick, *Productivity Trends in the United States* (Princeton, 1961), pp. 259 ff., 310.

Employment, with Selected Services Omitted. For the U.S.S.R., employment in the selected services totals 15.3 millions. This includes employment in health care and education, 8.3 millions; in government administration, including internal security, 2.7 millions; in the armed forces, 3.3 millions; and in housing, 1.0 million. For health care and education, see *Narkhoz, 1961,* p. 568. For education, reference is only to "education . . ." as given in the latter source, though probably many of the workers employed in "science . . ." should also be considered. For government administration, including internal security, employment is calculated by reference to total labor earnings and average wages, as given above, pp. 366–67. For the armed forces, see above, p. 368. For housing, I take employment to be one-half of that in "housing-communal economy," as given in *Narkhoz, 1961,* p. 568.

For the U.S.A., employment in selected services totals 13.1 millions. This comprises employment in health care and education, 5.1 millions; in government administration, 4.4 millions; in the armed forces, 2.5 millions; and in housing 1.1 millions. Essentially I rely here on the *Survey of Current Business* (July 1961), p. 27. For health care and education, I refer to employment in these fields as given in this source: "medical and other health services"; "commercial and trade schools . . ."; "educational services, n.e.c."; and "state and local-general government: public education." For housing, I take employment as given in the same source for "hotels and other lodging places" together with one-half that also given for "real estate."

Employment, Hypothetical. This is obtained through two adjustments of employment as initially calculated:

	U.S.S.R.	U.S.A.
Workers engaged, million	97.4	67.4
Workers engaged, adjusted to male equivalent, million	85.4	61.8
Workers engaged, adjusted to male, eighth grade graduate equivalent, million	83.7	71.7

To begin with the first adjustment, among wage earners and salaried workers employed in the U.S.S.R. in 1960, 29.3 million were women. See TSU, *Zhenshchiny i deti v SSSR* (Moscow, 1961), p. 120. In 280-day man-years, employment on the collective farm and in related activities in 1960 was taken above to total 19.7 million. Some 49 per cent of this number, or 9.7 million, were females: ibid., p.

129. Above, I also took employment on workers' and collective farm homestead plots as 11.1 million 280-day man-years. I assume that 80 per cent of this, or 8.9 million, consisted of female labor. See Eason, *Soviet Manpower,* p. 164, and TSU, *Zhenshchiny i deti v SSSR,* p. 55.

Thus, of the total number of workers in the U.S.S.R. in 1960, some 47.9 million, or 49.2 per cent, were women. For the U.S.A., I take the corresponding figures to be 22.2 millions, or 33.3 per cent. See U.S. Bureau of Labor Statistics, *Labor Force, Employment and Unemployment Statistics 1947–61* (October 1961), p. 5.

Following Denison, pp. 80 ff., I assume that one female worker in the U.S.A. in 1960 was equivalent to .75 of a male worker. I assume this rate also applies in the U.S.S.R. in 1960.

Having translated workers engaged into male equivalent, I translate them further into their equivalent in terms of eighth-grade graduates by reference to the data in Table B.2. In his "Costs and Returns in Education in the USSR" (dissertation, Harvard, 1962), pp. 136, 275, Dr. Nicholas DeWitt compiles data on the distribution of gainfully em-

TABLE B.2.

Assumed Distribution of Workers Engaged by Schooling, and Corresponding Labor Adjustment Coefficients, U.S.S.R. and U.S.A.

	U.S.S.R.			U.S.A.		
Schooling, Soviet	Schooling, U.S. Equivalent	Workers Engaged, percentage	Labor Adjustment Coefficient	Schooling	Workers Engaged, percentage	Labor Adjustment Coefficient
Literate, with 6 years or less	4 years	56.7	.83	Elementary		
				1–4 years	5.67	.79
Partial secondary	9 years	25.0	1.04	5–7 years	12.08	.88
				8 years	16.55	1.00
Complete secondary	12 years	13.8	1.24			
				High school		
Partial higher education	2 years, college	1.4	1.39	1–3 years	18.90	1.09
				4 years	29.45	1.24
Complete higher education	college graduate	3.1	1.81	College		
				1–3 years	9.32	1.39
				4 or more years	8.03	1.81
Total		100.0	.98	Total	100.00	1.16

ployed of 15 years and over in the U.S.S.R. by years of schooling. In Table B.2, I take Soviet workers engaged to be distributed by years of schooling correspondingly. I also accept DeWitt's translation of Soviet into U.S. years of schooling. For the U.S.A., the distribution of workers engaged by years of schooling is taken to be the same as that of the population of 20 years and over, exclusive of illiterates, as given in U.S. Bureau of the Census, *Current Population Reports,* Series P-20, No. 99 (February 1, 1960).

The labor adjustment coefficients are intended to represent the economic worth of workers of different years of schooling relative to one who is a U.S. eighth-grade graduate. Such a scale of coefficients is derived for the U.S.A. in Denison, pp. 67 ff. In Table B.2 I show the Denison scale for the U.S.A. and a corresponding scale for the U.S.S.R. adapted from the Denison scale to relate to years of schooling listed for that country.

On the foregoing basis the average worker engaged in the U.S.S.R. is equivalent economically to 0.98 of a U.S. eighth-grade graduate and that in the U.S.A. to 1.16 of such a graduate. In adjusting for differences in schooling I use these coefficients. Somewhat illogically I apply them to the data on workers engaged adjusted to male equivalent.

As we stated in the text, use of a very different scale for the U.S.S.R. does not affect the results perceptibly. In the alternative scale, differential economic worth compared with that of an eighth-grade graduate is everywhere increased 40 per cent. With little effect I also experimented with another way of translating Soviet into U.S. schooling. For the U.S.S.R. reference is made simply to the number of years of school attendance. For example, a Soviet high school graduate previously was taken as equivalent to a U.S. high school graduate. In the alternative computation, he is taken as equivalent to a U.S. worker who has completed two years of high school.

In adjusting employment where selected services are omitted, I apply the same factors as are used where selected services are included. Judging from incomplete information, I believe the sex structure of the employed labor force in each country is essentially the same in the two cases. No

Output and Factor Inputs

data are on hand to permit judgment of comparative educational attainment in the two cases.

Reproducible Fixed Capital, Net: U.S.S.R. The figures are derived from corresponding ones for January 1, 1960, on the assumption that the stock of reproducible fixed capital on July 1, 1960, was 104.8 per cent of that on January 1, 1960. See *Narkhoz, 1961,* p. 68. As for that on January 1, 1960, the derivation of the ruble and dollar figures on this may be explained by reference to Table B.3.

TABLE B.3.

Reproducible Fixed Capital of the U.S.S.R., January 1, 1960
(billion of July 1, 1955, rubles)

	GROSS ASSETS			DEPRECIATION		
	Total	*Buildings and Structures*	*Producers' Durables*	*Total*	*Buildings and Structures*	*Producers' Durables*
All sectors	2,826.7	2,185.4	641.3	706.6	504.9	201.7
Farm	281.2	177.5	103.7	81.2	43.0	38.2
Nonfarm						
Total	1,604.0	1,066.4	537.6	408.9	245.4	163.5
Industrial	800.1	490.6	309.5	200.0	107.2	92.8
Other	803.9	575.8	228.1	208.9	138.2	70.7
Housing	941.5	941.5	. . .[a]	216.5	216.5	. . .[a]

	NET ASSETS		
	Total	*Buildings and Structures*	*Producers' Durables*
All sectors	2,120.1	1,680.5	439.6
Farm	200.0	134.5	65.5
Nonfarm			
All	1,195.1	821.0	374.1
Industrial	600.1	383.4	216.7
Other	595.0	437.6	157.4
Housing	725.0	725.0	. . .[a]

a. All assets taken to be buildings and structures.

The data on net assets follow from those on gross assets and on depreciation. As to those on gross assets, essentially I show here the results of the recent Soviet capital census, as set forth in Norman Kaplan, "Capital Stock," in Bergson and Kuznets, eds., *Economic Trends in the Soviet Union*. Thus for all assets I cite data from Kaplan, p. 104. For all sector and for farm assets, I deduct from the indicated sums the estimated amount of livestock herds included: 138 billion rubles. See Kaplan, p. 117.

On buildings and structures, see Kaplan, pp. 104–05. For farm buildings and structures, account is taken of information in Kaplan, pp. 113–14; *Narkhoz, 1961,* pp. 420–21; and A. Beliakov, "Ob itogakh pereotsenki osnovnykh fondov kholkhozov," *Vestnik statistiki,* No. 1 (1963), 6–7. Buildings and structures in all nonfarm and other nonfarm branches are calculated as residuals. Given the volume of buildings and structures in each sector, the corresponding volume of producers' durables is calculated as a residual.

Depreciation is calculated in the light of the relation of accumulated depreciation to reproduction cost in Kaplan, p. 106, and *Narkhoz, 1961,* p. 425.

The foregoing calculations lead to an estimate of net, reproducible fixed capital in all sectors on January 1, 1960, in July 1955 rubles. A corresponding estimate in 1955 dollars is obtained by application of these dollar-ruble ratios:

	Buildings and Structures	*Producers' Durables*
Farm	$ .14	$ .22
Industrial	.16	.35
Other nonfarm	.14	.28
Housing	.14	...

I use here ratios corresponding to or calculated from parities for the Soviet fixed capital investment ruble given in Central Intelligence Agency, *A Comparison of Capital Investment in the US and the USSR 1950–59.*

U.S.A. The derivation of the figures on net reproducible fixed capital may be explained by reference to Table B.4.

Reproducible Fixed Capital of the U.S.A., December 31, 1958,
and July 1, 1960
(billions of 1955 dollars)

	GROSS ASSETS			NET ASSETS		
	Total	*Buildings and Structures*	*Producers' Durables*	*Total*	*Buildings and Structures*	*Producers' Durables*
			December 31, 1958			
All sectors	1,590.5	1,297.4	293.1	934.1	760.4	173.7
Farm	62.9	29.9	33.0	31.7	15.6	16.1
Nonfarm	886.2	626.1	260.1	517.1	359.5	157.6
Housing	641.4	641.4	. . .ᵃ	385.3	385.3	. . .ᵃ
			July 1, 1960			
All sectors	1,662.5	1,357.7	304.8	976.7	795.9	180.8
Farm	62.9	29.9	33.0	31.7	15.6	16.1
Nonfarm						
Total	926.1	654.3	271.8	540.4	375.7	164.7
Industrial	310.6	182.6	128.0	153.4	87.0	66.4
Other	615.5	471.7	143.8	387.0	288.7	98.3
Housing	673.5	673.5	. . .ᵃ	404.6	404.6	. . .ᵃ

a. All assets taken to consist of buildings and structures.

The data for gross capital are shown for reference; they
were not needed for the derivation of those for net capital.
In the table, the data for both gross and net capital on
December 31, 1958, are essentially Raymond Goldsmith's.
Thus in his *The National Wealth of the United States in
the Postwar Period* (Princeton, 1962), pp. 119, 123, 206,
215, he presents data for December 31, 1958, on the gross
and net stock of reproducible fixed capital by sector and
type in U.S. dollars of 1947–49. These figures of Goldsmith's were translated into dollar prices of 1955 by reference to price index numbers implied in corresponding figures in 1947–49 and current prices, in Goldsmith, pp. 121,
123, 215.

For all sectors, farm, and all nonfarm, corresponding

data for July 1, 1960, are obtained by extrapolation. I take account here of investment data in *Survey of Current Business* (July 1961), p. 8. As for the stock of fixed capital in industry, the net stock in manufacturing on July 1, 1960, is taken to have been $111.1 billion in 1954 prices. This is interpolated from end-of-the-year data in Daniel Creamer, "Recent Changes in Manufacturing Capacity," National Industrial Conference Board, *Studies in Business Economics*, No. 79, p. 44. For all industry, including mining and electric power, I take the net stock of fixed capital to be 35 per cent greater than that for manufacturing, or $150.0 billion in 1954 prices. I take account here of data in Kaplan, pp. 141–44; Creamer, "Postwar Trends in the Relation of Capital to Output in Manufactures," *American Economic Review*, *48S* (1958), 253; Goldsmith, pp. 75–77. Finally, I allow for a price increase of 2.3 per cent from 1954 to 1955. See Goldsmith, pp. 117, 119.

By letter of March 6, 1963, Creamer informs me that the gross stock of fixed capital in manufacturing at the end of 1959 amounted to $222.7 billion in 1954 prices. Extrapolating by reference to corresponding trends in net fixed capital, I find the gross stock amounted to $224.9 billion in 1954 prices on July 1, 1960. For all industry the gross stock in 1955 dollars is obtained by use of the adjustment factors applied in proceeding from the net stock in manufacturing in 1954 dollars to the net stock in industry in 1955 dollars.

In the foregoing I take Creamer's data to represent reproducible fixed capital, although they also cover a small amount of site land.

For industry as a whole, gross and net stocks are assumed to be divided between buildings and structures and producers' durables in the same proportions as obtain for private reproducible fixed capital, other than housing, as given in Goldsmith, pp. 117, 121. Nonfarm capital stocks, other than industrial, as of July 1, 1960, are calculated as residuals.

From the foregoing calculations I determine the gross and net stocks of reproducible fixed capital in all sectors on July 1, 1960, in 1955 dollar prices. The corresponding magnitudes in ruble prices of 1955 are obtained by application of these ruble-dollar ratios:

Output and Factor Inputs

	Buildings and Structures	Producers' Durables
Farm	7.0 R.	7.0 R.
Nonfarm		
Industrial	6.2	4.0
Other	7.0	9.0
Housing	7.0	...

These ratios are taken from or compiled from data in the CIA study referred to above.

Where selected services are omitted, for the U.S.S.R. I deduct from the gross and net stocks of fixed capital these magnitudes:

	Gross	Net
In 1955 rubles, billion	1,249.4	966.4
In 1955 dollars, billion	174.9	135.3

These magnitudes for July 1, 1960, are derived from corresponding figures for January 1, 1960, on the assumption that the stocks in question increased 4.5 per cent during the half-year, or by about the same amount as did "nonproductive" fixed capital, according to *Narkhoz, 1961,* p. 68. The volume of the gross and net stocks in question on January 1, 1960, is calculated as the sum of the corresponding stocks in housing and in other selected final services. Stocks in housing on January 1, 1960, are derived above. In ruble prices of 1955, the gross stock in other selected final services is taken to equal that in "public health, education, . . ." as given in Kaplan, p. 104, together with one-half of that in "municipal services" as given ibid. The corresponding net stocks are obtained by reference to data on depreciation, ibid., p. 106. The gross and net stocks of fixed capital in other final services in dollar prices of 1955 are calculated by application of the dollar-ruble ratio of $.14 to one ruble, as was done for housing.

For the U.S.A., I deduct from the gross and net stocks of fixed capital these magnitudes:

	Gross	Net
In 1955 rubles, billion	6,796.3	4,132.1
In 1955 dollars, billion	970.9	590.3

377

These magnitudes are calculated by summing corresponding figures for fixed capital in housing and in other final services. The gross and net stocks of fixed capital in housing are derived above. As for the gross and net stocks in other final services, these are obtained by summing the following items as given in Goldsmith, *The National Wealth of the United States in the Postwar Period*, pp. 204 ff.: nonmilitary, nonresidential structures and producers' durables of federal, state, and local governments. I also include one-half the corresponding assets of nonprofit institutions as given ibid. Goldsmith's data for December 31, 1955, in 1955 dollars are extrapolated to July 1, 1960, by reference to his corresponding figures for 1955–58 in 1947–49 dollars. Gross and net stocks in other final services in ruble prices of 1955 are calculated by application of the ruble-dollar ratio of 7.0 to 1.0, as was done for housing.

Nonfarm Inventories. By interpolating from end of the year data in *Narkhoz, 1961*, p. 70, we calculate nonfarm inventories in the U.S.S.R. as having amounted to 63.6 billion new or 636 billion old rubles on July 1, 1960. This represents the stock of inventories at acquisition prices. Considering probable general price trends during 1955–60, I take the corresponding figure in 1955 rubles to be 592 billions (i.e. 636 ÷ 1.075). At 1955 ruble factor cost, the stock is estimated to be 74.7 per cent of this or 442 billion rubles. The relation between factor cost and prevailing rubles is taken to be the same as obtains for the GNP. On the latter, see Bornstein, in *Comparisons*, pp. 380, 385. Finally, the corresponding figure in 1955 dollars is obtained by application of a dollar-ruble ratio, $.221, implied by the data given above on the Soviet GNP in dollars and in ruble factor cost.

From data in Goldsmith, pp. 117, 119, 206, I calculate that U.S. nonfarm inventories at the end of 1958 amounted to $97.7 billions in prices of 1955. The corresponding figure for July 1, 1960, is taken to be $105.2 billions. See *Survey of Current Business* (July 1961), p. 8. The corresponding figure in ruble prices is obtained by use of a ruble-dollar parity, 8.57, that is implied by the data given above on the U.S. gross national product in dollars and ruble factor cost. As was implied in Table B.1, where selected services are omitted no deduction is made for the very limited inventories employed in the provision of these services.

Cultivated Arable Land; Cultivated Arable Land, Hypothetical. On the former, see *Narkhoz, 1960,* p. 384, and *Statistical Abstract of the United States, 1962,* p. 621. Reference for the U.S.S.R. is to "cultivated arable land" on November 1, 1960, and for the U.S.A. to "cropland used for crops" in 1959.

In his "Agricultural Production," in Bergson and Kuznets, eds., *Economic Trends in the Soviet Union,* p. 225, Professor D. Gale Johnson informs us that:

> In an earlier study, I made a detailed analysis of the climatic and soil conditions of the Soviet Union and of North America to determine areas in North America with conditions similar to those prevailing in each major grain-producing area of the Soviet Union. Five states (North Dakota, South Dakota, Nebraska, Montana and Wyoming) and the Prairie Province of Canada include most of the climatically comparable areas.

For the five states referred to, an acre of farm land, together with associated buildings, had in 1959 an average value of $49.68, or 43.2 per cent of the corresponding figure for the U.S.A. See *Statistical Abstract of the United States, 1962,* p. 614. With the exclusion of buildings, an acre of farm land in the five states was worth $43.65 or about one-half of the corresponding figure for the U.S.A. See Agricultural Research Service, U.S. Department of Agriculture, *Farm Real Estate Market* (May 1959). Also, Professor Johnson informs me that if account were taken of differences between the U.S.S.R. and the five states in the nature and uses of farm land, an acre of cultivated Soviet crop land on the average might be worth in terms of the U.S. price structure more than half as much as an acre of cultivated U.S. crop land. For present purposes, I nevertheless take an acre of cultivated Soviet crop land to be equivalent qualitatively to .5 of an acre of cultivated U.S. crop land.

Input Weights. As represented by factor shares, the alternative weights employed in aggregating inputs are shown in Table B.5. As is appropriate here, in the case of each vari-

Appendix B

TABLE B.5.

Weights Used in Aggregating Factor Inputs

	RUBLE FACTOR SHARES, WITH 20 PER CENT INTEREST ON CAPITAL			RUBLE FACTOR SHARES, WITH 8 PER CENT INTEREST ON CAPITAL		
	Billion Rubles	Percentage, with Land Omitted	Percentage, with Land Included	Billion Rubles	Percentage, with Land Omitted	Percentage, with Land Included
Employment	753.3	58.6	53.3	753.3	78.0	69.0
Reproducible capital, including nonfarm inventories	532.8	41.4	37.7	213.1	22.0	19.5
Cultivated farm land	126.1		8.9	126.1		11.5
All, excluding land	1,286.1	100.0		966.4	100.0	
All, including land	1,412.2		100.0	1,092.5		100.0

DOLLAR FACTOR SHARES

	Billion Dollars	Per cent, with Land Omitted	Per cent, with Land Included
Employment	261.6	78.6	77.8
Reproducible capital, including nonfarm inventories	71.4	21.4	21.2
Cultivated farm land	3.1		.9
All, excluding land	333.0	100.0	
All, including land	336.1		100.0

ant the share of any factor is supposed to represent the income that would be attributable to it in 1960 at 1955 earnings rates.

The two sets of ruble factor shares differ only in respect to the share assigned to capital. Here the alternative magnitudes indicated are obtained simply by applying to the 1960 net stock of reproducible capital in 1955 rubles alternative hypothetical interest rates of 20 and 8 per cent. For employment, the magnitude indicated represents the product of the earned income of Soviet households, exclusive of imputed rent, in 1955, and the ratio of the number of workers engaged in 1960 to those engaged in 1955. The earned income of Soviet households, exclusive of imputed rent, in 1955 was 704 billion rubles. See Hoeffding and Nimitz, *Soviet National Income and Product, 1949–55,* p. 4. The number of workers engaged in 1960 was derived above. The corresponding figure for 1955, 91.0, is obtained by use of the same methods and sources as were used in

obtaining the 1960 figure. By implication, employment in
1960 was 107.0 per cent of that in 1955. Agricultural rent
in 1955 is taken to have totaled 60 per cent of farm labor
income. The latter amounted to 206 billion rubles. See
ibid., p. 4. The factor share considered here is taken as
2.0 per cent greater than the 1955 agricultural rent in view
of the increase from 1955 to 1960 in cultivated arable land.
See above, and *Narkhoz, 1956,* p. 109.

As for the weights corresponding to dollar factor shares,
I find that the total income attributable to labor, including
entrepreneurial wages, in the U.S.A. in 1955 was $251.58
billion. Also, private property income other than agricultural rent in the U.S.A. in 1955 amounted to $61.5 billion,
yielding a rate of return of 6.6 per cent on private capital,
exclusive of farm land. U.S. agricultural rent in 1955
totaled $3.25 billion. Essentially, I use here the same
sources and methods as were employed in a previous study
in calculating U.S. factor shares in 1929 and 1954. See
Bergson, "National Income," in Bergson and Kuznets, eds.,
Economic Trends in the Soviet Union, pp. 29–30.

The dollar shares shown for different factors in the table
are obtained from these data. Thus, that for employment
is obtained by adjustment of the 1955 labor income to
allow for the 4.0 per cent increase in the number of workers
engaged from 1955 to 1960. See above and U.S. Department of Commerce, *U.S. Income and Output,* p. 214. That
for reproducible capital is obtained by applying to the 1960
net stock in 1955 dollars, as previously estimated, the calculated 1955 rate of return of 6.6 per cent. That for cultivated farm land is simply the agricultural rent of 1955
after adjustment for the 3.3 per cent decline in farm land
from 1955 to 1960. See *Statistical Abstract of the United
States, 1962,* p. 621.

I have been referring to input weights employed when
selected final services are included. When selected final
services are omitted, the input weights used are shown in
Table B.6. For employment for each country, I deduct
from all labor earnings the earnings of labor in the different final services as previously computed. For housing, for
the U.S.S.R. labor earnings are calculated as the product
of employment as previously estimated and average wages
in 1955. The latter are taken to be 8,520 rubles, or the

Weights Used in Aggregating Factor Inputs,
with Selected Services Omitted

	RUBLE FACTOR SHARES, WITH 20 PER CENT INTEREST ON CAPITAL			RUBLE FACTOR SHARES, WITH 8 PER CENT INTEREST ON CAPITAL		
	Billion Rubles	Percentage, with Land Omitted	Percentage, with Land Included	Billion Rubles	Percentage, with Land Omitted	Percentage, with Land Included
Employment	627.2	64.9	57.4	627.2	82.2	70.5
Reproducible capital, including nonfarm inventories	339.5	35.1	31.1	135.8	17.8	15.3
Cultivated farm land	126.1		11.5	126.1		14.2
All, excluding land	966.7	100.0		763.0	100.0	
All, including land	1,092.8		100.0	889.1		100.0

	DOLLAR FACTOR SHARES		
	Billion Dollars	Percentage, with Land Omitted	Percentage, with Land Included
Employment	214.0	86.9	85.8
Reproducible capital, including nonfarm inventories	32.4	13.1	13.0
Cultivated farm land	3.1		1.2
All, excluding land	246.4	100.0	
All, including land	249.5		100.0

same as in the economy generally. See *Real SNIP,* p. 422.
For the U.S.A., labor earnings are computed similarly from
employment as previously estimated and an average wage
rate of $2,750. See the earnings in "real estate" and
"hotels . . ." in U.S. Department of Commerce, *U.S. Income and Output,* p. 213.

Factor shares for capital are calculated as before, except
that reference is now made to the interest on the stock of
capital employed other than in selected final services. The
factor shares assigned to land in the two countries are the
same as before.

INDEX

lished delivery quotas for, 196;
average size of, 198; quality of
management of, 198–200, 202,
208–09; shifting of industrial
personnel to, 208–09; and individual holdings, 211–13, 222–23;
compared to state farms, 234–36;
sources of inefficiency in, 336–37.
See also Agriculture

Combines, 30, 35 n.

Commission of Soviet Control, 39–
40

Committee for the Coordination
of Scientific Research, 39

Committee on the Economics and
Organization of Production of
the All-Union Central Council
of Trade Unions (VTSSPS), 252

Committee on Labor and Wages,
38–39, 116

Committee on Standards, Measures, and Measuring Equipment, 292

Communist Party: new program
of, 7, 323–24; in economic administration, 43–44, 196, 205,
208, 229, 235; overseeing of plan
fulfillment by, 90–91, 199–200,
208–09; and First Five Year
Plan, 322–23. *See also* Central
Committee

Competition, economic, with capitalist countries, 323–25, 326 n.

Congress of Soviets, 28, 44

Consumers' cooperatives. *See* Cooperatives

Consumers' demand, Soviet determination of, 277–80, 297–302

Consumers' goods, distribution of,
49 ff.; rationing of, 51, 276;
economy in inventories of, 69 n;
availability of and taxation,

120 n.; assortment and quality
of, 287–91, 296–99. *See also* Consumption, household

Consumers' preferences (vis-à-vis
planners' preferences), 7 ff., 338–
40, 350–53; and disposition of
consumers' goods, 67–71; and
labor recruitment and utilization, 120 ff.; and supplies and
allocations of industrial materials, 170 ff.; and use of resources in agriculture, 230 ff.;
and choice of technology, 268 ff.;
and structure of household consumption, 279–80, 297–302; and
capital formation, 321–26; and
economic merit, 327–29

Consumers' welfare, as standard
of resource use, 7 ff. *See also*
Consumers' preferences

Consumption, communal, 50, 310,
317

Consumption, household: structure of, 275 ff.; plan fulfillment
in, 282–86; per capita, 286, 313–
17, 326; rational norms for, 299–
302, 339; as share of national
income, 308–312; per employed
worker, *314*–15; and nonfarm
real wages, *314*. *See also* Capital
formation; Consumers' goods

Cooperatives: ownership of, 17–24;
administration of, 44–47; consumers', 47, 54–55, 57–58, 73;
producers', 55, 58

Cotton cloth, plan fulfillment in
(*1932–62*), *84*

Council of Ministers, all-union, 27,
28, 30, 31, 32; and Gosplan, 35–
36 n.; and Central Statistical Administration, 37–38; and Committee on Labor and Wages,

38–39; aid to technology by, 39; and Commission of Soviet Control, 39–40; role of in price formation, 56; direction of industry by, 72–73, 81; plan formulation by, 103, 116, 136, 251; operating reserves of, 140; role of in industrial materials price formation, 169; role of in collective farm administration, 180–81; and plan targets for investment, 319–20

Council of Ministers, republican, 32, 33; control of enterprises by, 101–02; plan formulation by, 145–46; and quality standards for consumers' goods, 292–93

Council of Ministers, RSFSR, 157

Council of the National Economy of the U.S.S.R., 33, 150; and Gosplan, 37 n.

Council of People's Commissars, 28

CRE method, 253–65, 270–71; and efficiency rules, 255–65

Creamer, Daniel, 376

Credit: organizations for supply of, 38; and control of industrial enterprise, 78

Crop schemes, 214–22, 337; for wheat, 216–19; for corn, 220–21

Crops, industrial, 179 n.

Cult of personality and investment allocation, 271–72

Cultivated arable land, U.S.A. and U.S.S.R., 348 n., 379

Cultural fund (collective farms), 188

Davies, R. W., 361

Denison, E. F., 347 n., 369, 371, 372

Depreciation charges in project appraisel, 258–61

Dewar, Margaret, 118 n.

DeWitt, Nicholas, 50–51 n., 329 n., 372

Dinerstein, H. S., 183 n., 189 n., 205 n.

Dividend allotments (in collective farm system), 179–97 passim; in kind, 184–86; in money, 186–87, 235–36; effects of on incentives, 190–97; changes in determination of, 193–96, 235–36; variations in among farms, 196, 236; for managerial personnel, 198–200

Eason, Warren, 239 n., 313 n., 371

Economic calculation, Soviet principle of. See *Khozraschet*

Economic competition with capitalist countries, 323–25, 326 n.

Economic councils, regional, 29–30, 31–34, 87; control of enterprises by, 101–02, 251; plan formulation by, 145–46, 150, 157; and quality control of consumers' goods, 293

Economic efficiency, comparative, U.S.A. and U.S.S.R., 340–58

Economic inefficiency, Soviet, sources of, 329–40

Economic law, in U.S.S.R., 12–13, 70, 122, 270, 325. See also Value theory, Soviet

Economic ministries, 30–31; and success criteria in industry, 74, 76–77, 79, 87; control of enterprises by, 101–02, 116; role of in plan formulation, 136, 137, 142, 144, 251

Economic rationality, 11–12; and economic merit, 327–28. See also Consumers' preferences

Education, 50, 365–67, 369–70

Efficiency rules, 12; for retail

Index

trade, 52–53, 67–71; for industrial labor recruitment and allocation, 104–05, 117–23, 125 n., 229–30, 237–38; for industrial materials supply, 130–33, 150–51; for industrial materials price formation, 159–61, 167, 169–72; for agriculture, 202, 209–10, 213–15, 222, 224 n., 229–31, 237–38; for technological choice, 160–61, 245–49, 255–74; for structure of household consumption, 276, 297–98; for capital formation, 321–22

Electric power, plan fulfillment in (*1932–62*), *84*

Employment: determination of in industry, 93 ff.; freedom of choice of, 94–99, 104–05, 121, 227–28; determination of in agriculture, 225–30; data on, 368–73

End products, defined, 127–28

Enterprise fund, 78, 109

Enterprises, industrial, 30, 31, 34–35; status of, 42–43; success criteria in, 73 ff., 88–89, 288–90, 297, 334–36; plans for, 74 ff., 105–06, 134 ff., 251–52; per-unit costs in, 77, 79, 166, 167, 289; profitability of, 77–78, 88–89, 162; administrative responsibility within, 90–91, 100, 116; occupational structure within, 100–04; wage determination in, 106–18, 122, 125–26; role of in plan formulation, 136, 137, 142, 160–61, 251; materials input norms for, 137–44, 147, 150, 161; subsidies to, 162–63, 165; inventory norms for, 177

Erlich, Alexander, 267 n.

Extrabudgetary organizations, 42–43

Factor inputs, weights used in aggregating, 379–82

Factor productivity, U.S.A. vs. U.S.S.R., 341–54, 363–82

Fainsod, Merle, 27 n., 205 n.

Farm machinery associations, 46

Feshbach, Murray, 368

Field, Mark, 50–51 n.

Fifteen-year plan, 74

Finance, Ministry of, 38; control of enterprises by, 101–02

Firms, 34

First Government Ball-Bearing Factory, 150

Five Year Plan, First, 52; employment under, 95, 105–06; and determination of wage scales, 111; and collective farm members' income, 191; transfer of labor from agriculture to industry under, 227–28; GNP and household consumption under, 309–10, 313; investment under, 321; as projected by Communist Party Congress, 322–23

Five Year Plan, Second: labor flow under, 95–96; investment under, 308; per-capita consumption under, 314–15; consumption per employed worker under, 315

Five Year Plan, Fifth (*1950–55*), 89; increase in per-capita consumption under, 315

Five Year Plan, Sixth (*1956–60*), 89

Five-year plans: and open market distribution, 52; results of for selected industries, 83–85; budgetary requirements under, 119–20; and centralized decision making, 173; and expansion of

Index

223, 336; for managerial personnel in collective farms, 198–200, 202; vs. rapid growth, 304–05, 318, 322

Income, national, growth and allocation of, 306–26

Income, household. *See* Money income, household

Income, inequality of, 328. *See also* Dividend allotments; Wage determination

Income tax: on industrial workers, 119, 123–24; on collective farm members, 187, 190, 195; on private holdings in collective farms, 211–12

Indivisible fund, in collective farms, 187, 190, 195

Industrial Bank of the U.S.S.R., 38

Industrial materials: determination of supplies and allocations of, 127 ff.; funded goods in supply of, 143–44; categories of, 143–44, 146–47, 150; concern for economy of, 151–54, 157, 160–61, 167; substitutions among, 158–61, 164–65; formation of prices of, 166 ff.; inefficiency in allocation of, 332

Industrial ministries, 30–31; liquidation of, 31–32, 251

Industry: types of ownership in, 16–17; organization of, 29 ff.; reorganization of (*1957*), 31–34, 86–88. *See also* Enterprises, industrial

Input-output analysis: and industrial materials supply, 129–30, 131–32 n., 159, 174–76; in determining structure of end products, 243–47, 299

Institute of Economics of the

Academy of Sciences of the U.S.S.R., 252

Interdistrict Territorial-Production Administration (TPU), 46–47, 205–06, 222

Interest costs, use of in project appraisal. *See* Technological choice

Inventories, nonfarm, U.S.A. and U.S.S.R., 378

Investment. *See* Capital formation; Technological choice

Investment goods, inefficiency in allocation of, 332

Italy, consumption in, *286*

Jasny, Naum, 85 n., 189 n., 203 n., 211 n., 213 n., 223 n., 234 n., 239 n.

Johnson, D. Gale, 191 n., 313 n., 348 n., 379

Kahan, Arcadius, 191 n., 313 n.

Kaplan, Norman M., 250 n., 319 n., 367, 374, 376, 377

Karcz, Jerzy F., 184 n., 189 n., 193 n., 196 n., 211 n.

Kaser, Michael, 86 n.

Kendrick, John W., 369

Khachaturov, T. S., 250 n., 264 n., 270 n.

Khozraschet, 43, 204; and consumers' goods, 50; in industrial enterprises, 73–74; in industrial materials supply, 132; as a source of inefficiency, 334

Khrushchev, N. S.: reforms in bureaucratic structure by, 28; and Seven Year Plan (*1959*), 89; decentralization under, 174, 221–22; and collective farms, 198, 199–200, 205–06, 209; and administration of agriculture, 207–

08, 232; on decision making under Stalin, 215–19; reorganization of agriculture by, 220–22; on party functions in industry and agriculture, 229; on quality control in industrial goods, 293–95; standards of consumption under, 317; as "satisficer," 318; statement by on party economic program (*1961*), 323–25; criticism of Gosplan by, 332
Kirsch, Leonard, 106–07 n.
Kulchycka, Lydia, 368
Kuznets, Simon, 317 n., 346 n.

Labor, agricultural, question of surplus of, 238–40
Labor, Ministry of, 38
Labor, nonfarm, recruitment of from agriculture, 225–30, 239
Labor cost economy, in industry, 74–75, 77 ff., 99–106, 153–54
Labor day system in collective farms, 179–83, 197, 203, 223, 235–36; for managerial personnel, 198–200
Labor force, comparative, U.S.A. and U.S.S.R., 346–48, 349–50, 368–73; by sex distribution, 347, 370–71; by schooling, 347, 370–72; by unemployment, 349–50
Labor reserve schools. See Vocational training
Labor Reserves, Chief Administration of, 39
Labor theory, in U.S.S.R., 13, 70–71. See also Economic law; Value theory, Soviet
Labor turnover: in industry, *95–99*; in agriculture, 224–25
Lange, Oscar, 330 n.
Lenin, V. I.: views of on central-

ized economic organization, 173; on small-scale production, 233
Levine, Herbert S., 89 n., 134 n., 138 n., 142–43 n., 147 n., 149 n., 161 n., 175 n., 177 n.
Liberman, E. G.: on reform of managerial incentives, 88; on decentralization, 174 n.
Livestock herds: by type of ownership, 18–*19;* individual holdings of, 211, 213
Lokshin, E.: on socialist planning in industry, 148; on localism in allocation of industrial materials, 155; on quality control of industrial materials, 156; on quality control and assortment, 296–97
Lorimer, Frank, 313 n.
Lump-sum tax, 118, 122–23

Machine-tractor stations (MTS), 21; financing of, 43; and collective farms, 45–46, 185–86, 189–90, 192–93, 202–07
Machinery enterprise, premium scales for managerial personnel in, 75–76
Marketings, farm, government concern for, 230–38 passim. See also Dividend allotments
Marx, Karl: on the nature of socialism, 6–7, 122; "law of value" of, 13; on use of compound interest, 270; on the downfall of capitalism, 357–58
Marxian tenets on anarchy of market processes, 173–74
Material input coefficients. See Industrial materials; Input-output analysis
Materials for own use, defined, 127–28

Index

Mendershausen, Horst, 5 n.
Migration, net rural-urban, U.S.S.R., *226*
Mikoyan, A. I., economic principles of, 70
Mining enterprise, wage scales in (*1958*), *108*
Mishan, E. J., 12 n.
Money income: household, and distribution of consumers' goods, 9, 50, 69; Soviet accounting for sources and disposition of, 66; and taxation, 118–20, 125, 328; of collective farm members, 187, 194, 211–12, 223, 235–36; inequality of, 328–29
Money income of collective farms, U.S.S.R.: by use, *187;* per 100 hectares of arable land (*1960*), *197*
Moorsteen, Richard, 308 n., 311 n., 346 n., 350–51 n.
MTS. *See* Machine-tractor stations

Nash, Edmund, 329 n.
Nemchinov, V. S., 175 n.
Net national product: share of net investment in, U.S.S.R., *312;* comparative, U.S.A. and U.S.S.R., 341, *342*–43, 363–68
New Land Program (*1934*), 18–19, 235
Newth, J. A., 211 n.
Nimitz, Nancy, 119 n., 184 n., 189 n., 193 n., 194 n., 195 n., 202 n., 207 n., 213 n., 220 n., 223 n., 224n., 234 n., 235 n., 366, 380
Norms and Conflicts Commission (RKK), 91
Nove, Alec, 73 n., 134 n., 157 n., 179 n., 183n., 190 n., 195 n., 195–96 n., 205 n., 211 n., 220 n.,
235 n., 245 n., 250–51 n., 260 n., 287 n., 291 n., 293 n., 319 n., 335 n.
Nutrition Institute of the Academy of Medical Sciences of the U.S.S.R., 300
Nutter, Warren, 292 n.

Ob'edinenie. See Combines
Occupational rates, for managerial and technical personnel, 112–*13*
Oil industry, plan fulfillment in (*1932–62*), *84*
Output mix, desirability of, U.S.A. vs. U.S.S.R., 350–51
Ownership, forms of, 15 ff. *See also* Collective farm ownership; Cooperatives; Private Ownership; Public Ownership

Party-State Control Committee, 39–40
Per-unit costs in industry, 77, 79
Piece work: in industry, 109–10, 112, 117; in collective farms, 181–82
Plan formulation: Gosplan role in, 41; in industry, 74 ff., 102, 103; safety factor in, 81–85, 88–89, 177, 293; in industrial materials supply, (pre-*1957*) 134–44, (post-*1957*) 145–50; in collective farms, 180–82, 200 n., 205–07; in agriculture, 214–22; for structure of household consumption, 276–82, 287–92, 297–302; in capital formation, 319–26. *See also* Technological choice
Plan fulfillment: in industry, 83–85, 89; in selected industrial products and employment (*1932–62*), *84;* in allocation and use of industrial materials supply, 150–

391

Index

Sales tax. *See* Turnover tax

Samuelson, Paul A., 248–49 n.

Savings accounts, 38

Schroeder, Gertrude, 352 n.

Schwalberg, Barney, 239 n., 369

Schwartz, Harry, 5 n., 193 n., 213 n.

Schwarz, Solomon M., 73 n., 94 n., 97n., 224 n.

Seton, Francis, 308 n.

Seven Year Plan (*1959–65*), 83–84, 89

Smolinski, Leon, 267 n.

Social insurance, 96

Socialism, the U.S.S.R. as an example of, 6–7, 355–58

Sovnarkhozy. See Economic councils, regional

Speculative operations, 71

Stalin, I. V.: reorganizations after death of, 48, 178, 206–07, 212, 213, 236–37; economic principles of, 70; and trade unions, 91, 117; retreat from centralization after, 174; determination of collective farm dividend under, 183–93, 199; changes in determination of collective farm dividend after, 193–98; decision making under, 215–19; project appraisal under, 262; and cult of personality, 271–72; standards of consumption under, 315, 317; as "maximizer," 318; investment under, 321

State Bank, 38, 42; as self-financing government institution, 43; as source of working capital, 78, 79, 80

State Committee for Materials Supply, 36 n.

State Economic Commission, 36 n.

State farms: output of, 213; allocation of labor among, 225; compared to collective farms, 234–36. *See also* Public ownership

State Planning Commission. *See* Gosplan

State Scientific-Economic Council, 36 n., 37

Statistical data, U.S.S.R.: compiling of, 37–38; reliability of, 207–08, 291, 321

Steel, plan fulfillment in (*1932–62*), *84*

Stroibank. *See* Bank for Financing Capital Investment

Stumpage fees, 168 n.

Success criteria, in industrial enterprises, 73 ff., 88–89, 288–90, 297; as a source of inefficiency, 334–36

Supreme Economic Council of the U.S.S.R.: control of publicly owned productive assets by, 29, 41; liquidation of, 30; revived, 32 n., 33, 35, 150; and Gosplan, 35 n., 150; aid to technology by, 39

Supreme Soviet, 28

Swearer, Howard, 205 n.

Taxes: relation of to worker income, 118–20; effect of on incentives, 123–24, 187–88, 190–91, 195, 210, 303–04, 336. *See also* Income tax; Lump-sum tax; Turnover tax

Taylor, Fred M., 330 n.

Technical-industrial-financial plan. *See* Tekhpromfinplan

Technological choice: and materials inputs, 160–61; nonfarm, 249–65, 269–72; and efficiency rules, 255–65, 268–72, 330, 334; nonfarm vs. farm, 265–68, 272–74